SHOW BIZ KIDS

Also BY The Author:

"Scattered Moments"

Coming Soon By The Author From Barclay House:
"Beware of A Man Who ..."
"Beware of A Woman Who ..."

SHOW BIZ KIDS
How To Make Your Kid A Film, Television or Recording Star
(Ages Infant - 18)

Ruthie O. Grant

With An Insert by Show Biz Teens:
*Salim Grant (from NBC's Saved By The Bell)
and Ebonie Smith (Lethal Weapon I, II & III)*

**Barclay House
New York**

A BARCLAY TRADE PAPERBACK
Published by Barclay House, a division of the Zinn Publishing Group:
ZINN COMMUNICATIONS / NEW YORK

Copyright (c) 1995 Barclay House
All Rights Reserved. No part of this book may be reproduced or transmitted in any form or by any means, electronic or mechanical, including photocopying, recording, or by any information storage retrieval system, without the written permission of the Publisher, except where permitted by law.

ISBN: 0-935016-36-8

Printed in the United States of America

Library of Congress Cataloging-in-Publication Data

Grant, Ruthie O., 1954-
    Show biz kids : how to make your kid a film, television, and recording star / Ruthie O. Grant.
    p. cm.
    ISBN 0-935016-36-8 (pbk. : alk. paper)
    1. Performing arts--Vocational guidance--United States.
    2. Child actors.   I. Title.
PN1580.G73 1995
791.4'023'73--dc20
                                                                                                                           95-46116
                                                                                                                             CIP

Real Magic, Copyright 1992 by Dr. Wayne W. Dyer. All Rights Reserved. Reprinted Courtesy of HarperCollins Publishers.

The Measure of our Success, Copyright 1992 by Marian Wright Edelman. All Rights Reserved. Reprinted Courtesy of Beacon Press.

The L. A. Agent Book, Copyright 1990 by K Callan. All Rights Reserved. Reprinted Courtesy of author.

Zoe F. Carter, *"Baby, It's You"* Copyright 1991. All Rights Reserved. Reprinted Courtesy of the author.

Kyle Counts, *"The Search For Appealing Kids"* and *"Discovering Kids Willing To Make a Commitment"* Copyright 1990. All Rights Reserved. Reprinted Courtesy *The Hollywood Reporter.*

Mark Kenaston & Dana Alan LaFontaine, *"Only Love Is Real, Marianne Williamson on A Course In Miracles"* Copyright 1992. All Rights Reserved. Reprinted Courtesy of Bodhi Tree Bookstore.

Harry Medved, *"Close Up, Brock Peters Interview"* Copyright 1991. All Rights Reserved. Reprinted Courtesy *Screen Actor Magazine.*

Nancy Randle, *"A New Generation of Stage Mothers"* Copyright 1990. All Rights Reserved. Reprinted Courtesy *The Hollywood Reporter.*

This Book Is Dedicated To:

Salim and Crystal, my very own show biz kids. Their self-sufficiency during the long hours I spent writing and editing made this book possible; and my mother, ***Louella,*** who taught me, by example, the true meaning of unconditional love and the importance of faith in fulfilling any major life quest.

Special Thanks To:

David Zinn, for having the vision to include the second edition of ***Show Biz Kids*** in his new Hollywood book line. May we sell millions! ***Diane Ronngren,*** who encouraged me to put my hard earned experience into words that might benefit others attempting to blaze the show biz trail. I wanted to wait until I had the time to write the book. She insisted that if I waited, I would never get around to meeting my destiny. ***Carrie See,*** the children's photographer who believed in and supported this project from day one; ***Horace Grant,*** for his original input on the outline and for proofreading the final manuscript. ***Rhoda C. Fine*** for her detailed review of the chapters on Child Labor Laws and Studio Teachers, and ***Andrew Leranth*** for his editorial comments.

For a list of national **workshops and seminars** conducted by the author send a self addressed, stamped envelope to Ruthie O. Grant, 859 Hollywood Way, Suite 175, Burbank, California 91505. For personal consultations or to book the author for lectures and speaking engagements call 800-507-0950

TABLE OF CONTENTS

FOREWORD

INTRODUCTION 1
Visions of Hollywood

CHAPTER 1
STAGE MOMS: MYTH V. REALITY 7
The Future Has Never Looked Brighter ... 9
A Word of Caution About Unrealistic Expectations 12
An Inside Look at Beginning Salaries 14

CHAPTER 2
WHAT AGENTS AND CASTING DIRECTORS LOOK FOR 17
Commercials 18
Print Work 20
Newborns and Toddlers 23
Theatrical Work 24

CHAPTER 3
BECOMING MONEY IN THE BANK 30
For The Older Child Just Starting Out 31
Learning to Develop Instant Rapport 32
Nurturing Your Child's Strong Suit 34
Interviewing Successfully With an Agent or Manager 35
Sending The Child In Alone On Interviews 38
Avoid Manipulation and Duplicity 39
Following Through and Honoring Commitments 40

CHAPTER 4
MANAGERS 44
Realistically, What Can One Expect From A Manager? 44
What Not To Expect 45
Why Agents Work With Managers 46
Why Some Agents Won't Work With Managers 47
Managers and Split Representation 48
My Approach To Management 49

Do I Need a Manager?	51
Hints for Finding a Manager	52
Making a Personality Assessment	53
Management for Singers	54

CHAPTER 5
GETTING READY TO GET AN AGENT — 56

Seeking Approval From Within	57
It Takes Money To Make Money	57
The Importance of Strong Reading Skills	58
Ways To Develop Stronger Reading Skills	60
Finding The Right Instructor	61
Photographs For All Age Groups	63
Getting Duplicate Photos	65
Professional Photography Fees	66
Now That You've Done Your Homework	68
Agency Fees	69
Seminars and Workshops	69
My Story	70
Being a No Limit Person	74
Younger Siblings Often Follow Suit	76
Samples of Winning Resumes and Headshots	80

CHAPTER 6
PREPARING FOR AUDITIONS AND CALLBACKS — 81

Essential Items To Keep In Your Car:	
(1) Headshots	81
(2) Thomas Guide Map Book	82
(3) Healthy Snack Packs	83
(4) Parking Money	85
About those Polaroid Pictures at Auditions	86
Smooth Riding To and From Auditions	87
Help Your Child Cope With Discord In The Family	88
Callbacks (Commercial and Theatrical)	89
Practice Your Lines (i.e., Sides)	90

CHAPTER 7
POSITIVE GOAL SETTING AND AFFIRMATIONS — 93
Avoid Negative Commands — 95
Listening to Motivational Tapes — 97
Using Affirmations — 98

CHAPTER 8
COMMON PARENTAL FEARS ABOUT SHOW BUSINESS — 104
Studio Teachers — 105
Dealing With Difficult Teachers — 108
Enmity from Peers — 109
Performing Arts Schools: Proceed With Caution — 110
The Hollywood Brat Syndrome — 113
The Non-Show Business Sibling — 115

CHAPTER 9
CHILD LABOR LAWS — 119
SAG Rules Regarding Work Hours For Minors — 120
Music Videos — 121

SPECIAL TEEN SECTION

ABOUT BEING SHOW BIZ TEENS
(Written By Salim Grant and Ebonie Smith)
Introduction — 125
Was There Life Before Show Business? — 125
The Audition — 126
Dealing With Disappointment — 127
The Competition — 128
The Balancing Act: School and Work — 129
Surviving Puberty:
   What Happens When You're Not Cute Anymore? — 130
Staying Grounded — 131
Association Breeds Assimilation — 132
The College Years — 133

CHAPTER 10
TEENAGERS
Modeling For Teens   135
Teen Male Models   136
Teens, It's Not How Old You Are ...   137
Entering That Awkward Stage   138
Early Maturity   139

CHAPTER 11
EDUCATIONAL ALTERNTIVES   *142*
Emancipation and Early High School Completion   143
The Studio Academy (North Hills Prep)   143
Independent Study Programs   143
Supplementing Your Child's Education With A Computer   144

CHAPTER 12
EARTHA ROBINSON DISCUSSES DANCE   *146*
DANCERS: REACHING A POINT OF READINESS   *149*
An Inside Look At Those Dynamic Dance Auditions   150
Learning To View Setbacks As Opportunities   152
Auditions Add To Experience   153

CHAPTER 13
INTERVIEW WITH LOU ADLER, A MUSIC LEGEND   *156*
SINGERS: IN PURSUIT OF A RECORD DEAL   *162*
But Can The Child Sing?   163
For Children With More Desire Than Talent   163
Preparing To Go Pro   165
Session Work As A Background Vocalist   166
Getting Ready To Audition For A Record Label   166
The Importance of Learning to Harmonize   167
Helpful Hints For Learning To Harmonize   168
Vocal Coaches and Practice Tapes   169
Putting Together Performance Routines   170
Singing With Choreography   171
Hanging out at the Hottest Dance Studios   171
Industry Professionals Spot Talent at Dance Studios   172
Seize Every Opportunity   173

Back-up Dancers	173
Creating A Look	175
Groups vs. Going Solo	176
Finding the Right Producer	177
Master-Apprentice Frustrations	178
Puberty and Male Vocalists	180
Getting Music In The Right Key	183
Paying Up Front v. Demo Spec Agreements	183

CHAPTER 14
WARDROBE: INVESTING IN TOOLS OF THE TRADE — *187*

Creating A "Look" For Your Child	187
Set Aside Specific Outfits For Auditions Only	188
Consult Your Agent on Appropriate Audition Attire	192
Getting to the Audition on Time	192

CHAPTER 15
NOW THAT YOU'VE BOOKED A JOB — *195*

Sharing Your Good News	195
Protect Your Child From Vicious Competitors	196
Playing it Safe to Avoid Accidents	198
Packing Basic Items to Take On The Set	199
Create a Check List The Night Before	201
On the Set: What to Expect	203
Avoiding Celebrity Hounds and Groupies	205

CHAPTER 16
RULES WERE MEANT TO MAKE LIFE EASIER AND MORE ORDERLY, NOT MORE DIFFICULT — *207*

SAG-AFTRA Rules Regarding Siblings On The Set	209
Too Many Rigid, Non-Thinkers In Charge	211
Dealing With The Assistant Director From Hell	211

CHAPTER 17
DEVELOPING COPING SKILLS ON THE SET — *215*

There is no Substitute for Self Esteem	215
Positive Problem Solving on the Set	218

Empowering Your Child By Setting Boundaries	219
The Best Defense Is No Defense	219
Those Brave Enough To Do The Right Thing	222
Believing In A Power Greater Than Yourself	223

CHAPTER 18
THE COMPETITION LIES WITHIN — 225

There Are No Actual Overnight Success Stories	226
Focus on Your Own Assets;	
Quit Worrying About The Competition	227
The Power of a Smile	228

CHAPTER 19
SLOW PERIODS: WORKING THROUGH THEM — 231

The Games People Play	232
So What Have You Done Lately?	232
Seeing Slow Periods As A Seam	
In The Cycle of Success	234
Creating Work On Your Own	235
Using Benefit Work To Create Your Own Facade	237
Working Your Way Out of Limbo Land	237
How Do I Handle Waiting Jitters?	239
Make Each Audition An Adventure	240
It's Easy To Become Jaded or Disillusioned	241

CHAPTER 20
MAKING THE MOVE TO L.A. — 244

Preparing For Our Summer In Los Angeles	245
Deciding to Make That Move	248
Necessities Once You've Arrived In The City	250
Housing	251
Cultivating the Right Attitude Towards The City	252

CHAPTER 21
WHAT IF I'M A SINGLE PARENT? — 255

How I Made It As a Working Mother	256
Yes, Some Single Stage Parents Work	257

Audition Drivers/Set Sitters	258
Hollywood Screen Parents Association	***259***
Guardians On The Set: Pitfalls To Look Out For	259

CHAPTER 22
CONTRACTS: WHAT TO ASK FOR UP FRONT — **262**

Small Considerations Can Become Major Issues	263
Billing and Screen Credits	264
Day Player v. Principal Player	265
Singers: Demo Spec Agreements	265
Singers: Production Company Contracts	266
Singers: Points, Merchandising and Publishing	269
Duration of Management Contracts	270
Oral Contracts & Canceling Contracts	271
Weigh All Offers Carefully	272

CHAPTER 23
THINKING ABOUT CHANGING AGENTS? — **275**

Remember To Do Your Part To Help The Agent Help You	277
Does Your Agency Make You Feel Like A Small Fish In A Big Pond?	279
What If The Agent Won't Take My Call?	280
Practical Considerations Before Changing Agents	280

CHAPTER 24
YES, RACISM IS ALIVE AND WELL — **284**

Too Apathetic To Do Anything	285
Two Shades Too Light, Or Two Shades Too Dark	287
Times, They Are A Changin'	288
Racism Within Races	289

CHAPTER 25
HOLLYWOOD CASTE SYSTEMS — **297**

Disregard For Mothers On The Set	297
Extras, Your Voice Deserves To Be Heard	300

CHAPTER 26
Roz Stevenson, Sr. Publicist, Universal Pictures
  Hollywood, Reveals Valuable Insights
  on Publicity For Children In Film   303
PUBLICITY AND PUBLIC RELATIONS   *307*

CHAPTER 27
BRACES, WORK PERMITS AND
UNEMPLOYMENT BENEFITS FOR MINORS   *311*
Clear and Removable Braces   311
Flippers   311
Work Permits For First Timers   312
For Renewals   313
Unemployment Benefits For Minors   313

APPENDIX   *314*
Hollywood Screen Parents Association   314
Performing Artists Unions (SAG and AFTRA)   314
On Location Education   314
The Studio Academy (North Hills Prep)   314
Performing Arts Programs (Los Angeles)   315
Recommended Reading List (Books and Tapes) 318
Glossary of Terms   320
Agents List (SAG Franchised for Los Angeles Area) 327

FOREWORD

Hollywood, the original creator and innovator in entertainment, continues to set trends that the rest of the world follows. Due to the global impact of advertising and the popularity of television and film, every major city in the U.S. and abroad is involved in some aspect of the entertainment industry (i.e., commercials, fashion, theater, local television and film). The material presented herein can be applied, for the most part, to any major city in America or abroad, and is not limited to Hollywood, unless specifically stated.

In order to create a book that went beyond simply *how to get started* in show business, I found myself wearing several hats composed of the following viewpoints: (1) the personal stage mom's perspective, with its concern for the child's self-esteem and emotional well being; (2) the manager's mindset, with its overriding interest in the child's potential for success; and (3) the experienced, inside industry observer of policies, unspoken rules, or idiosyncrasies. On occasion the viewpoints might appear to oppose each other. For instance, the stage mother might react differently to a situation involving her child than a manager would; whereas, an industry professional would view the same situation differently than a parent or manager. I worked to diffuse the potential for confusion by being as specific as possible.

For newcomers, industry terms are in bold within the chapter and defined in the glossary at the end of the book.

Regarding age levels: Unless specifically spelled out, the information provided in this book pertains to all age groups. When it applies to a specific age group such as infants, teenagers, young adults, etc., I make particular note of it.

With the exception of direct quotes, the views in this book are expressly, entirely and explicitly my own. I hope the reader will use this information in the spirit in which it is intended: to create positive, supportive and nurturing environments at home, school and work for child actors, in particular, and children in general.

Introduction

VISIONS OF HOLLYWOOD

The real Hollywood where people live and work and the Hollywood created in the minds of adoring fans are worlds apart in conception and reality. The bridge between the two is delicate and difficult to traverse.

Before moving to Los Angeles to further the acting careers of my two children, the perceptions I had of Hollywood were indistinct and enigmatic, clouded by images I had seen on the silver screen or read about in books, magazines and newspapers. Writers use an array of colorful and descriptive adjectives that paint vivid images of Hollywood such as: gossipy, glamorous, insecure, fantastic, incredibly rich, and magical. Some call it a "singularly secretive town." Although fascinated by the entire illusion, it was this *secretiveness* encircling the entertainment capital of the world that intrigued me most.

After accumulating over a decade of experience working with children in the industry, I felt compelled to dispel much of the secretiveness surrounding Hollywood by writing a book designed to pave the way for parents of aspiring and experienced child actors. I was motivated by the realization that the closest many hopefuls would ever get to the real world of entertainment is a whistle stop tour aboard the Universal Studios tram. *Show Biz Kids* allows readers to journey inside the lives of young performers who are well on the way toward realizing their dreams.

Even stage parents whose children have been working in show business for a while still experience confusion from time to time about how to find the most direct route to success in the entertainment field. It took a few years for me to work my way through the maze of Hollywood. Even now I find it easy to lose my way whenever I inadvertently step away from the straight and narrow path. When that happens it can take a lot of positive self talk and support to get back on track.

Until a parent or young performer accepts that the shortest distance between two points really is a straight line, the quest for success in Hollywood can become a long circuitous journey filled with road blocks and too many stops to ever get anywhere. For those determined, however, to seize an opportunity to become a part of the magic, myth and madness of Hollywood, this book provides light, insights and inspiration along the way.

The image that Hollywood created was larger than life and so unlike most towns in America that people became excited about its infinite possibilities which prompted many to answer the call to "Go West, young man" long after the Gold Rush was over.

My career as a children's manager began in Houston when I wrote an article titled, "Show Biz Kids...How to Get Your Child Started." At the time, my son and daughter appeared pretty regularly in print, on stage, and in television commercials in Texas. With growing confidence in the abilities of my two children, their agent began calling me looking for other kids in different age groups and categories who were *triple threats* (i.e., can sing, dance and act). After a few successful referrals, I earned a reputation for spotting and developing talent. Keep in mind that agents usually do not have time to advise or coach clients. An agent counts on parents to create and maintain a competitive edge for their children by teaching them at home or enrolling young performers in acting, dance, or voice lessons, where appropriate.

In due time I found myself inundated with strangers, friends, acquaintances, and relatives who wanted my help or advice in getting their child an agent. Parents who already had a talent agent conferred with me on how to sharpen audition skills so that their children could *book* more jobs. All too often, conversations and encounters with parents turned into marathon information sessions where I found myself giving out the same advice or answering the same questions over and over to each new parent. It did not take long to end up in a dilemma between my desire to help others and a lack of time in which to do so on an individual basis. Trying to help new parents find their way through the entertainment maze took up an inordinate amount of time, of which I already had little to spare, between a full time position at a law firm and part-time writing, teaching and editing assignments. I came to the conclusion that writing an article was the shortest distance between two points for me.

A few years later I found myself in the same predicament all over again after moving to Los Angeles. In particular, after the children and I appeared on *"Hard Copy"* and *"Inside Edition"* in segments entitled *"Twinkle, Twinkle Little Stars,"* and *"Child Stars."* Requests for information inundated me. People who recognized us from television stopped us on the street, in public places, or at auditions asking questions. Since my article needed to be updated and expanded I could not hand out copies in Los Angeles the way I did in Houston. That's when I made up my mind to set aside time at night to write a book for parents and young performers based upon my experiences.

With the incessant negative media focus on stage children who have gone wrong, I thought it might be a switch to hear about show business from the perspective of a Stage Mom/Children's Manager who has two hard working young performers of her own: Salim, a 17 year old college student who has co-starred in major feature films; appears as a series regular on NBC's "Saved By The Bell," has an international group album to his credit and is writing and producing his own a solo album. Thirteen year old Crystal co-starred in the feature film "Lawnmower Man 2." Her face has adorned magazine covers, billboards, and television. She also has a couple of dozen national and international commercials to her credit along with an international group album, and a soon to be released solo album. Crystal wrote and arranged the melodies to over half the songs on her debut solo album.

In *Show Biz Kids* I called upon the courage to tackle issues often brushed under the rug or only spoken of in hushed tones, bringing to the surface the prevalence of stereotypes, bias and discrimination against children and minorities in Hollywood. Not from a powerless explanation of: "here's this huge machine that controls, extorts and takes power away from us," rather, from the perspective of empowerment. The reader can choose to either learn from the situation or avoid the hazard entirely.

As a parent, I felt compelled to take a stand and speak out against situations that might destroy or diminish a child's self esteem or self-worth and examine situations that present pause for concern.

As an humanitarian, I found it important to address the existence of a caste system among actors and extras that would upset the sensibilities of anyone who correctly assumed that feudalism disappeared with the Dark Ages.

There were moments during the first draft of *Show Biz Kids* when I thought how valuable it would have been to have such a book available when we first arrived in Los Angeles. Knowing little of the city's subtleties or unspoken rules, in the beginning I found myself clueless and unsure where to turn for advice or help. Ultimately I had no choice but to rely on my own common sense. Naturally, I made a few mistakes along the way that I would rather have avoided. By piecing together and sharing my wisdom and experiences—both good and bad—I hope to help others avoid unnecessary headaches, hard-knocks, and stumbling blocks.

One of my primary objectives in *Show Biz Kids* was to recount important personal experiences that would provide the neophyte with an inside glance at the mechanics involved in the real world of children working hard to "make it" in show business. I wanted to present a step-by-step examination of how it is done without exaggerating or glamorizing the realities. In the process, I did not want to traumatize or dissuade aspiring amateurs.

Show Biz Kids was also designed to encourage parents and children who have struggled long and hard with little or no success, by pointing out ways that young performers might change their thinking or fine tune their approach in order to reap the rewards of their hard work and sacrifice.

Show Biz Kids moves the reader a few steps beyond the material currently available on the topic of children in show business. The book goes beyond simply telling how to get started in show business. That is not enough. After getting into the business, one needs to acquire survival skills in order to make it and stay successful in show business.

Show Biz Kids Quest for Success also allows the reader to gain practical insight from my knowledge as a "Stage Mom" and children's manager. The book is candid, open and honest. It is written in a friendly, conversational tone, filled with positive, informative, practical and helpful ideas designed to lessen the learning curve, mitigate fear of the unknown, and encourage those that are daring, resourceful and undaunted.

After completing this book readers should find themselves knowledgeable enough to decide if: (1) their child is suited for this business; (2) the parent can make a commitment; or (3) the family is willing to make the sacrifices necessary to support a child in the business until he or she becomes self-supporting; which can take a while sometimes.

After completing this book, the newcomer should disseminate enough information to discern whether or not he or she is simply a curiosity seeker, or someone who possesses the necessary dedication, selflessness, and love for the entertainment profession to give their child a realistic opportunity at success in Hollywood.

Above all, I hope that readers will complete *Show Biz Kids, Quest for Success* with a new found appreciation for how irrefutably parents and children must work together, and what a wonderful achievement for the entire family when a child succeeds in spite of the odds in favor of failure.

Chapter 1

STAGE MOMS: MYTH VS. REALITY

Mothers are frequently put in a position of taking an unpopular stand in order to protect their kids. It's one of the reasons they get a bum rap. -Diane Schroder, Rick Schroder's Mom ("The Hollywood Reporter" Nov. 12, 1990)

Unfair and inaccurate myths continue to persist that haunt and frustrate many "Stage Mothers." The mere title tends to dredge up images of a "Mommy Dearest" beating her child to make the innocent abused go on stage and perform. There also exists a common belief that the child does not want to enter show business at all; that the mother is living vicariously through the child, or that the parent is creating self-fulfilling fantasies through the little actor or actress. The most damaging image of all is that of a parent exploiting and mismanaging the child's money. Nancy Randle in an article entitled "A New Generation of Stage Mothers," ("The Hollywood Reporter,"11-12-90) found that *"One of the most common ulterior motives attributed to stage parents is greed. It is a belief that has been reinforced by some high-profile lawsuits."* Randle found that *"Like all negative stereotypes, this one deprives these women of their individuality. It denies the complicated* nature of the parent's commitment and it can muddy the truth by assuming that the motivations of a few bad parents apply to each one."

Kevin McDermott, who runs an acting workshop for kids in Los Angeles, supports Randle's viewpoint in the following quote: *"everyone gives parents a bad rap, but most of them would not be doing it if their kids hadn't bugged them."* (see Zoe F. Carter's *Premiere Magazine* article "Baby, It's You")

Los Angeles children's agent Judy Savage points out that *"there's never been a successful child actor who didn't have at least one committed adult—either a mother, a father or a manager—behind them."* Savage, in tracing the origins of the negative image stage moms must combat anytime the subject of child actors comes up, says that *"It started in the days of the big studios, when Shirley Temple and a very small group of child stars existed."* However, once an individual gets past the media hype, or becomes personally acquainted with stage parents, they are likely to agree with Judy Savage that the negative image of *"stage mothers is inaccurate. It's a small percentage of bad parents that get the publicity. I have found over the last 20-25 years that 99% of them are really terrific parents who have their child's best interest at heart."* (see Nancy Randle's article)

Mary Grady, who has over thirty years experience as a children's agent, feels that *"We have a more intelligent group of mothers"* today. One of the reasons that the negative stage mom image continues to persist, however, has to do with the fact that *"Mothers are frequently put in a position of taking an unpopular stand in order to protect their kids. It's one of the reasons they get a bum rap,"* says Rick Schroder's mother, Diane Schroder. (See Nancy Randle's article)

Once a child becomes a star, Hollywood would have the world believe the child got there all by himself or herself with the family as nothing more than a nuisance to be tolerated, if not dispensed with all together. More often than not, the movie studio or t.v. network would prefer that parents relinquish all parental authority while on the set, allowing the producer or director to have complete control. That's where conflict often enters. Not so much because of parental inter-ference on the set, but because of the fact that parents are often treated like an extra leg that's in everybody's way.

For the most part, stage parents that I've observed tend to keep a respectful distance on the set, stepping in when the situation calls for parental input or assistance. Those parents who do make a nuisance out of themselves (by getting in the way, becoming too demanding or pretentious) soon receive a call from the child's agent complaining about the situation.

Ironically, it would amaze most people to find out how much parents have to sacrifice, in terms of careers and savings accounts, to get their children into the business and the stressful choices one must make in order to accommodate other family members when a child has to go on location to film a movie.

In actuality, the stage mothers that Nancy Randle interviewed all stated that what they wanted most was their children's happiness. With that in mind Randle concludes: *"perhaps it is time to open our minds and peel back the layers of the stage parent stereotype to explore what lies beneath."*

THE FUTURE HAS NEVER LOOKED BRIGHTER FOR SHOW BIZ KIDS

The demand [for kids] is greater than ever before. Practically every show has a kid in it. Producers want kids to watch television, and kids love to watch kids. -Meg Liberman, Casting Director (from "The Hollywood Reporter" Nov. 12, 1990)

Over the past decade, movies featuring children have become booming business rather than the exception to the rule. The list of films featuring children continues to grow, including: *Angus, Lawnmower Man 1 & 2, The Little Rascals, The Little Princess, The Secret Garden, Home Alone 1 & 2, Problem Child 1 & 2, Mikey and Me, Sidekicks, Forever Young, Curly Sue, Radio Flyer,*

The Mighty Ducks 1 & 2, Uncle Buck, Parenthood, Ghost Dad, Hook, Stand By Me, Goonies, The Boy Who Could Fly, Harrison Ford's Indiana Jones series, etc. Like *The Never Ending Story*, the good news is we don't have to worry about an end in sight for films featuring children as long as there is money to be made at the box office. Moreover, the exceptional event of an eleven year old winning a 1994 Oscar for Best Supporting Actress in the film "The Piano" only increased the search for more Academy Award Winning child performers. Hollywood is ever ready to capitalize on success. Anytime a movie is a box office smash one can almost count on a sequel and/or a television series based on the movie.

The fact that historically only a small percentage of child actors transitioned successfully into adult roles made it difficult to find examples of young performers who had not been sensationalized by the media for taking a bad turn in life once they grew up. In Zoe F. Carter's "Premiere Magazine" article, cited earlier, the writer found that if you *"ask almost any producer, casting director, agent, or parent what happens to former child stars, they'll say, 'Look at Ron Howard. Look at Jodie Foster."* Carter found it difficult to get anyone she interviewed to come up with names of other high profile child actors who had fared well after the fame. America watched on television and film as Ron Howard went from a successful child and teen actor to a sought after director with hit movies to his credit such as "Parenthood," "Cocoon" and "Apollo 13." A precipitating factor in his success, however, was the fact that as a teen, Ron was fortunate enough to land a role on a second hit televison show, "Happy Days" which allowed him the venue to grow into an adult on television. Jodie Foster had similar luck that enabled her to progress from child actor to adult star in movies like "Silence of The Lambs" and "The Accused."

Traditionally there simply have not been enough television shows featuring teens in order to accommodate young actors as they grew up. Fortunately, more pilots that feature teens and kids are being written, produced and picked up by networks, providing far more transitional positions today than ever before for child actors to continue working into adulthood.

Examples of other child actors who have fared well include: Kim Fields, from the television series "Facts of Life," who now stars in the adult sitcom "Living Single." Michael J. Fox made it big in television and film. Drew Barrymore made a triumphant comeback as an adult film star after her struggle with childhood alcoholism. Brooke Shields never really stopped working as she matured. Tony Dow and Jerry Mathers from the original "Leave It To Beaver" went on to star as adults in the new television version of "Leave It To Beaver." Tony also produces and directs for television. But more importantly, after hailing from one of the most popular television shows of its era, Tony Dow and Jerry Mathers grew into fine young adults. My point is: who's to say that those child stars who went bad would not have chosen that path anyway?

Jackie Briskey, casting director for "Growing Pains" believes that *"there's much more work for kids these days...than when I started in this business...I think it's due to the success of movies like 'The Breakfast Club and 'Sixteen Candles'—the whole Brat Pack thing ... that's what really started the youth trend in television."* (Kyle Counts, *The Search For Appealing Kids, The Hollywood Reporter* Nov. 12, 1990). Joy Stevenson, agent for Herb Tannen and Associates, agrees with Jackie Briskey: *"It's an exciting time for children and young adults."* (Kyle Counts, "Discovering Kids Willing To Make A Commitment," *The Hollywood Reporter* Nov. 11, 1990). Brian Reilly, one of the producers of the movie, "Don't Tell Mom The Babysitter's Dead," adds that, *"We baby boomers are always looking for entertainment to take kids to and I think you'd have to have your head in the sand not to realize that there is a huge interest in those projects with kids in them."* (see, Zoe F. Carter's article)

Increased demand as well as opportunities for children generates a steady influx of "wide-eyed wonders" whose parents haven't a clue as to the real world of show business. They come to Hollywood uninformed, eager and ill-prepared; full of "Great

Expectations" about money and opportunities. Usually, these ideas have little basis in the harsh realities of the industry.

A WORD OF CAUTION ABOUT UNREALISTIC EXPECTATIONS

We tend to expect that one window of opportunity will launch you. Well, I learned that it usually doesn't happen that way. It just didn't happen for me. So I kept pounding the pavement until opportunities began to happen. —Brock Peters, Actor (from "Screen Actor" magazine, The Screen Actors Guild, Summer 1991, Vol 30, No. 1)

The common belief among newcomers to the business in instant stardom and riches can bring with it disillusionment or disappointment if success does not happen right away. Usually such people come to Hollywood thinking that they are going to make it big in a couple of months. Often success takes time.

Movie studios and production companies are in business to make money. Each movie venture is an expensive gamble based on calculated risks. It would not be a smart move financially for a studio to invest heavily in an unknown when millions are lost each year on highly bankable names.

Of course sometimes the unexpected happens. Who could have guessed that "Home Alone" would become such a global phenomenon? *"Home Alone' has been called a wish fulfillment movie for both kids and parents, just as 'Pretty Woman' was a wish-fulfillment movie for men and women who fantasized about romance,"* says Pat Jordan in her article "Mac Attack" ("Special Report on Personalities" magazine, Winter, 1991).

No doubt studio executives at Universal regretted not signing Macauley Culkin for a second movie after "Uncle Buck," which, according to a Los Angeles newspaper, only earned Culkin five figures. As a result, Universal's oversight and loss became 20th Century's gain when they signed Culkin for "Home Alone." The point is, it wasn't Culkin's first movie "Uncle Buck," nor his second,

"Home Alone" that made him rich. It was the sequel to "Home Alone" that made Culkin rich. And he did quite a few other movies in-between the sequel. If Culkin's agent had been able to surmise what a success he would become after "Uncle Buck" it certainly wouldn't have taken a sequel for Culkin's salary to reach four million, which might seem an implausible jump considering that he only earned $150,000 for the first "Home Alone" movie.

Often actors are too eager to dispense with common sense, ignoring that, as in any business, one must "pay dues." Granted, success many come swiftly at times. But more often than not, it doesn't. Usually success ensues after many small accomplishments that eventually lead to "the big break" all actors strive for. Or, success may consist of a string of several notable achievements that add up to one huge sensation.

Actor Brock Peters, after winning the Screen Actor's Guild 1990 Achievement Award, appeared in an interview in the Screen Actor's Guild quarterly magazine, "Screen Actor." He pointed out that *"we tend to expect that one window of opportunity will launch you. Well, I learned that it usually doesn't happen that way. It just didn't happen for me. So I kept pounding the pavement until opportunities began to happen."* Peters was referring to his role in the successful release of the movie, "Carmen Jones." Later, after he was cast as Crown in "Porgy and Bess," he felt more optimistic. *"After that film, I thought, well, surely now I've got a really good opportunity, a springboard in this."* But there was virtually nothing until "To Kill A Mocking Bird." And even after that powerful and successful movie, Peters again found that *"it was still rough sledding from one role to another."*

Lou Gosset, Jr. commented, in a television special about blacks who have paved the road to Hollywood, that he had never been so disappointed or so out of work after he won an Oscar for his role in "An Officer and A Gentleman." Receiving a wonderful accolade, such as an Academy Award, does not necessarily signify that one has reached the pinnacle of success. No such condition exists in this business. Everybody wants to know what you've done lately ... *as in the last few weeks.* Human nature compels the actor or actress to expect offers to come pouring in after such acclaim. Unfortunately, and particularly if one is a minority, it does not always happen. Eventual rewards are reserved for those who stick it out.

Naturally, exceptions do occur and it is wonderful when that happens, but don't count on it. Nobody in Hollywood has been able to come up with an accurate indicator of public tastes and which "sleeper" will become the next box office success.

AN INSIDE LOOK AT BEGINNING SALARIES

Unfortunately, salaries in show business are not attached directly to the caliber of performance and are not distributed equitably. Everything is negotiable and a performer's price depends on how "hot" he or she happens to be at the time. The salaries of Jaleel White (i.e., "Family Matters"), Elijah Wood (i.e., "Huckleberry Finn") and Macauley Culkin are exceptional for child actors. For example, Many co-stars of top rated television shows and films earn only a fraction of what the stars make even when their roles are pivotal to the success of the star's performance. For television; ratings and the star of the show count; for movies, it's box office dollars and the star of the movie. Any way you look at it, it's about the mighty dollar.

For actors or actresses who are SAG eligible performers (i.e. Screen Actor's Guild), regardless of their age, beginning base salaries for a television series or a feature film range anywhere from current SAG minimum of approximately $1,800 per week, to about $8,000 per week. The wide range has to do with whether the role is regular, recurring, lead or supporting and how much the child earned on the last job or offer received. For instance, if your child made it to the final screen test for a television series, network will require that you sign a contract that locks your child into a specific salary, for example, $5,000 per episode. Even if the network decides to go with someone else, that contract sets a precedent and the next time your child goes up to network (whether it's the same network or a different one) for the same type of show (i.e., either a prime time drama, comedy, talk show or a Saturday morning show) they have to match or exceed your last offer. If the last offer, however, was for a prime time drama and your child is up for a Saturday morning show, then the rule does not apply because all shows are not equal -- prime time pays premium prices. With a television series, the pay scale rises each season and is based on 13 or 26 weeks of filming, depending on how many episodes the network picks up.

Pay scales vary greatly from one medium to another. For commercials, SAG performers recieve approximately $500 per day; whereas, *print work* (i.e., magazines, billboards, and newspapers) is about $125 per hour in Los Angeles, with about one hour the average for most shoots. If it's a national billboard or print ad children usually get a flat fee somewhere between $1,000 and $3,000 for that job.

Session singers are not covered under SAG guidelines. Their pay scale is governed by The American Federation of Television and Radio Artists (AFTRA), which has a slightly lower pay scale than SAG. For example, singers who do group session work on albums often average about $40 to $60 per hour, with pay based on a sliding scale -- the more people, the less pay. Solo session singers receive in excess of $100 per hour, or a flat rate of between $300 to $600 per song. AFTRA provides a list of pay scales for members. There is a small fee for non-members.

Hollywood tends to undervalue a child's right to earn the same pay as adults, which can keep a child earning SAG minimum for a while. That is, until he or she gets a hit movie, album, or t.v. show. Still, the allure of fame and riches keeps people pouring into Hollywood. They arrive to claim their piece of the dream, their star on the Walk of Fame, or their moment of glory when the folks back home call, bubbling over with pride and excitement over seeing someone they know on television or the big screen.

POINTS TO PONDER:

1. Today, there are more opportunities available for children in television, film and commercials than ever before in the history of Hollywood.

2. A child should become an entertainer because he or she has talent and enjoys performing for others — not just for the potential financial reward or glory. The business of entertaining the public should be a reward in and of itself.

3. Beginning salaries for children tend to be lower than adults in the entertainment field. Initially, income is sporadic and rarely enough to live on. Many young actors do succeed, however and make considerable amounts of money, which is the lure that keeps so many people coming to Hollywood each year; an attraction similar to the Gold Rush of 1849.

4. For Stage Parents, the good news is that negative stereotypes against them are gradually changing as a result of positive support by agents and managers along with a new breed of stage moms who now refuse to accept inappropriate treatment.

5. The bad news is that there still exists a significant enough amount of bias in the industry against Stage Parents to merit mention.

Chapter 2

WHAT AGENTS AND CASTING DIRECTORS LOOK FOR

In Hollywood, there's a man many call king. Some think he's crafty and ruthless. Others say he's a brilliant visionary, destined to control realms beyond the movies. -Alan Citron- from "Unraveling the Myth of Super-Agent Mike Ovitz" (LOS ANGELES TIMES MAGAZINE, July 26, 1992)

Whenever children express interest on their own about getting into show business industry professionals take delight in seeing their eyes light up into bright excited little smiles. The same thing applies if an agent or manager asks children directly if they would like to be in pictures. On the other hand, no one wants to risk signing children who walk in the door with their head fixed on the floor, with a finger in the mouth, or who respond to questions in monosyllables or a shrug of the shoulders. Although each agent, casting director and manager differs in terms of what they specifically look for or expect in talent, as the following comments reveal, they all share common professional ideals and expectations.

Suzi Smith, formerly with MGA and The Bobby Ball Agency, now head of the children's department for TGI-Bloom, says that, *"naturalness is the key."* She prefers children who have self-initiative and can *"think for themselves ... not just say what their parents tell them to say."* Moreover, when she interviews a child, she likes it when they can *"walk in a room, start a conversation with an adult and carry that conversation, possibly adding thoughts of their own."*

Vicki Light of The Light Co. said that *"If a young person is really confident, excited and dedicated to doing this, then [representation] is something you just gamble on."* Estelle Hertzbert, who heads up Twentieth Century's youth division, revealed that she seeks out kids with *"high energy, lots of spark and out going personalities--kids who are willing to make a commitment."* Mary Grady, owner of The Mary Grady Agency (MGA) says that she looks for children and young adults with *"warmth, honesty and natural performing ability. I look for real, sincere kids, not the kind who pose through their interviews."* (Kyle Counts "Discovering Kids Willing To Make A Commitment," *The Hollywood Reporter*, 11-12-90)

COMMERCIALS:

"Beyond having an identifiable LOOK that makes them easy to cast, children and young adults looking to make their mark commercially and theatrically need to possess character traits that have nothing to do with white teeth or high cheekbones."
(Kyle Counts)

Bonnie Ventis, children's commercial agent at JHR, in her interview with Kyle Counts, agrees with the view expressed above. She feels that in order for a child to be successful in this business he or she needs to possess *"the same kind of qualities that people need to have in life to be successful. They should be fairly intelligent, hard workers, very gregarious and they should enjoy what they do."* Bonnie's partner, Jody Alexander, who handles the children's commercial division for JHR added that a child needs *"a belief in one's own ability, an inner strength and determination. I

What Agents and Casting Directors Look For

believe the healthier and happier an individual is, the more willing they are to bite the bullet and go for it."

Bob Preston, children's agent at Cunningham, Escott, Dipene (CED) agrees on the importance of a child having a healthy attitude. *"He or she has got to, at all times, be up, confident and positive -- otherwise he's going to get shot down."* In this book, I have devoted an entire section to the importance of having good self-esteem and a healthy attitude towards success and competition. (See Chapter 17, "Developing Coping Skills On The Set," subsection, "There Is No Substitute for Self-Esteem").

At commercial auditions I've seen many parents shake their heads in resignation over determining what criterion casting directors and their clients use to select children for commercials. Sometimes casting directors and their clients do not actually know what they want until they see it. The exception involves commercials requiring a special skill, such as dance. Even then, a child's ability in that area may or may not be a decisive factor. Let me explain:

My daughter filmed a shoe commercial with five other children, all of whom had to perform solo dance steps during the filming. All but one of the children were excellent dancers. By accident I discovered why they chose the non-dancing child. I over heard the producers talk while the little girl filmed her solo dance scene. They were absolutely delighted by the child's earnestness and inhibition. The little girl's wild, uncoordinated, jerky dance movements were executed with such zest, sincerity and total abandon that one could not help but giggle while watching her. She did not resemble the typical child who could not dance and knew that she could not dance. There was no way you could have convinced this child that she couldn't dance.

In another example, my son filmed a commercial with a group of five kids who had to learn a dance combination from a choreographer the morning of the shoot. The mother of one of the children was concerned because her child was not a dancer. Again, that did not stop this little boy. He imitated the steps as best he could and performed them with a big, wide-eyed smile that every one found charming.

Elissa Fisher, head of the children's commercial and print division at It Kids, specializes in "exotic" talent (i.e., her client list includes a high ratio of racially mixed children) and goes after a "LOOK." She searches for *"kids you wouldn't normally see on T.V.,"* children who have *"something different"* about themselves. Moreover, she knows *"immediately"* if the child has what she's looking for. Otherwise, she won't take him or her, because she *"can't push for a child unless [she's] head over heels about him."* Once Elissa finds that perfect, hybrid blend, she puts everything she's got into promoting her talent. She finds that, *"it's a great feeling when advertisers ask for traditional looking children, but end up booking not so traditional, [racially] mixed kids. They spice up the commercial world."*

In Kyle Counts' article, Natalie Rosson, of the Natalie Rosson Agency says that *"a good percentage of [a child actor's success] is timing."* Timing may refer to a child being the right age, look and type for a particular part when it hits the market, or timing, as in knowing when and where to pause for effect in delivering ones lines. Ruth Hansen, head of the children's division, at the Harry Gold Agency says that she is drawn to children with *"a lot of personality, the kind that light up the room."*

Once a child has an agent, the most important point for the parent to remember is what agent, Evelyn Schultz said: "No agent, no matter how well connected, can guarantee their talent a job." The agent's primary responsibility involves setting up the audition. The child has to go in and convince the casting director that he or she is the best candidate for the job. (See Kyle Counts' article)

PRINT WORK:

With models, a popular misconception exists regarding the fact that they have *"no need for personality"* as long as they've got the *"look."* Stacy Burns, who formerly ran the children's print department for JHR, begs to differ. *"As in commercials,"* she says, *"the child needs to possess something special that will come across in print -- especially in the eyes or in the smile -- a certain charisma or energy"* that will give them an edge in the competitive print market.

Remember that print work tends to be somewhat seasonal with a tendency to peak during Christmas time, back to school, and Easter. In addition, certain areas of the country tend to focus more heavily on national print work that others. New York City heads the list, with Chicago, Los Angeles and Dallas making significant contributions. Orlando is beginning to create a noticeable impression on the children's print market. Keep in mind that all major cities run large editorial print ads in the Sunday newspapers, with advertisements for local department stores; so there's always some work to be found in every city. The difference is the amount of pay, which is significantly lower for regional print ads. For example, an ad in a local newspaper might pay only $50 to 100 per hour, whereas an ad in a national magazine could pay in excess of $1,000 for the same amount of work and time as the regional ad.

No agent, no matter how well connected, can guarantee their talent a job. -*Evelyn Schultz, L. A. Children's Agent (from "The Hollywood Reporter" 11-12-90)*

All print agents have certain clients who will call them exclusively to book talent through their agency. This means that clients signed to that agency do not have to audition for the job because the agent selects the models according to size, age, ethnicity or gender. Otherwise, "go sees" can involve a lot of running around, displaying a portfolio or trying on clothes without booking a job. And when a model does book a job, unless its a national ad, most print jobs only pay for one or two hours of work, which does not add up to a lot of money when one counts driving time and the number of "go sees" involved in booking the job.

With that in mind, if one wants to focus on modeling, to the exclusion of commercials or theatrical work, sign with an agency that specializes in fashion, editorial and product print. Look for an agent who also has a strong client base and a long standing reputation in the print field. This type of agency will be able to offer significantly more jobs that the client can book directly without having to run around all over town on "go sees." Moreover, if one is truly serious about modeling he or she should build up a portfolio with regional or local ads first, then send copies of the portfolio to print agents in New York. (Call the Screen Actors Guild in New York and get a list of agents from them). After getting a New York agent one should consider making a move to the East Coast in order to maximize the most of a career based exclusively on modeling.

Craig Schulze of the Colleen Cler Modeling and Talent Agency, which is the largest and most prominent children's modeling agency in Los Angeles, reminds parents that they need to start early because *"by the time a girl grows out of a size 10 and a boy out of a size 12-14, there is very little editorial or fashion work available to keep the child busy or the parent happy. In particular for girls. At that point some product print work is still available in girls sizes 12, but very little."*

Once a girl or boy outgrows their size, the natural progression is for the agent to focus on commercial or theatrical work, which can tide youngsters through their teen years provided they do not grow awkward or overweight. Colleen Cler pointed out that with long term clients, she rarely has to worry about extra weight during puberty because those *"parents whose children have been with me for a while are conscious of the importance of good diet and exercise."* Moreover, Colleen's clients know that after children outgrow their sizes very little print work is available for them until they're older. It's the new parents who come in to interview with Colleen who do not know the importance of maintaining a *"healthy looking weight"* (i.e., not *"too thin"* or *"too heavy"*). In addition, Colleen added that *"some new parents bring children in to interview with me fresh off the playground, dirty and unkempt. This does not present the child in the best possible light and certainly does not make a good impression on the agent."*

Of the many new faces that they see, Colleen Cler *"only signs about 1% of them because we already have a large client base of over 500 children in all age groups and categories, each of whom work regularly. Even though this number may sound alarming to some parents who fear their child might get lost in the shuffle* within an agency our size, we are a family owned business and have a personal relationship with each of our clients. We know every parent and child on a first name basis."

Craig Schulze, Colleen's husband, points out that when they do sign someone new it's "*due mostly to attrition that results when a child has out grown a category, or someone has moved, leaving a spot available.*" Moreover, their agency receives an excessive number of telephone inquiries each week from parents "*calling to ask if we received the pictures, or to request that we return the photos when we're done because the pictures are special or unique.*" In their anxiousness to hear if the agent is interested, such parents fail to realize that if the agent is interested they will call. In addition if a parent wants photos returned they should include a self addressed stamped envelope for this purpose.

NEWBORNS AND TODDLERS

It is somewhat easier to start toddlers and pre-school children out modeling, as opposed to commercials or theatrical work first, because so little is required of them: a nice clean look, cooperativeness, a good temperament, and the ability to smile, mimic and follow basic directions. For the most part, all that's expected of an infant is contentment, curiosity and cuteness because crying babies are easy to find.

Craig points out that although the Colleen Cler Modeling and Talent Agency takes babies from newborn on up that they do not "*require that the parents bring a baby in until they're at least six months of age--snapshots will do.*" He also emphasizes that "*very few calls come in for babies under six months of age.*" When such calls do come in their agency usually calls managers to help them find babies in the newborn to six month category.

WHAT CASTING DIRECTORS LOOK FOR

THEATRICAL: There does appear to be more precision or predictability in casting talent for theatrical roles in film and television as opposed to commercials. Actual acting ability, experience and the right look account for a large part of the decision making process. **Breakdowns** for commercials are not very descriptive and include little more than age range, ethnicity and sex of the child. Whereas for theatrical calls, the **Breakdown Service** usually provides a more detailed physical description of the character type as well as the personality. As a result, fewer people actually make the initial elimination process to audition for T.V. and film than for commercials.

As for special skills in theatrical work, the same criterion used for commercials seems to apply. For instance, the movie, "Ghost Dad," required that the young boy have a magician's skills. When my son got the part the director simply hired a magician to teach Salim the magic tricks he needed for the role. There were young hopefuls that auditioned for the movie who already had magician skills. Salim, however, had the requisite amount of experience and fit the type they were looking for, making skills secondary.

There's usually really only one child that's right for the part. Mali Finn, Casting Director (from *"Baby, It's You"* by Zoe F. Carter, *Premiere Magazine*, Nov. '91)

Regarding making the right casting decision, Finn paraphrases John Schlesinger [the director should be able to] *"determine the essence of the character and then find the actor who embodies that essence."*

Writer Zoe F. Carter, found that *"casting directors usually begin by looking at kids in the business--the ones who already have an agent and some work experience."* In keeping with the no hard and fast rules in this business, however, there are those directors who prefer to hire unseasoned talent, *"especially in commercials or sitcoms,"* says Carter. Such directors feel that some children who have worked a lot no longer have the *"unadulterated child like quality from which a pure and naturalistic performance can be carved."* Michael Gross, producer of the movie "Beethoven" told Zoe F. Carter in her article that *"you can get a lot of ruined ten-year-olds in this business."*

What Agents and Casting Directors Look For

Casting director, Robin Lippin, who casts for "Saved By The Bell" and "Carol & Company" revealed that *"producers are looking for personalities, whether they're ethnic or non-ethnic. They want someone different."* Lippin does not make a distinction between the process she uses for casting a young adult role (i.e. over the age of 16) or a kid's role. She says that she *"looks for that actor who's interesting, bright, and takes a different approach to a part. You want him to be really appealing, someone you think people would want to watch week after week. If it's a comedy, you look for somebody with great timing who makes you laugh."* (See Kyle Counts' article)

Susan Vash, casting director for "Ferris Bueller," in Kyle Counts' article said that she likes to keep *"an eye out for kids who have something a little quirky, something special--not your average, run-of-the-mill, commercial-looking cute kid."* Many people in Hollywood rely on their intuition, instincts or initial reaction to a child in making their decision. Vash says that, *"the second that somebody special walks in the room, I get this excited feeling in my stomach that tells me I know they're going to be good ... there's a sparkle, an energy and a kind of charisma that not that many people have. It's what makes a star."* Kyle Counts says that *"while triple-threat moppets were once the rage, casting directors today look for authenticity in the kids they hire."* For instance, when Lippin cast the lead in the movie "Bingo" she looked for someone *"who had an orphan-like quality and who was a little bit of a misfit. We didn't want a perfect looking kid; we wanted someone who was appealing, yet had a quirkiness about him."* Of course the change in trend regarding triple threats, which Counts refers to, seems to apply more for dramatic or character roles. It is not only helpful, but necessary, in other areas of the industry, such as musicals, commercials or theater, that a child have the ability to sing, dance and act.

Joanne Kohler, casting director for "Full House" and "The Family Man," stated in Kyle Counts' article that she is attracted to "real' kids. She adds that she has *"never really cared for cutsey, stagy, plastic children."* She prefers *"kids who are unaffected by the business and who look like the kids I met at my friend's house over the weekend."* Meg Liberman shares this viewpoint. She says that her producers tell her that they *"don't want a sitcom kid,"* they want *"to see something they can relate to."*

Counts found that *"casting a little girl for a lead in a feature film can be trying."* For instance, in "Curly Sue," Janet Hirshenson of the Casting Company, stated that *"we didn't need just a cute little girl, we needed a very smart, funny kid who could really act."* Hirshenson confirmed that *"Cute in commercials is one thing, but often what they're looking for in commercials is exactly the opposite of what we're looking for."* Of course, this does not mean that the industry excludes cute kids, because Hirshenson adds that: *"We're always looking for cute people who can act. They don't have to be devastatingly handsome or gorgeous, but you're looking for a sparkle there. I'm more likely going to need that more than a plain kid that can act."* Hirshenson's partner, Jane Jenkins, clarifies that, *"a pretty face is not enough."*

One point I always have to remind parents of is the fact that children do grow, mature and change. Just because the child cannot act, sing or dance this year, does not mean that he will be unable to do so a year or two from now. Especially if the child takes classes around other talented kids or associates with them. Children tend to rise to the occasion and keep up with their peers. Valerie McCaffrey, director of feature casting at Universal Studios, agrees with this position. In Kyle Counts' article, Valerie McCaffrey revealed that it is *"important to see kids every so often; even if you think they may not be exactly right for a role; they may just walk in and blow you away six months later."* Joanne Kohler agrees that *"some kids get much better as they get older."*

It used to be difficult to make the transition from television to feature films. In the industry, film is considered more prestigious work. Casting directors like McCaffrey, feel that *"familiarity plays a significant role"* in casting feature films with roles for young adults. She feels that it has to do with *"recognizability factor, and the fact that producers sometimes feel more secure with someone who has had a lot of experience, as opposed to going with someone unknown."*

What Agents and Casting Directors Look For

Familiarity and recognizability in a television sitcom in and of itself does not insure that your child will be cast in a feature. Joanne Kohler points out further that a child's resume does not impress her. It's the performance she gets from him when he comes in to audition. She says that she's *"seen kids on a TV series who are just wonderful, that I read at one time and didn't think much of. Kids have good days and bad days, like everyone else."*

Kim Door, who worked for nine years as a casting director for The Arthur Company, finds that the same qualities she looked for as a casting director carry over in her selection process as head of the children's department at The Bobby Ball Agency. Kim looks for children who are *"focused,"* not someone *"who is more interested in what's on my desk or outside the window."* The question that Kim asks herself is whether or not *"the child is present (in the audition) and able to remain in the moment,"* as opposed to some one who is *"too easily distracted."* For auditions, Kim recommends that parents *"teach their children to listen and respond with their whole bodies, not just their ears and voices; eyes are important."* To aid in this process, she adds that parents should encourage *"children to take note of whom they are speaking to as well as who is speaking to them."* Moreover, children should learn to participate in and *"watch life around them."* Because it is *"the child's imagination that we want to capture, not merely his ability to mimic adults."* Kim suggests that parents encourage children *"to read, use their imagination and enjoy being a child."*

Kimberly Hardin, Casting Director for Jackie Brown-Karman & Associates states that the needs of each particular role dictate what they look for in a child. For example, when her office auditioned boys to play Michael Jackson at different ages in the television movie, The Jackson Family, "An American Dream" they not only looked for boys *"who could sing and dance, but ones with dramatic acting ability as well."* For children too young to read, they try to find a child *"who follows directions well."* Young children also need to *"assimilate, understand and mimic the director's instructions."*

In Counts' research on finding appealing kids, he concluded that *"the challenge remains to find fresh, new, unspoiled talent.*

Depending on the role involved, looks may be less important than the special quality."

This special quality was captured well in E. Jean Carroll's article "Try Out Blow Out" for "Special Report on Personalities" magazine (Winter 1991) where she describes a **cattle call** covered as a reporter. During this audition, Carroll and the people in charge, became captivated by a little two year old African-American child who possessed a *"madly captivating deep voice and a wiggly little body."* The child was dressed in a cute, trendy little outfit and completely at ease in the moment. When she was asked to repeat something the child turned out to be a perfect mimic. In fact, the writer related that the little girl *"jumps up and down and chuckles when she says"* her lines. Carroll adds that the directors become so taken with the child that they *"look as if they are about to throw themselves at the feet of the annihilatingly adorable little thing and worship her as the female Buddha."* What impressed Carroll most about the child, however, was that the little girl turned to her, spoke and asked: *"What's your name?"* Carroll explains that the significance of the little girls question was the fact that *"she's the only child out of 328 to remark on the existence of another person on the planet."*

What Agents and Casting Directors Look For

POINTS TO PONDER:

1. *Commercial auditions rarely specify more than age, ethnicity and gender, making it difficult to determine what casting directors and their clients want.*

2. *In general, commercial casting directors search for a look, a sparkle in the eyes, animated facial expressions or a particular energy level in actors who audition.*

3. *Theatrical breakdowns specify personality and detailed character descriptions making them easier to prepare for.*

4. *In many instances theatrical casting directors search for actors who embody the essence of the character.*

5. *Acting coaches and managers are helpful in preparing for theatrical auditions.*

6. *Those interested in modeling only should consider moving to New York City, which has the largest market for national editorial, product and fashion ads. First, however, build up a portfolio from your hometown with local and regional print ads.*

Chapter 3

BECOMING "MONEY IN THE BANK"

As dirty as it gets, it's the best thing that's ever happened to me.
Jeremy Miller of "Growing Pains" when asked the question: "Knowing what you do about this industry, do you want to keep acting?" (Special Report On Personalities, "It's A Jungle Gym Out There" by Stephen Talbot, Winter '91)

Acquiring an agent or manager on your own can "challenge" the parent and child's staying capacity. To make the search go smoother and faster, work on building your child's courage and confidence before setting up interviews. Problems tend to minimize themselves when viewed as challenges as opposed to obstacles.

Although workshops and seminars attended by agents are good opportunities, they offer no guarantees. If your child is not chosen the first time, try again. Persistence pays off. Keep in mind that part of the agent's selection process includes a child's look, age, ability to establish instant rapport upon entering a room, and how far above average the child stands among his or her peers.

Whether a newcomer or a veteran to show business, take time to learn the intimate history of Hollywood by searching out and reading as many books and articles in print about kids in the entertainment field. Encourage your child to follow suit. Autobiographies such as Shirley Temple Black's book, **CHILD STAR,** can shed light on many misconceptions about the history of children in

Hollywood. Moreover, subscribe to trade magazines in the industry such as **Drama Logue, Casting Call, Variety**, and **The Hollywood Reporter,** to name a few. These magazines not only stay abreast of what's happening industry-wise, but most have casting notices in them.

The Hollywood Screen Parents Association keeps an updated bibliography of books and articles published about children in show business. There is also an Appendix located in the back of "Show Biz Kids" with a recommended reading list.

For older children who lack a strong track record, it can be a challenge to get an agent or manager to take on the risk of a novice who has to compete with children that have been working for years. The answer often entails making your child more bankable. On the set of one movie we worked on, each time someone performed to the level of the star's liking, (himself included) he gave that actor a high five and then exclaimed: "Money in the bank!" That expression is an excellent metaphor for show business. It also represents a fairly clear reflection of Hollywood's value system. "Money in the bank" includes box office dollars, merchandising, advertising, or gold records. Unless an actor, singer, screenplay, television show, etc. falls in the category of "money in the bank;" then, by default, it ends up in the bankrupt or overdrawn category. Sound like a Catch 22? True.

FOR THE OLDER CHILD JUST STARTING OUT

Acquire or develop one or more of the following:

1. Specialty skills such as stand up comedy, martial arts, gymnastics, dance, musical ability or singing;

2. Strong acting ability, including improvisational skills; (study under several reputable or well respected acting schools and/or coaches); musical and community theater training;

3. *A distinctive character look such a nerd, jock, intellectual (weight and beauty is not a prerequisite in this category. Jaleel White of "Family Matters" created a furtune out of his "Urkel" character.*

4. *A wholesome, "boy or girl next door" look with even teeth, a charming smile, healthy hair and good skin and a slim, toned, well proportioned figure is always an asset*

The question remains, however, what can one with no experience, or very little, do to increase the odds of getting an agent or manager?

LEARNING TO DEVELOP INSTANT RAPPORT

The key to developing instant rapport with others is attentiveness, keen observation skills, and automatically mirroring the rate of speech or body language of the person communicating with you. Many times, instead of actually listening to the other person, our mind wanders out in left field, focusing on details such as how we are coming across; what we want to say next; whether the person likes us; or, what's for dinner. Crowding one's subconscious with unrelated concerns inhibits one from consciously focusing on the simple task of paying complete attention to the speaker.

Anthony Robbins, motivational speaker and author of "Personal Power," says that *"the present moment is the point of power."* Which means that we need to experience each moment NOW, without projecting our thoughts into the future, focusing on imagined concerns, or dissipating our energy worrying about a past that one has no control over anyway. Children are innately acquainted with this concept. They live in the eternally present moment. The concept of time is a mere abstraction to them. It evolves out of man's need for control over his life.

Furthermore, children are naturally curious in new surroundings. Parents would do well to imitate them by taking notice of the agent's or manager's office while waiting for the interview, or during breaks in the conversation. Office decor can tell a lot about the individual. What's more, these details can add fuel to a conversation, as does observing how the other person talks and dresses. Also, pay attention to personal preferences that the agent expresses -- they hold the key to an individual's value system.

Sometimes one simply needs to use the same semantics, rate of speech, voice inflections, etc. in order to communicate effectively with others. For example, if an agent speaks rapidly, or is extroverted and gregarious, then one can pretty much bet that if you are reserved, soft spoken and speak in short, clipped sentences, that particular agent will not feel that the two of you "hit it off." On a conscious level the agent or manager may not be able to articulate or put a finger on why the two of you did not "click." Often all the agent needs to intuit is that you probably would not be able to work well together. That would be enough for the agent not to sign a marginal chile or one who did not interview well. When the scales are uneven, establishing good rapport can tip the scales in your favor.

Children who are encouraged to maintain their natural ability to mimic (which is how children learn to talk anyway) automatically adjust their body language and speech to match the person spoken to. That is, until teachers or parents shame or criticize them out of this instinctive, unaffected inclination towards rapport with others.

Many people are afraid to venture out and become acquainted with those who are different from themselves. Human nature is such that we tend to feel more comfortable surrounding ourselves with those most like us or who share similar values. Learning to develop rapport is an important aspect of making remarkably new or different friends who are capable of broadening our horizons.

NURTURING YOUR CHILD'S STRONG SUIT

With children, a great deal tends to hinge on timing and recognizing when they've reached their own personal point of readiness. Any teacher knows that it is infinitely more practical to develop a child's strong point as opposed to struggling with a weakness. The average child has one particular area of the entertainment field that he or she is innately more talented in, or attracted towards. For instance, movies as opposed to commercials, singing rather than dancing, or gymnastics as opposed to dance.

For peace of mind, or for objectivity's sake, parents may want to seek outside opinions on whether their children have natural singing ability, for example. Teachers, friends and relatives are quick to point out how accomplished a child is in a particular area, such as: singing, basketball, dancing, acting, or whatever. Evaluate their opinions against yours then consider how driven or inclined your child is in that area. At that point decide if singing, for example, might not be the area best suited for your initial investment of time and energy. In the end, the precipitating factor in the decision making process should be common sense and your gut instinct as a parent coupled with the child's express desire and natural abilities. A wise person once said that natural talent is doing easily what others find difficult. So let that be a yardstick for measurement.

Moreover, children do not keep their natural abilities a secret-- a child who loves to dance will learn every new step he or she sees, or one who enjoys singing does so at every opportunity. Keep in mind, however, that it is much easier to develop one particular talent first before attempting to become a triple threat in several areas simultaneously. That can become a long term goal. In any area of a child's education or development, the child builds upon previous experience.

Be realistic. Not every child can be a triple threat. Be grateful if he or she has one strong talent. Always encourage your child to maximize the chance for success through practice and hard work. The saddest thing in the world is a parent pushing a child to pursue an area where the child has absolutely no talent and even less inclination to develop it. Usually in such instances the parent has not listened to professional advice nor taken note of the reaction or, more importantly, the lack of reaction the child receives when performing in public.

Avoid the other extreme of parents who have children with in- credible singing voices or dance ability, yet insist that they pursue acting instead. This approach automatically forces the child's first love to take second seat to an ability he or she might not have mastered yet or one that requires hard work and discipline for mastery. Of course I'm not saying that one cannot develop other talents. Only that one might consider enhancing and developing the child's natural ability first. This approach would allow the child's singing or dance ability to open up opportunities later for acting. Many singers and dancers make natural transitions into movie careers.

Similarly, I have met simply beautiful children who would make incredible models, but do not yet possess enough pizzazz or personality for commercials or theatrical work. Such a parent would do well sticking to modeling until that child's abilities grow in other areas.

INTERVIEWING SUCCESSFULLY WITH AN AGENT OR MANAGER

More deals find fruition over dinner, at parties or on the golf course than in the office. If you are meeting with someone in their office for your interview, do your part to turn it into a pleasant, social event. The following hints are helpful:

1. Reserved or overly quiet children may end up the teacher's pet, but they will not win brownie points with an agent or manager. In show business, shyness is sudden death. Personality sells products. This does not mean create a disturbance in the waiting area just to get attention; simply learn the difference between good behavior and children being too quiet for their own good.

2. As a parent, be relaxed and anxiety free. This will help your child relax. Also, avoid allowing insecurities or selfishness to shine through under a weak mask of self confidence. A seasoned agent or manager can see through this.

3. Be informative without bragging excessively about your child or allowing the child to do so. Let the agent ask what the child has done, read it on the child's resume, or hear through someone else. Remember that the child's personality and how candidly he or she responds to the agent's questions or commands play a big part

in the success of an interview. Similarly, a parent should keep in mind that the agent is interviewing both parent and child.

4. As mentioned earlier, encourage good listening skills and let the child know how important it is for him or her to take an interest in the person interviewing. Even if the child thinks the agent or manager is boring, unattractive or simply "strange looking," he or she should refrain from negative criticism or statements. Some children have a habit of commenting unkindly to others regarding their physical appearance, speech pattern, or manner of dress. Teach your child to find something nice to say about others, especially the person conducting the interview. If a sincere compliment is not possible, at least find something interesting in the office to compliment or inquire about. People love to hear about themselves and take pride in their possessions. Besides, we are our own favorite topics of conversation. Believe me, children have a clear grasp of this concept.

One key person that many parents fail to recognize as important is the receptionist or casting assistant. Sometimes the receptionist may actually be one of the agents in the office who happens to be providing relief on the switchboard. In many situations the receptionist may have the duty of screening parents in the waiting room. Later this receptionist will relay input to the agent on the parent and child that could affect the agent's decision to sign the child. Colleen Cler says that Kathy, the receptionist in her office, *"plays a valuable role. Often her opinion will be the decisive factor for me."*

The bottom line is, if an agent decides that the parent or child is rude, unruly or has no interest in others, the agent will be more apt to write YOU and your child off.

In the effort to establish rapport, look for something interesting about the interviewer such as office ambiance, books, decor, or dress. Moreover, if the interviewer wants to discuss personal interests, hobbies, or family, by all means pursue and develop that end of the conversation. You may learn something about the person that comes in handy later in understanding how they operate their business. I have found that my most successful interviews (in getting an agent to sign my clients or to appear at one of my workshops) have been those where we talked about everything BUT the project or client.

Don't hesitate to ask questions. I do not mean insincere or inane questions. The average person can readily see through that. Ask the agent or manager's opinion about things you might do to improve your child's pictures, appearance or audition techniques. Or inquire about the agency, how it got started, how long the agent has been there, etc. Before the interview, go over possible questions the child might ask the agent.

It may surprise one to know that very few clients bother to ask the agent about themselves. Human nature is such that we tend to wrap ourselves up in our own needs and concerns. Allow and encourage the agent or manager to talk at length about personal issues, preferences or tastes. If you or your child does not happen to be one of those who genuinely care about others, practice pretending interest until such practice allows one to grow to the point where taking an interest in others becomes an actual part of the personality. Of course, I am not advocating coming across totally "Hollywood" or a phony. Rather, I truly believe it is simple, common courtesy to express interest in others. Even the most boring person has a story with a lesson lying hidden somewhere. Many times that lesson may merely involve how not to act.

REMEMBER: What others feel about you is in direct proportion to what they perceive that you think of them, which is why arrogance is often so self-defeating. If the child takes no interest in the interview, acts put off, impatient or rude towards the agent or manager, do not expect favorable results. The same goes for parents. A child may do well in an interview only to have the parent destroy his or her chances by speaking unfavorably about the business, indicating a fear or negative bias against agents and managers or by not paying adequate attention during the interview.

On the other hand, if the child did not do exceptionally well, a parent can compensate by allowing the agent to take the lead in the conversation during the parent's interview. Simply follow suit. For instance, if the agent or manager points out weaknesses in the child, instead of becoming defensive, ask for suggestions on how to overcome them. Express a willingness to spend extra time on your own to work with the child or to take classes to make the child more bankable.

Some agents do not interview the parents on the first visit, only during the callback. Colleen Cler, of the Colleen Cler Modeling and Talent agency, is one of those agents. She explained that her *"first interview is usually very short; five or ten minutes."* When a child comes in to interview, Colleen states that *"an alarm goes off if I spot a child who is incapable of walking through the door without crying. After all, child actors are expected to go into the casting director's office alone."*

SENDING YOUR CHILD IN ALONE ON THE INTERVIEW

Many new parents are unaware that the child must go in on the interview unaccompanied. In today's climate of rampant child abuse, asking your child to go in alone on an audition goes against everything we currently teach children about protecting themselves from strangers. Since it is customary for the child to go in alone at an audition, a climate of trust should be created ahead of time to make the child feel comfortable enough to proceed in this unknown arena. To make the child feel more secure about this process explain that you are right outside the door and that all he or she has to do is call for you if the person inside requests an act that the child does not feel comfortable with. For a measure of reassurance, I might add that in all my years of working with agents and casting directors in Texas and California, I have never encountered, nor had a parent complain to me about an indecent situation or proposal involving children and an agent or casting director.

Since sending a child in alone may feel a little uncomfortable the first time around, agent Colleen Cler says that she leaves *"the door to [her] office open."*

Teach your child to "slate" his or her name, age and agent before going out on an interview or audition. If it's an interview with an agent or manager, practice the child smiling and saying: "Hi, I'm Jane Doe and I'm six years old." For auditions: "Hi,

I'm John Doe, I'm eight years old and my agent is ABC." Make sure the child looks at the person or camera straight on, does not squirm, look down at the feet, or stare off into space. Work with your child at home on this simple technique until mastered. More importantly, explain to the child before the interview why he or she is going, so that if the agent pops that question the child won't feel thrown off guard.

AVOID MANIPULATION AND DUPLICITY

It's in poor taste to try and con an agent or manager into hiring you or your child by using reverse psychology, or pretending not to be interested in the business. Besides, why would an agent want to hire someone who has no enthusiasm or genuine interest in the business? Moreover, if you really feel that way, why waste everyone's time? No one wants to bother with someone who isn't absolutely sure about what he or she wants to do.

I have found that one usually does not have to worry about parents who are up front and honest about the sacrifices they make. They will admit that they want their kids to have every advantage or any edge possible. Generally, this type will go about the process through appropriate channels. The other type will stab you in the back, walk over your dead body, and then shove your child in front of a speeding car if you get in the way. In the end this parent would tell everyone what a horrible accident it all was. The old Bette Davis movie: "Whatever Happened To Baby Jane" might have been specifically about sibling rivalry in show business, but the tactics remain the same. Jealousy and excessive ambition know no bounds. The most important thing to such parents (and it rubs off on the child, too) is getting their child the job at all costs, or out shining the other children the parent views as competition.

My experiences with such people taught me a valuable lesson about heeding warning signs. Even though I have always been able to spot potential problem personalities, at times I have let my guard down and suspended disbelief, inspite of my inner instincts screaming caution! Now I've learned to pass over passive-aggressive personalities whose behavior is oddly incongruent with what they say and to heed the counsel of a wise person who once said: "avoid loud and aggressive people for they are a vexation to the spirit."

FOLLOWING THROUGH AND HONORING COMMITMENTS

Before taking children to interview with an agent, make sure they understand that signing with an agent entails an agreement to show up for auditions unless impossible to do so. Children need to know that once an agent schedules an audition, unless the child is sick or injured, the agent expects the child to honor the commitment by making every effort possible to show up for the audition. Moreover, an agent always expects the child to show up for callbacks. Once a job is booked, the child then has an obligation to complete the job, health or circumstances permitting. On the other hand, allow children the freedom to quit the business or put their career on hold at anytime, but only upon proper notification to the agent.

At the age of nine my son learned a valuable lesson in honoring commitments. Salim was the only child in a musical play. Eyewitness News called the Director and wanted to film song and dance clips of the show at the television studio. The Director called me and asked if Salim could appear at the television studio the following day to perform his solo tap routine.

At this point we were still in rehearsal for the play and Salim had just learned the routine the day before. He had not had a chance to rehearse it and I was not sure if he had actually learned it since the choreographer had only worked with him for a half hour. I told the Director I would check with Salim and call her back later that day.

When Salim came home from school I told him about the television show and asked if he felt ready to perform the routine he had just learned on television tomorrow. He was eager to do the television show and quickly agreed. So I called the Director of the musical and confirmed Salim's appearance. That night we rehearsed the routine in preparation for the following day and he did just fine.

At the television studio Salim waited until he had been introduced to the news people and bragged about by the Director, before telling me, all of a sudden, that he could not remember the routine. Mind you, I had just watched him rehearse it only moments before and he knew all of the steps. I asked him to do the steps for me. (He was apparently turning nervous jitters into lack of confidence). As he reluctantly demonstrated the steps to me on the tile floor, Salim made himself fall (conveniently on his behind) so he could have an excuse to cry and get out of taping the show.

After facing his first big fear and walking through it, he realized that on the other side stood success. One simply has to cross over in order to embrace it.

Since Salim already had a habit of jumping from one project to another without finishing what he started, I knew this would happen again and again if I allowed him to manipulate his way out of a commitment. I did not want him to allow nervous jitters or fear to sabotage his success. Especially after he had already committed to doing the show and had voluntarily passed up an opportunity to say no ahead of time without any penalty involved.

In that instant, I could see Salim as an adult telling someone he would show up for an interview then standing up the host at the last minute. I felt it important for Salim to face his fears and move past them. So, I let Salim cry, then took him outside into the hallway and explained how he had been given an opportunity to say no, without any pressure from anyone. Then I reminded Salim of our rule that once he started something he had to finish it, unless to do so would harm or injure him in any way. This was not an audition, it was a commitment, which was not optional.

I also stressed to Salim that he needed to let me know now if he was setting a trend. If that was the case, I had no plans to participate further. Moreover, I would no longer take time from my job, nor spend anymore of my money pursuing and developing a career that he had chosen. I explained firmly and clearly that if he backed out at this point, then I would also back out, which meant that he would have to wait until he was an adult to pick up his acting career. From the tone of my voice Salim knew I was serious and would move on with our lives without a backwards glance at his stab at an acting career.

Once Salim was presented with a choice, along with the consequences of his actions, he dried his eyes and decided to go ahead with his performance. And he did a great job.

Now, you can bet that after that incident, anytime I ask Salim if he is ready to do something, he does not hesitate to admit when he is not. Furthermore, he realizes that he should opt out of a situation if he does not feel adequately prepared, but that he should do so when the opportunity presents itself, not afterwards.

Fortunately, the foregoing was the one and only incidence of stage fright that Salim has encountered. After facing his first big fear and walking through it, he realized that on the other side stood success. One simply has to cross over in order to embrace it.

POINTS TO PONDER:

1. *Develop strategies for your young actor or entertainer designed to make him or her more bankable.*

2. *Nurture your child's strong suit first rather than have the child struggle with a weakness. This approach develops self-esteem and self-confidence.*

3. *Learn the art of sincere, professional small talk. Try to be interested in others and listen to what they have to say.*

4. *Most people appreciate honesty, sincerity and straight-forwardness. Avoid duplicity or manipulation tactics.*

5. *The first few times that a child goes on an audition, reassure him or her that although the child should follow the instructions of the casting director or agent, he or she should not do anything that feels uncomfortable. Moreover, assure your child that you are right outside the door should he or she need you.*

6. *Teach your child to follow through and honor commitments for auditions, callbacks and bookings.*

Chapter 4

MANAGERS

It's more important to study and be ready ... A lot of people aren't ready to audition yet. They've never auditioned and they wouldn't know what to do if they went into an audition room.
Arthur Toretzsky of The Gores-Field Agency (from "The L.A. Agent Book)

REALISTICALLY, WHAT CAN ONE EXPECT FROM A MANAGER?

Basic managerial responsibilities encompass grooming the artist to get an agent, (including photographs, creating a marketable look, and insuring that the child gets proper classroom training), then finding the client an agent. Once the child has an agent, the manager advises the parent about career decisions, makes himself or herself available and visible to agents; monitors the client's growth and reports that progress to the agent to insure that the agent remembers the client when the right audition comes along. After all, managers know that agents have a choice of many actors to send out on each audition. Many managers also submit clients for jobs or receive direct bookings through personal contacts.

Anything beyond the above pretty much falls under the optional category, or manager's discretion. Mind you, many managers do go above and beyond the call of duty while others only get the child an agent.

WHAT NOT TO EXPECT

Clients should show consideration and respect for a manager's personal life; in particular, phone calls. Restrict phone calls to business hours, respecting the manager's evenings and weekends. Remember that within the Los Angeles area, toll calls cost as much as long distance calls. In order to eliminate telephone tag and cut down on excessive toll calls leave a complete message so that the manager can call you back and relay the information you need on your answering machine in the event you are not in when the manager returns your call.

Many clients fail to consider that all expenses incurred in their behalf initially come out of the manager's pocket. Some manager's bill for every out of pocket cent; other's only bill for big expenses such as an airline ticket. Normally, managers will bill clients for extraordinary expenses like long distance and toll calls, meals purchased for the child, or travel expenses on the child's behalf. To keep the manager from incurring out of pocket expenses, send meal money with your child, have the manager call you collect or when the manager calls, hang up and ring the manager right back so that the call is on your bill. For travel, purchase airline tickets yourself, or use your car when traveling on behalf of the child. Such acts keep you in control of expenses and prevents the manager from having to bill you for out of pocket expenses. Keep in mind that the manager does not get paid for all the time spent working with clients until that actor books a job, which can take a while in many cases.

It is also unrealistic to expect your manager to accompany you to each audition, or to provide transportation to auditions. Think about it, how can a manager effectively manage your child's career if the manager has to be in ten different places at once? Sometimes a manager will show up when a client auditions for an agent, or for a major role. Furthermore, even though some manager's also serve as acting coaches, the parent has a responsibility to get the child to the manager in enough time to go over the lines.

Never page a manager with a routine call. Anytime that happens the manager drops everything to return the call. For example, my children were taping a local television show when my beeper went off. It was after 8:00 p.m. on a Friday night. Earlier that day one of my children had gone on a callback where a decision was expected that night. When I did not recognize the number, I thought it was the agent paging me from her home. Upon discovering that it was a new client, whose children I had tentatively accepted from photos in the mail, I could not believe she beeped me to find out when we could meet in person. Guess what? I never met with this mother.

WHY AGENTS WORK WITH MANAGERS

Many children's agents in L.A. prefer to work with managers because they can save the agent a lot of leg work by referring children that are ready for auditions, complete with pictures, previous training and/or work experience. Further, for children under the age of three, agents in L.A. like working with managers because babies and toddlers change too rapidly to keep track of their growth. Babies, in particular, grow in and out of age categories too quickly for agencies to keep current photos on them. Furthermore, when casting directors and photographers call for an 18 month old baby, they do not mean a 13 month old. Further, for newborns, they want a baby from two to six weeks of age; not two or three months old.

Agents also use managers because it saves time if a call comes in at the last minute from a casting director requesting, for example, the agency's thirty best kids. (Some casting directors will call one agent exclusively because they have come to rely on that agent for quality talent.) When the agent has less than an hour to contact thirty kids, placing a call to several managers can save the day because the agent only has to make two or three calls, as opposed to thirty.

WHY SOME AGENTS WON'T WORK WITH MANAGERS

During my career as a children's manager I have personally encountered a few agents who do not like working with managers. One case in point involves an adult agent (who shared offices with a children's agent that I worked with). This agent either ignored me or was unduly rude when I came by the office. Over a period of time he softened and became surprisingly nice. Eventually the agent explained that he did not like managers because the ones he had worked with before were unreliable; he could never get in touch with them when he needed them. During his confession, this agent explained that the only reason he changed his mind about me was because he was able to see for himself how hard I worked for my clients. When I was there in the office he observed me respond quickly and efficiently to last minute castings by helping the agent put submissions together for delivery under a last minute deadline. Often, if we missed the deadline, I would drive the submissions over to the casting office myself, in the middle of rush hour traffic on the other side of town.

One children's agent I know only worked with managers selectively because she resented the fact that they receive a higher fee than an agent. (The standard Agent's commission is 10%, while managers receive 15%). She felt insulted by the fact that an agent has to pay for bonding, contracts from SAG, plus city and state licensing fees while a manager only has to pay a city licensing fee, unless he or she joins the organization of managers and pays their membership dues.

One very prominent children's agent who wanted to sign my two children, along with a couple of others that I managed, decided to tell me, when I called, on the day I was scheduled to sign the contracts, that she HATED MANAGERS and DID NOT WORK WITH THEM. Guess what? I respectfully declined her offer which deeply offended this agent. She reminded me what a legend she was in this town. Well, I wasn't impressed.

MANAGERS AND SPLIT REPRESENTATION

In Los Angeles one can only have a single agent in each area of the entertainment field (i.e., commercial, theatrical, print, dance and music). This situation makes a manager helpful in convincing an agent to split representation among those areas. Agents in L.A. have to agree to work with each other. Some will not **split representation** and work with another agency in much the same way that kids handle their toys: some will share, most won't. In L.A., dividing up representation has its advantages because it provides the energy of more than one agent working for you. As a result, when one agent isn't on the job, the other one takes up the slack. Plus, if things go sour with one agent, switching representation over to the other agent can happen without losing transition time involved in finding an entirely new agent.

Should a parent choose **split representation**, he or she may find that dividing the child among two agents can be difficult at times, due to scheduling conflicts, primarily because agencies no longer specialize. Until a few years ago, modeling agencies only handled models. Now, finding a modeling agency in LA. that has not opened up a commercial division is almost an anomaly. As a result, one can practically forget about finding a print agent who will sign talent for print only.

Most modeling agencies now insist on commercial representation simultaneously, unless the client already has a dynamic portfolio that insures them the child will work a lot in print. Even so, many print agents now focus more heavily on their commercial division than their print department because commercials are simply too lucrative for modeling agencies not to capitalize on that market; especially since New York continues to hold a monopoly on the fashion market. A successful model in Los Angeles has to do a lot more waiting around for work than one in New York. Moreover, commercials pay residuals. Most print work only pays a one time fee or a reuse fee whereas residuals from commercials come in steadily during the life of that commercial. Most print jobs are buy-outs, anyway, without reuse fees attached.

In keeping with the trend towards ***multi-service agencies,*** providing a child is ready for representation in all areas, most agencies prefer to sign talent across the board. The only time agents will consider making an exception is if an actor already has a good track record. Only then can the agent justify signing the actor in a limited capacity. The agent has to believe that the child is strong enough in commercials, for instance, to make money in that area, which is a valid consideration since most kids do better in one area "only," as opposed to several. This is why one will hear agents refer to children as "commercial" or "theatrical."

In a situation where one wants or needs multi-representation, having a manager would then be helpful because the agent might be more willing to deal with inevitable scheduling conflicts that result from split representation because they know they can rely on the manager to handle this conflict for them.

MY APPROACH TO MANAGEMENT

Each manager sees and performs the job from a different perspective. One may be willing to execute certain functions for a client while unwilling to perform services that other managers might be perfectly willing to take on. How much responsibility a manager wants to take on varies. With that in mind, I decided to write this section based on my own experiences as a manager while adding information about managers in general.

As a manager I become a mentor, teacher, advisor and friend. Initially I size up my clients' assets and deficiencies, then work on figuring out a way to balance them. Usually this involves minimizing the inadequacies by strengthening assets.

For instance, if I find a child who has a charming, pleasant, and outgoing personality, but a look that's too rough around the edges for marketability, immediately I go to work on polishing the child's appearance and honing the talent into a three minute showcase. At times this entails creating a cute little character look that works with the child's overall features. At the same time, I labor on developing a dynamic audition piece designed to get the agent delighted with the child. Sometimes what I have to do to create a diamond out of the rough often comes to me immediately upon meeting the child. At other times I have to see the child more than once in acting or dance classes before the right idea comes to me.

Keeping track of each client's growth and progress as an actor, model, or simply as an individual, enables me to effectively sell my clients to agents and casting directors. For instance, once a child learns to skate board, roller blade, ski, etc. I keep the agent abreast of such progress. As a result, whenever the agent asks me if a child is competent enough at a particular task to audition for a job I can answer without lying or stretching the truth.

I meet with clients once a week at their dance class to chat with the parents, observe the children's progress and interact with them after class to measure their self-confidence and self-esteem levels. The time I spend with these children every week gives me a clear idea of their abilities and level of commitment. Moreover, from dance class I choose new dancers on a rotating basis, to perform with my son and daughter during stage or television appearances in order to help build the resumes of newcomers.

Along with dance, I also require that all clients take an acting class or workshop. Even veteran actors receive encouragement to study under a new instructor, just to sharpen acting skills. Observing children in acting class enables me to determine the child's ability to deliver lines, remember them and follow directions. Dance classes, on the other hand, permit a certain level of freedom and abandonment that acting classes cannot; thus, allowing me to see how the client handles pressure and competition.

I point out to all clients in the beginning that most auditions require dance, gymnastics or specialty sports. Therefore, a child not currently involved in any type of sports or extra-curricular activities finds himself or herself limited in the number and type of auditions the child can go out on. Further, casting directors are quite specific about skill levels. If a manager takes a chance sending someone out on a call requiring a skill the client does not have or has not mastered, the manager places his or her reputation at risk. For instance, if a casting director asks for children who can "Double

Dutch" and your child cannot even jump rope, sending that child out would prove a waste of everyone's time.

I find that in the beginning most parents willingly enroll their children in classes. After getting an agent, however, they tend to drop the class before the child acquires a sufficient level of mastery to give him or her the confidence needed for an edge at auditions. Moreover, these very same parents complain about their child going on audition after audition without booking a job. Furthermore, some parents will find out about auditions through other children that the manager works with and show up there even though the child's skill levels are not adequate for the level of competition. For a singer or dancer who is not up to par, such a ploy can backfire because the child will audition against the best dancers or singers in that age group. Nine times out of ten, the better dancer or singer gets the job, thus, prompting the child who dropped out of classes to complain about not getting the job. Which brings me to:

An important thing I learn from attending dance class is how healthy the child's attitude is towards their peers. Either the child becomes totally intimidated by others, or the youngster jumps into the class feet first and works twice as hard until he or she reaches the same level as the other students. I watch for those who appear nice on the surface, yet as soon as they think the choreographer is not looking, will trip other children or step on their feet if they pick up the steps faster. In such a situation I have no choice but to drop such children from my list for posing an insidious threat to harmony within the group.

DO I NEED A MANAGER?

The answer to whether one needs a manager depends on whom you pose the question to: a manager, actor, or agent. In Los Angeles, even within a particular agency, one will find mixed reactions. For instance, one agent there may work almost exclusively with managers while another agent in that office will not, or does so only on a selective basis. In New York, however, one needs to have a manager because agents work almost exclusively through them. Mothers who live on the East Coast accept that having a manager is a must. Mothers from Chicago say the same thing. In New York an actor can have more than one agent in a particular area or specialty. Therefore, having a manager who works with the best agents in town can insure that an actor never misses a call. In New York clients use a first come, first serve basis to determine which agent gets credit for sending the client out on the audition.

As stated earlier, if one lives on the East Coast, a manager is indispensable. However, here on the West Coast, a manager's services are considered optional. Before answering the question, "Do I need a manger," one should probably take a personal personality assessment. Examine the status of your child's career. Clearly define, ahead of time your expectations. Often, your expectations and the reality may not line up; especially if you fail to spell out your desires to the manager early on or as they develop and change.

For those who have never had an agent, who have tried unsuccessfully on their own to get an agent, or who do not know where to begin, a manager might prove your best move. Keep in mind that many people find it easier to get an agent than a manager. I know from my own experience as a manager, I'm quite selective about the talent I take on because of the considerable amount of time and energy that goes into developing new talent. Now that I spend so much time writing, rarely do I take on new clients out of my desire to do a good job with the few that I kept. Instead, I refer clients to agents and other managers through seminars and workshops that I conduct.

HINTS FOR FINDING A MANAGER

(1) When searching for a manager, ask someone who already has one if they would recommend you to theirs. Or if you meet that person's manager in person, ask for a card then call the manager and let that person know how impressed you are with the job he or she is doing with your friend. Then make the manager aware that you are looking for someone like him or her to represent you.

(2) Again, workshops, seminars and acting classes often invite agents and managers to visit their classes, offering an excellent opportunity to audition based on your ability and/or a recommend-

ation from the speaker or instructor. As mentioned before, do not become discouraged if passed over the first time. Try again, or go to other workshops until you find an agent or manager looking for someone like your child.

(3) Managers prefer parents capable of following instructions, who are eager, enthusiastic and cooperative about auditions.

For the novice, not quite ready for presentation to an agent, a manger can be an indispensable item in helping the child reach a point of readiness.

MAKING A PERSONALITY ASSESSMENT

A strong manager will continually strive to sell the client at every available opportunity. For an introverted type of parental personality, having an out-going manager can readily release such a parent from the burden of selling the child to others, thus freeing the parent to focus on developing the child's creative talents.

A manager can also prove helpful if the parent only wants an agent for the child, yet feels quite capable of handling the child's personal development and public relations. In that case, state this desire up front to avoid misunderstandings or hurt feelings later. In the alternative, request a one year contract. On the other hand, one could also strike an outside agreement to give the manager a referral fee on the first three jobs booked through the agent, or something of that nature. This would, of course, depend on how involved one wants the manager to become. Moreover, the scenario assumes that your child already has headshots, ability and training and all you need is an agent. Under such circumstances, a manager would be more inclined to give you a one year contract because he or she does not have to spend six to nine months developing the child to a point of readiness for an agent.

For well established child actors who already have agents yet feel that a manager might give their career the boost or direction it's lacking, parents could propose a 90 day trial period with a manager. Sometimes the child may simply be going through a slow period, prompting the parent to wrongly decide that a manager can speed things up a bit. With a three to six month trial period, if things do not happen the way one hoped, the child gets out of the contract and no one's feelings are hurt in the process.

A reminder for miserly parents: do not take advantage of or waste a manager's time if you know very well up front that when the time comes to pay a commission to the agent and manager, you will either resent doing so or not do it at all.

MANAGEMENT FOR SINGERS

If you, as the parent, have invested the time and money into grooming and developing your child to get him or her ready for a record deal, (in effect, taken on the role of manager) weigh carefully and consider whether you are actually willing to turn your child over to a more high profile manager or production company to shop the record deal for you. Keep in mind that, as parent, after putting together the demo, wardrobe, choreography and stage experience, you've already done the hard work. All a manager or producer has to do is walk into a record label and present the package for you -- something you can, in actuality, do for yourself.

Remember that after your child has an offer from a record label, before closing the deal, the record company will want a manager assigned to the child. Since management is an important personal issue, the parent would be wise to take control of the selection process ahead of time by choosing an experienced, reputable music manager that he or she feels comfortable with before shopping the deal.

In the music industry, managers and production companies take from fifteen to fifty percent of their client's gross earnings, with fifty percent pretty much standard for production companies. Music managers, however, take twenty to twenty five percent. Depending on the particular music manager, a higher percentage may come into play. Just remember that percentages are not fixed in the music industry and everything is subject to negotiation.

POINTS TO PONDER:

1. *In Los Angeles many children's agents like to work with managers because it saves them time; in particular with babies and toddlers. Managers also refer children to agents who have training or established track records.*

2. *In Chicago and New York, managers are a must because clients can have more than one agent. Here in L.A. talent can have only one agent in each area of representation (i.e., print, commercials and theatrical) making managers optional.*

3. *Basically managers prepare a client to sign with an agent, then monitor the client's progress to insure that he or she goes out as often as possible on the right calls. Through personal contacts, managers may book additional auditions for the client.*

4. *Choose a personable manager who values your child, easily establishes new contacts, and works hard.*

5. *Be honest, clear and specific about expectations before signing with a manager. You may not need one.*

Chapter 5

GETTING READY TO GET AN AGENT

Success in the entertainment industry, particularly that portion that uses actors, involves enough paradoxes and variables to prevent anyone from telling anyone else that he/she doesn't have a chance. Lawrence Christon, "The Glut of Actors--Enough Already" THE LOS ANGELES TIMES, November 15, 1987 (from "The L.A. Agent Book")

Parents who presume to have naturally talented children that sing, dance or act, who have no need of training to sharpen their skills, should take time to sit in on auditions or talk to parents of children performing regularly in the business. One would not believe all the years of training that go into having "naturally" talented children. Moreover, I do not know of anyone so skilled they cannot learn something new or different. With proper training a child can learn to harmonize or hold a simple tune, provided the child is not tone deaf. For those children who walk with two left feet, tap teaches rhythm; jazz teaches movement; and, ballet teaches form.

SEEKING APPROVAL FROM WITHIN

After deciding to involve a child in show business and disclosing that intent one will quickly find out who remains in the category of real friends and supporters. For instance, members of my husband's family opposed Salim becoming an actor and dancer, proclaiming it an expensive waste of time. One even declared that it would only make a "sissy" out of him. Such comments by close relatives put a damper on Salim's enthusiasm. Luckily, I helped my child realize that no one's opinion of him was as important as the one he held of himself and that pursuing his goals and dreams should never be contingent on the approval of others. With the unwavering encouragement and support of my mother and me, it did not take long to convince Salim that the only approval necessary was his own. Interestingly enough, those who criticized the loudest were the first to jump on the bandwagon of success when Salim began booking jobs right away.

IT TAKES MONEY TO MAKE MONEY

No; dance, voice, acting lessons and the corresponding wardrobe are not free. And I do not advocate families going without necessities in order for the budding child star to obtain the proper training or outfits. A parent might simply consider creating a new budget that includes classes in the future. In the alternative, try involving sympathetic grandparents, godparents and friends who believe in and support your child; which may not be as easy as you think. Other options include scholarships for the child, or volunteering your parental talents, time or services to local performing arts schools in exchange for free classes. There are many non-working mothers who barter for the biggest part of their children's expenses.

THE IMPORTANCE OF STRONG READING SKILLS

Since children naturally grow more articulate with age and develop stronger reading skills each year after the age of six, four and five year olds who read well or who possess excellent memories fall in the exceptional category. Between the ages of six and ten, agents and casting directors *expect children* to know how to read and deliver their lines well. Before that age, however, industry professionals express surprise and delight any time they find a child with strong acting or reading skills.

By the age of six, the ability to read, memorize lines (called *sides*) and deliver them with naturalness and ease becomes a decisive factor in whether or not a theatrical/commercial agent or manager will represent the child. Sometimes, if an agent is taken by a child's personality or look, inspite of the fact that verbal skills are weak, the agent will accept the child under the condition that the parent enroll the youngster in a *cold reading* class, commercial workshop, or acting class.

Cold reading classes are important because children receive unfamiliar sides at commercial auditions that can run several pages in length. Not only must the child be able to read aloud with expression and animation while sounding like he or she is engaged in a real dialogue or monologue; but, while in front of the casting director, a young performer must deliver the lines in pretty much the same manner as a newscaster working from a script. That is, glancing down at the sheet and reading the lines, then looking back up at the casting director to deliver those lines while using complete sentences or phrases. Moreover, after delivering a line the child has to glance back down at the next sentence or group of sentences without losing his or her place on the sheet, which requires good hand-eye coordination. After glancing up and down, young children tend to lose their place on the script. The technique also calls for good manual dexterity in order to keep one hand on the sheet of paper while the index finger of the other hand moves down the line as the novice reads and delivers the material. Through practice, children quickly lose the need to keep place on the page with their index finger.

In addition to their own natural qualities, child actors also need to be able to memorize lines, take direction and feel comfortable around adults. ("Baby, It's You" by Zoe F. Carter)

Young children who have great memories often do exceptionally well at auditions before they acquire the ability to read. Some parents make the mistake, however, of relying too heavily on the child's memory as opposed to moving ahead to develop strong reading skills at the appropriate age.

The story of a seven year old child that I managed best illustrates my point. The mother brought me videotapes of work the child had done since the age of three. The little girl had an impressive resume and had worked steadily since the age of three. Her mother came to me in distress because, in the several months since they had moved to Hollywood the child had not booked a single job during that time. She decided that the new agent must be at fault. Based on the child's track record her verbal skills and how quickly she caught on in dance class I agreed that the first order of business was to place the child with a new agent.

Normally I have all new clients do a cold reading immediately, but this little one was reciting monologues and singing and dancing like a prodigy, so I did not feel compelled to do so. Moreover, getting the little girl a new commercial agent was easy for me because she recited her ***monologue*** and did a song and dance number that totally captivated the agent.

Fortunately, before scheduling the audition for a new ***theatrical*** agent (i.e., movies and television shows), I pulled out a couple of scripts for the child to read aloud. The little girl's inability to sound out words caught me completely off guard. Moreover, the child's reading vocabulary was barely a dozen words.

The little girl's mother had a hard time accepting that the child's ability to memorize was utterly useless unless the script was short and there was adequate time for her to learn the lines. Before, the child had been able to memorize all of her lines with the mother's help. However, audition scripts for a seven year old can be quite extensive and unless the child had adequate time to learn new or unfamiliar words, the child would be up a creek without a paddle. I explained to the mother that here in Hollywood, one is lucky to have a whole day's notice on a theatrical audition, while ten or fifteen minutes is considered adequate for a commercial audition.

In effect, this child had reached her level of incompetence. She could no longer cover up for poor reading skills. Moreover, the little girl had a lot of catch up work to do in that area before she would become a competent reader within her age group and not enough time to do so. Overwhelmed by their financial situation, the child and her mother ended up going back home inspite of the fact that with a few months of intensive reading therapy the little girl was bright enough to close in the gap. This is a story I have seen repeated over and over by exceptional and naturally talented children who come to Los Angeles between the ages of seven and ten with weak or poor reading skills.

Not only should a child have strong reading skills but he or she needs to read with the type of expression, humor and drama that makes words come alive. Nevertheless, the necessity for memorizing large amounts of material in a short time span is still a valuable asset. On the first audition it is acceptable to read the material aloud during delivery, but for callbacks the casting director expects the actor to have the material memorized. At that time, for reassurance, the actor may, however, bring the script inside. During the *screen test*, the actor should have the material memorized to act out in front of the camera. Casting directors expect actors to know the material by that time.

WAYS TO DEVELOP STRONGER READING SKILLS

Reading aloud to your child at night from a very early age will instill a love for reading. In order to make story time interesting for your child, read the lines with expression and excitement, encouraging the young reader to mimic lines from the story. While reading aloud, point out simple words in the book to create site recognition. As your child's vocabulary grows, take turns reading aloud one page then allow the child to recite the next page until he or she graduated to reading an entire chapter. In the mornings, have your child read aloud to the family from an inspirational or self-help text. Time set aside daily for reading aloud is the best investment a parent can make to ensure strong verbal skills, and the best part is that the entire process requires less than an hour a day.

FINDING THE RIGHT INSTRUCTOR

When looking for a dance school, vocal coach, or acting workshop ask parents with children in the business where they go for instruction. Not all parents are helpful or willing to share information, so keep asking around until you find one who will. With that in mind, I've included a list of dance studios and acting coaches for the Greater Los Angeles area at the end of this book. For those outside of California, consult your local chapter of the The Screen Actors Guild, the State Labor Commission, or your Yellow Pages. Agents can also provide referrals. When cold calling on schools, remember to ask for the teacher's credentials along with the names of any students who have gone on to prominence.

Once the child has been enrolled in classes for a year or more try to avoid becoming blindly devoted to one particular school or dance studio, especially if it no longer serves your needs or the growth of your child. For example, if your child is a quick study it may not be necessary to stay with one program for more than a year or two. Each child is different, however, so get to know your child's learning curve and work within it. If a school stays on the cutting edge of the industry, then it may not be necessary to change to another school. However, do not allow a teacher to make you feel that you're being disloyal when the time does come to move on. Dance studios commonly compete with each other, which explains why one may feel pressure from a studio to take all classes from them, when in fact, their strong suit may only involve tap. Make an effort to find the best jazz or ballet school for the child, even if it means going to more than one school.

One should always be cautious and practical about money spent on training for your child. Family funds would be better utilized on teachers with a reputation for producing successful children and on getting your child into a program where the instructor allows students to progress at their own pace. It can be quite discouraging for a child to have a teacher who will not allow students to develop as rapidly as they would like. Similarly, do not stick your child with a teacher who pushes children beyond their abilities; and certainly not with a teacher who has a sour temperament. Children progress much more rapidly in a class that they find enjoyable.

After a child achieves a certain level of proficiency in one area, the parent should then diversify and move on to music and voice lessons, for example. That is, unless the youngster wants to take several classes simultaneously in the beginning. A child's level of confidence grows considerably when he or she feels good at something. This process promotes a healthy self image and good self esteem, which fosters a sense of confidence that can motivate a child to develop other talents in the future.

Usually, children who sign with an agent by the age of three (and work regularly) require less training. Experience is the best teacher. Work in front of the camera substitutes for classes. Normally instructors will not accept children in acting classes until they've reached the age of six, while most dance studios will accept three year olds.

A large percentage of children do not receive an introduction to the entertainment field until the age of six or seven; most much later, because many parents do not feel that children have enough maturity or focus for such a discipline until they're over the age of ten. Others wait for the teen years when youngsters begin to make their own decisions. Personally, I have found that early dance, gymnastics or martial arts classes provide a level of discipline that children may have difficulty attaining on their own. In addition, group interaction is great for developing interdisciplinary skills.

Furthermore, acting classes allow children to express themselves in front of an audience, which promotes poise and confidence in public. On the other hand, every child matures at different ages, and interests change from year to year, so just because a child is not interested in music or dance at the age of six does not mean he or she won't be a few years later.

Since children tend to mentor easily, younger siblings generally benefit from what the older sibling learns in class. As a result, I have had to spend very little money on training for my daughter because she learned so much vicariously by interacting with and imitating her older brother. Moreover, I was able to teach her from what I learned over the years working with my oldest child.

PHOTOGRAPHS FOR ALL AGE GROUPS

Most agents will submit snapshots of children under the age of five to casting directors because children in that age group grow and change significantly each year before the age of five. Moreover, during the submission process, agents will also set up an interview with the child based on snapshots received in the mail.

Once a parent has submitted snapshots and found an agent, at that point he or she will have to get a professional ***headshot*** taken by a reputable photographer who specializes in black and white photos. A headshot is an 8"x10" black and white photo of the face that usually does not extend beyond the bust. *(Please turn to the end of this chapter for samples of photographs).* Go to a specialist, not a photographer whose medium is color photography, or one who primarily does still shots, sports photography, action photos, or weddings.

Currently the trend with commercial agents is three quarter length headshots, (i.e., a vertical picture that includes the top two-thirds of the body with borders on the right and left side to accentuate the vertical pose). Modeling agents may continue to ask for a ***composite*** (an 8"x10" black and white photo with several different poses) because they need to see the entire body in different outfits.

Composites may also depict different types of character looks such as "scholar," "athlete," or "tomboy," or for modeling, different styles of dress.

This change from composites to three quarter length headshots for commercial agents is primarily due to the popularity of MTV. Most commercials are now patterned after MTV, with dance, action or gymnastics involved. The focus is no longer only on the actor's eyes and facial expressions. Unlike commercial agents, theatrical agents tend to prefer a simple headshot. You will find, however, that they, too, will accept three-quarter length headshots.

Please Note that it is not absolutely necessary to have a composite or headshot prepared before searching for an agent. It will not, however, hurt your chances, and in fact often enhances them, since the agent could then start submitting the child's pictures right away, once the agent has decided to represent the youngster. There is an advantage, therefore, in already having at least one *proof sheet* (a 36 exposure roll of film printed on an 8"x10" sheet with small black and white photos the size of the negative) to show the agent, or, in the alternative, at least a package of color snapshots. These photos allow the agent to can see how well your child photographs because photos are the single most important tool an agent has to sell her clients with. If a parent brings headshots to the interview an agent will recognize the parent's willingness to invest in a new career, which, like any other business, requires start up capital. Even if the agent is not crazy about the pictures you walk in with, unless they are really bad photos, usually the agent will use them until the child makes enough money to afford new pictures. Bear in mind that each agent has a particular photography style that they prefer, and most agents will want the parent to have pictures redone to suit their particular taste in photography, or done in the style of that agency. If nothing else, the agent will need to have their logo printed on the pictures or have you purchase agency labels to place on the headshots you bring in.

If the parent of a novice child (1) spends money on headshots from a photographer who does not work with children's agents; or, (2) does so without first determining if the child has a better than average chance of competing with his peers in show business then that parent should prepare for a possible loss.

Helpful Hints For Taking Your Own Photos. Photographers prefer taking photos outside during early morning or afternoon sunlight because the light is not so harsh during that time. For great outdoor backgrounds go to a park, flower garden, or the beach. Indoor pictures require a well-lit room with a white wall or solid color for a backdrop. Avoid including anything in the picture except the child (no friends or family). Try to get as close as possible for headshots, without distorting the face. For full body shots, do not stand too far away; this prevents the face from being featured clearly or prominently in the frame of the picture.

Snap candid, action poses. Have the child wear clean, simple, well fitting, comfortable outfits; avoid sunglasses or hats that hide or create shadows on the face. Make sure the child's face is clean: No photos with mud, dirt or food stains on the face. During my interviews I had agents complain about the number of such photos they receive in the mail with spaghetti or Cheerios stuck to the child's face.

Try several different hair styles (i.e., a ponytail, hair completely loose; a half pony tail; braids, etc., for girls. For boys, hair combed all the way back, then maybe parted on the side; tousled, wet or dry). Remember one hairdo may feature the face better than another and give the agent an idea of which "look" they can better work with. Moreover, the right hair cut or style can literally launch a child's career; highlighting the child's best features. I've had children come to me who had a hard time booking jobs until I came up with a cute hairdo and/or outfit. Often the new look acts as a confidence booster for the child.

GETTING DUPLICATE PHOTOS

There are several steps involved in getting a composite or headshot ready for the agent. The actual photo session comes first. This involves a separate fee in and of itself.

It's important to find a photographer accustomed to working well with children and one whose photos have gotten children work.

It saves time and money in the long run to shoot at least two to three roles of film on different occasions, if possible, in order to capture various attitudes and aspects of the child's character. Newcomers often have to grow accustomed to the photographer's commands or directions, requiring that the photographer show them how to pose, or coax them into following instructions until they strike upon a pose or expression that works. Often it takes the second role of film before the child relaxes or feels confident enough to give the photographer something to work with.

The most important reason to shoot more than one role of film is because the outfit or hairstyle that the child walks into the studio with might not flatter the child and the parent won't know until the proof sheet comes back. If able to afford only one role of film make use that the child changes outfits and hair styles half way through the roll. Since some photographers only allow one outfit per role have the child wear a layered look which can easily peel off right there in the studio. Taking off a jacket, vest or sweater can create an entirely new look. For girls, take pictures of the hair loose first before pulling it back; and, for boys, shoot the baseball cap last to keep from messing up the hair.

PROFESSIONAL PHOTOGRAPHY FEES

In Los Angeles, "average" photography fees range from $65.00 to $200.00 per roll. Most photographers will include in that price one 8"x10" enlargement, contact sheet and a roll of 36 exposure film. Others only include the film and proof sheet in their fee. The client has to pay for their own 8"x10's." In either case, the client has to incur the expense for additional photos that the agent may want enlarged. The fee for an 8"x10 can be minimal and is usually paid directly to the company that develops the film since most photographers do not develop their own pictures anymore. If a photographer offers to have the photos developed for you, remember that the photographer will most likely inflate the actual costs to make a profit and to pay for their time.

If you have the enlargements done directly by the lab, each 8"x10" will cost you anywhere from $6.00 to $12.00 per print. Again, keep in mind that if you go through the photographer for enlargements they will set their own prices for the 8"x10." Some photographers charge as much as $60.00 for one 8"x10" black and white while others are quite reasonable. Inquire ahead of time.

Most photographers will not release negatives to the client; which forces clients to order enlargement photos through the photographer. An unspoken rule exists that when a model poses for a photographer the photographer "owns" the negatives since they are tools of the trade used by photographers to obtain repeat business. Some photographers, however, will release the negatives.

The typical composite contains about four different photos. A headshot has one. However, for a headshot, the agent or manager usually requests enlargements of several photos in order to have different poses to choose from. Often flaws in a photo are not exposed until after the photo is enlarged (i.e., hairs in the face, one eye slightly squinted, a crooked smile, shadows that fall in the wrong place, clothing slightly askew, etc.)

After the requisite number of photos are enlarged and the final selections made, the last step is to take the final selections to a photo place for mass duplication. You will receive a separate fee to shoot an 8"x10" negative of each photo along with a separate charge to typeset the child's name and the agent's logo on the bottom border. These are one time fees, however. When the actor runs out of copies and needs more of the same picture one only pays for the actual copies.

Usually the agent will require at least 100 copies; you will need the same amount to take with you on auditions. By shopping around one can get three hundred copies for between $100.00 and $200.00. Remember that black and white glossy photographs cost more than black and white *lithographs*, which involves a type of printing process run on card stock as opposed to photography paper. Most agents use lithographs because they are less expensive than glossy photographs. Remember that publicity photos for magazines and newspapers use glossy photographs not lithographs because lithographs do not reproduce as well as glossies.

NOW THAT YOU'VE DONE YOUR HOMEWORK...

With over 200 agents in Los Angeles specializing in children, the weeding out process of finding the right one can be overwhelming. Confusion can set in when more than one agent wants to sign the child and the parent is not sure which one to choose. In that instance, it is best to rely on your first impression or gut instinct, in conjunction with the agent's reputation or proven track record. Ask for a client list.

For parents who send out pictures and receive no response at all, one might consider getting new pictures done by a different photographer with an entirely new hair style or "look" for the child. Again, pictures are the single most important selling tool an agent has to work with.

With no shortage of children's talent agents in the Los Angeles area, the question then, is what distinguishes a good agent from a mediocre one? Writer Kyle Counts feels that being an effective agent often *"boils down to hard work and serving the client's best interests in the form of individualized attention."*

Included in the index of this book is a list of children's talent agencies in the Los Angeles area. Remember that *franchised agencies* are licensed by the State and are prohibited from being connected with photography studios, modeling or acting schools, management companies, or any other venture construed as a possible conflict of interest. Franchised agents also cannot request their percentage up front and do not charge fees for signing a client.

Outside of California, to obtain a list of agencies licensed or franchised by your particular state, call the local Screen Actor's Guild or your state labor commission.

AGENCY FEES

Franchised agents get their *commission* after the client receives payment for the job. The standard agency commission is *10%* for *commercial* and *theatrical* work (this includes film, television and stage) and can go as high as *20%* for *print* work, which includes billboards, posters, magazines and newspapers. The commission is higher on print work, because it does not pay as much as commercial work and contains no provision for residuals.

If a parent wants to avoid the endless rip offs associated with the entertainment field, deal only with bonded, franchised agencies or managers who work with them. That way, you never have to wonder how much commission will be charged and "if" the pay check will actually come in since franchised agencies can lose their license by engaging in unethical behavior.

Moreover, look out for casting services who pose as agencies and charge a registration fee, or require excessive sums for photographs, modeling school or acting lessons. Licensed agents do not take money for classes or photographs. Moreover, legitimate agents will not demand or put pressure on a parent to use a particular photographer; they will only recommend or suggest.

SEMINARS AND WORKSHOPS

Attend seminars or workshops where agents are in attendance. If possible, choose one connected with an acting school, casting agency or someone who has a proven track record in the entertainment field. Fees for such workshops are usually quite reasonable: from $50 (for one or two hours) to $150 for a full day seminar. Keep in mind that some of the best acting schools rarely charge more than $150 per month out of regard for struggling actors. Some seminars run for a weekend and cost between $200 to $350. This type offers more hands-on training. Look for seminars or workshops that allow participants the opportunity to actually act and audition before agents and managers.

To find out about acting workshops or classes in your area, call and ask for recommendations from local children's agents or dance studios; look for advertisements in the Calendar section of your weekend newspaper; scan local children's weekly newspapers that are offered free at newsstands; or reputable national and local trade magazines such as "Variety," "The Hollywood Reporter," or "Drama Logue."

My son and daughter got a Los Angeles agent through an acting workshop. Linda Seto, Director of ***The Dallas T.V. and Film Workshop (i.e., "Young Actor's Space)*** contacted my son's agent in Houston looking for children to attend. Salim's agent chose him and four other children to participate. It took enrolling Salim in that particular seminar, along with a week long summer movie camp, and a second weekend workshop before Los Angeles agents Mary Grady and Bob Preston discovered him. My daughter was six at the time and not enrolled in the workshop. She was in the lobby when Mary Grady walked up to her and asked if she would like to come out to California with her brother for the summer.

MY STORY

When my son, Salim, first decided that he wanted to become an actor, he was pretty enterprising about coming up with ways to earn the money to pay for his classes and pictures. After going through numerous money making ventures, only to realize that none of them would net him the money needed to pay for his *composite* anytime soon, Salim soon struck a bargain with me: If I would invest the necessary capital to pay for his pictures and training; he would repay me from future earnings. Out of these earnings he also agreed to invest a part of this income into his own training and tools of the trade, such as specialty audition outfits and props. It turned out to be a good investment on my part. And as usual, I am glad I did not listen to friends and relatives. By the age of eleven Salim had saved up a sizable amount towards his college education.

Even though Salim does not hail from a show business family, my mother and most of her sisters have natural singing and dancing ability. At family get-togethers aunts and uncles always encourage the smaller children in the family to perform in front of adoring and applauding relatives.

My mother and sister, Betty, encouraged Salim to dance and sing before he could walk or talk. As an infant, they taught him to pop his fingers, rock and clap hands in time to the music. Salim was seven when my mother's younger sister Maeola, who is a great singer and dancer, moved on to our street. Weighing barely 100 pounds, Maeola can perform intricate, back-breaking dance moves with the energy of a teenager. Whenever my mother came over to visit, Maeola would come by and challenge Salim to outdo her dance moves or to master new vocal acrobatics from Jackie Wilson, her favorite singer. My mother taught Salim to sing the blues like Bobby "Blue" Bland and encouraged him to play the guitar like B.B. King and Hendrix. She always instilled confidence in Salim's natural abilities by telling him at every opportunity that he was a natural born star. And at Salim's performing arts school in Houston everyone was encouraged to be a Roger's Star. Since Salim's father sings and plays a couple of instruments and I also sing, our two children learned through association and assimilation at home.

Growing up in an environment that valued and nurtured talent in all it's stages of development, by the age of three, Salim thought it was show time whenever someone came over to visit. It did not matter if they were strangers, he would come in the living room, wait until my friends acknowledged him, and then ask if he could sing, rap, or dance for them. Of course no one turned him down.

Any musical show that aired on television was an event all the family looked forward to. Salim was five when cable television came to our area of Houston. He kept the channels on MTV (Music Television) or BET (Black Entertainment Television) to catch the latest music videos. Salim insisted that we videotape his favorite performances. In particular those from Michael Jackson's "Thriller" album, and "Motown 25," which Salim utilized to teach himself the "Moon Walk."

By the age of seven, Salim began asking us to videotape high school dancers at local talent shows so that he could learn their moves. Since Salim taught himself to dance from watching music videos (with the exception of a few tap classes in Houston), Salim did not take regular dance classes until the age of 12 (a couple of years after we moved to Los Angeles). Even then he would only enroll in Hip Hop or Tap classes because his father and grandfather convinced him that ballet and jazz was for the birds. Grateful that Salim's father had not discouraged him from dancing completely, I did not force the issue.

Listen to the mustn'ts, child, listen to the don'ts, listen to the shouldn'ts, the impossibles, and the wont's, listen to the never haves, then listen close to me -- anything can happen child, anything can be. --Shel Silverstein, Children's Author (from "The Measure of Our Success" by Marion Wright Edelman, Beacon Press)

Following the lead of his two older cousins, who sang and danced naturally, between the ages of three and five, Salim participated in school plays, local talent shows and fashion shows. By the age of five, Salim landed a commercial for "Sesame Street" and was performing every week at the Laff Stop in Houston with a professional children's musical troupe, called "Too Short for Prime Time." At the age of seven, Salim won the Jr. Dance Division of The Houston Talent Awards (along with his cousin) using a dance routine he choreographed from music videos. He went on to take top awards in every state and local talent competition he entered, even after his mentor cousin chose to quit performing.

All of this occurred before getting an agent for Salim, which did not happen until he was seven and a half. The thought of finding an agent might not have occurred to me if Salim had not fallen under the influence of Tracye Walker, a teenage girl he admired in his musical troupe who already had an agent. I sought advice from Tracye's mother, Philomene, who was quite supportive and helpful, then pulled out my Yellow Pages and began calling around.

After narrowing down the list of agents, I searched for the best photographer in Houston to shoot Salim's composite. Disapproving friends and relatives (on my husband's side of the family), who knew nothing about the business, discouraged me from taking this approach because they had heard on a television news program, that snapshots were a better alternative. I felt that having a composite would look more professional. I hired the best black and white photographer in Houston, V. Fairchild Bennett.

After making mass copies of the composite, I mailed them out to the three top children's talent agencies in town, along with a *resume* listing the work Salim had gotten on his own. *(Please refer to the end of this chapter for samples of winning resumes.)* I also enrolled Salim in his first musical theater class at Theater Under The Stars. In my desire for Salim to learn from the best teachers in town, the following year I sent him to Houston International Theater, and Chris Wilson's Studio for Actors.

Within a few days I received calls from all the agents I mailed packages to wanting to meet with Salim. The day after we interviewed with Actors and Models of Houston Salim *booked* a job on "Good Morning Houston."

After Salim signed with The Mad Hatter Talent Agency (his agent from Actors and Models of Houston left to take over the children's division of The Mad Hatter) I attributed many of the jobs he got to sheer beginner's luck. When it lasted, however, I had to adjust my viewpoint, especially when I realized that many children work with an agent for months without ever booking a job. More importantly, some do not book anything at all. In fact, writer, Zoe F. Carter, in her article for *Premiere* magazine titled, "Baby, It's You," found one mother who admitted that she *"went on 34 go-sees the first year without getting a job. Undiscouraged, she took him on 51 interviews the next year, finally snagging two commercials and a print job."* The following year this same mother took her child on *"95 interviews out of which he landed two commercials, three print ads and a regular role on a soap opera."* The average child goes on about 20 auditions before getting one callback.

Both of my children's track records tend to be higher than the average because we work together to maintain *The Eye of the Tiger* (i.e., roaring confidence, preparation and enthusiasm about each audition). Regular practice keeps audition skills sharp. And we strive to keep the right frame of mind by listening to motivational or self-help tapes that enable us to remain positively focused. Initially Salim booked one out of three auditions he went on in Houston. After we moved to Los Angeles, where there are more children going out on auditions than in Houston, he booked or received a callback on one out of every five theatrical and commercial auditions. His sister, Crystal, has a similar track record, booking more *commercial* jobs than *theatrical*, whereas Salim books more theatrical than commercial jobs.

BEING A "NO LIMIT PERSON"

I came to realize that one reason Salim's success rate ran higher than average was because I allowed him to keep his childhood belief in no barriers. With my training and encouragement Salim knew that the only person he competed against at an audition or talent show was himself. On each audition I encouraged Salim to strive to out do his previous best. No matter how crowded the room became with young hopefuls, he had a way of walking off into a corner by himself and practicing his song, dance, or lines as if no one else occupied his space. Totally focused, he never tuned into the nervousness or anxiety in the room.

Salim's near photographic memory also played a large part in his theatrical success. He could memorize anything after reading it a couple of times. Through her research, writer, Zoe F. Carter agrees that *"in addition to their own natural qualities, child actors also need to be able to memorize lines, take direction, and feel comfortable around adults."* These skills get better and sharper with practice, determination and application.

Salim also possesses a total belief in his ability to learn anything he sets his mind to...from tap dancing to fencing, to skate boarding.

As a mother I worried about accidents, but most of the time it exhausted me to keep up with him.

From the beginning, Salim had no fear of the unknown, rarely balked at hard work and was not intimidated by harsh realities or the dire predictions of others. He possessed total belief in himself and his ability to accomplish goals. Moreover, it only made him work harder to catch up once he discovered that many of the children his age, enrolled in his first musical theater class, were a few years ahead of him.

The basic problem for the actor is finding his own emotions and using them on stage at will. --David Groh (regarding the Lee Strasberg method --from "Special Report on Personalities")

When Salim's grasp exceeded his reach, he learned to climb on a foot stool to reach higher, constantly challenging himself. He saw the small time as something to work through on his way to the big time. Within a year and a half after getting an agent, Salim landed a starring role in a Disney Educational movie filmed at NASA in Houston. The casting people auditioned all types in his age group. Salim came home after the first audition confident he had the part. The other boys never stood a chance.

Salim's spirit of invincibility got him another educational film the very first week we arrived in Los Angeles, along with bookings almost every month that first year we arrived in L.A., despite dire predictions about how much stiffer the competition would be in Los Angeles, as opposed to Houston and Dallas.

Producers and casting directors told me that what attracted them was Salim's nonchalant politeness and dreamy-eyed intelligence, the very qualities that got him the movie "Ghost Dad." It was Salim's improvisational ability and knack for crying on command that landed him a dramatic role in the Japanese film "Asian Task Force," as well as the Chuck Norris movie "The Hitman." Although in the latter movie, Salim's resume was also a decisive factor. Originally, the part was written for someone much younger. But after an extensive search in the US. and Canada, they decided to go with an older, more experienced child who could handle the pressure of a tight shooting schedule and still do well in front of the camera. Each time a production company has to reshoot a scene unnecessarily they risk going overtime and over budget.

YOUNGER SIBLINGS OFTEN FOLLOW SUIT

As for my daughter, Crystal simply followed in Salim's footsteps as naturally as a fish swimming in water. Association does breed assimilation. Crystal found an agent, not because we were looking for one (I thought she was too young) but because she was always with me whenever I took Salim on auditions. Photographers and casting directors would see her and sometimes hire the two of them together or change their mind entirely about Salim and hire her instead.

Crystal never ceased to amaze me. She would tag along, totally disinterested, sucking on a pacifier (until she was five years old it hung on a gold chain around her neck). Whenever casting directors fixed their attention on her to ask if she wanted the job, I always held my breath expecting her to shake her head "No." When she would pop that pacifier out of her mouth and walk into the casting office all by herself, I was proud beyond belief.

I remember Salim's agent coaxing me to let Crystal do an *editorial print job* for the Sunday section of the newspaper a few months after she signed Salim. Since she was only three, I felt sure that Crystal would not work with a photographer alone. With the agent's urging, however, I agreed to that one job, just to see how Crystal would handle it and to test her wings.

When we arrived at the studio and the assistant came out to get Crystal, she happily waved good-bye. After grabbing the photographer's assistant by the hand, Crystal disappeared inside that large studio without once looking back.

While waiting in the lobby, I remembered a fashion show Crystal participated in at a large department store in Houston at the age of two. Again, this was a situation where the Director hand-picked Crystal as we walked through the large children's department store. When we arrived for the fashion show, the director asked me to walk down the runway with Crystal because all the other toddlers her age wouldn't do it without their mothers. Crystal, however, brushed my hand away and waltzed down the isle alone, with her clear pacifier in tow.

Even though Salim always loved to dance, until the age of nine, I could never get Crystal to take a lesson or even get her out on the dance floor. She was content to watch at dance class or rehearsal. However, once I auditioned a group of dancers to perform with Salim during stage and television appearances, Crystal announced that she wanted to join the group. I did not think she would stick it out so I made a deal with Crystal: If she learned the routine and kept up with the other trained dancers she could perform with the group. A few weeks later, when Crystal performed behind her brother at the ABC Entertainment Center in Century City, no one back home could believe that was Crystal on the videotape dancing in perfect step with professional dancers. Crystal did the same thing with singing. At the age of eleven she was offered her first group record deal. By the age of thirteen Crystal had her own solo record deal, writing most of the songs for her debut album. She learned it all from working with her brother who started writing and producing his own songs at the age of twelve.

As a mother, at one point I wondered if Crystal's rising successes might intimidate Salim, especially since he taught her everything she knew and Crystal booked more commercials and music videos than Salim. But her brother was always proud and genuinely happy whenever Crystal booked a job, mostly because none of us have ever gotten over how reserved Crystal used to be. I am sure, however, that one of the reasons Crystal's successes do not bother Salim is because he tends to book more theatrical jobs. In typical Crystal fashion, however, she is on the rise theatrically. They both have a way of challenging and keeping each other on their toes.

The moral of this story is that we, as parents, tend to limit our children by our concerns, fears and desire to keep them babies, (especially the youngest). Both of my children have taught me to believe in them and the things they affirm about themselves. Besides, who are we to decide how much talent our children do not have? I remember Wayne Dyer saying that when our children tell us they want to achieve something, instead of instilling limitations, we should simply say: "And why not?"

Our children know exactly how much territory they can conquer. Often, our job as parents entails getting out of the way while giving our children the tools to accomplish whatever they believe possible. At other times we have to take them by the hand and show them the possibilities because they have not yet discovered the depth of their own potential.

POINTS TO PONDER

1. Find out where your child's NATURAL abilities lie, develop that area first, then move on to the weaker ones.

2. Ask around, audit classes, and look for a teacher who encourages students to excel without having to browbeat the child in the process.

3. Examine the headshots of other children, ask for recommendations from franchised agents, then make your own decision on which photographer best suits your budget and child's personality.

4. Headshots are not necessary for children under the age of five; simple outdoor photographs with a good 35mm camera will do.

5. Theatrical and commercial agents take a ten (10%) percent commission AFTER booking jobs. A modeling agency can take up to twenty (20%) percent.

6. Seminars and Acting Workshops that invite agents to see their students perform are excellent ways to find an agent. Moreover, they are reasonably priced and offer a variety of industry speakers.

RESUME

CRYSTAL CELESTE GRANT

Solo Recording Artist "C.G." - International Group Recording Artist L.A.X

FILM CREDITS
LAWNMOWER MAN, II	Jade (co-star)	New Line Cinema
LISTEN UP, The Lives of Quincy Jones	Singer	Warner Bros.
MICKEY'S SAFETY CLUB	Lisa	Disney
JIM HENSON'S MUPPET BABIES	Guest	Warner Video
VISTALINE-The Computer	Lucinda (Star)	Westinghouse
TALKING WITH T. J.	Jill	Hallmark

TELEVISION CREDITS:
WHERE I LIVE	Dorinda	Disney-ABC T.V.
FBI The Untold Stories	Shannon (Guest)	MCA Television
POLLY, COMIN HOME	Singer	Disney TV Movie
HARDCOPY-TwinkleTwinkle Little Stars	Guest	Paramount T.V.
INSIDE EDITION - Child Actors	Guest	NBC Television
BLOOPERS & PRACTICAL JOKES	Guest	Dick Clark TV
LOU RAWLES PARADE OF STARS	Guest	PBS TV
SLAM IT OR JAM IT	Singer	Continental Cable
SOUL & SOUNDS OF WATTS	Singer	Continental Cable
THE UP&COMING RISING STARS	Singer	Century Cable
PROJECT LITERACY CAMPAIGN	Guest	ABC Television

MUSIC VIDEOS:
PARACHUTE EXPRESS	Sue	Disney Records
SHENICE WILSON	Dancer	Motown
STARR PARODI - Kenya	Dancer	Fresh Produce
QUINCY JONES - Tomorrow	Singer	Propaganda
TONY LEMANS - Forevermore	Guest	Paisley Parks
PRINCE	Guest	Propaganda

THEATER:
HIP HOP GOES BROADWAY	Singer	Palladium
THE VELVETEEN RABBIT	Doll	Will Rogers Theater
ANNIE	Orphan	Will Rogers Theater
ONCE ON THIS ISLAND	Little TiMound	Van Nuys H.S.P.A.

PROFESSIONAL TRAINING:
FILM ACTORS WORKSHOP (Richard Brander)	Acting for Film & Television
PROFESSIONAL ARTISTS GROUP (PAG)	Commercial Acting Workshop
REGINA'S SCHOOL OF PERFORMING ARTS	Funk & Street Dance Classes
UNIVERSAL DANCE (Paul Kennedy)	Tap & Funk Dance Classes

SPECIAL SKILLS:
Roller blading, roller skating, swimming, handball, softball & tennis

COMMERCIALS: List Furnished upon request
NOTE: It is customary not to include a list of commercials on the resume because advertisers compete with each other, which can cause **conflicts**. Many beginners, however, will list commercials on the resume to fill up space.

Getting Ready To Get An Agent

SALIM GRANT

FILM CREDITS:

ANGUS (w/Kathy Bates)	Mike (Co-Star)	Turner Films
THE HITMAN	Tim (Co-Star)	Cannon-MGM Films
GHOST DAD, Starring Bill Cosby	Danny (Co-Star)	Universal Pictures
LISTEN UP, THE LIVES OF QUINCY JONES	Singer	Warner Bros.
ASIAN TASK FORCE	Mickey (Co-Star)	Lumination Pictures
POLLY, COMIN' HOME	Singer & Dancer	Disney T.V. Movie
BARNEY AND THE BACKYARD GANG	Jason	Lyons Edutainment
MINNIE'S SCIENCE FIELD TRIP TO NASA	Matt (Star)	Disney Educational
MY SELF ESTEEM	Jeremy (Star)	Armstrong Pictures
MATH ROCK COUNT DOWN	Louis (Star)	Davidson Edu.
TODD ALLEN DIRECTOR'S REEL	Director	Hollywood Studios
FIRST AID FOR LITTLE PEOPLE	Lewis	Alfred Higgins Ed.
SAFETY FOR PUBLIC SCHOOLS	Student	Metropolitan Transit

TELEVISION CREDITS:

SAVED BY THE BELL	RJ-Series Regular	NBC Television
SISTER, SISTER	Darnell	Paramount TV
THEA	Eric	ABC Television
SINBAD	Singer	Disney Productions
FAMILY MATTERS	Featured	Lorimar Television
SALUTE YOUR SHORTS	Guest Star	Nickelodian
WONDER YEARS	Patkus	New World
HARD COPY "Twinkle, Twinkle Little Stars"	Special Guest	Paramount
INSIDE EDITION "Child Actors"	Special Guest	NBC Television
GENERATIONS	Andy	NBC Television
ARSENIO HALL SHOW (w/Quincy Jones)	Singer	KCOP Television
TODAY IN L.A. (w/All God's Children)	Singer	Local TV Show
TOTALLY HIDDEN VIDEO	Special Guest	Fox Television
HOLLYWOOD SQUARES	Guest	MCA Television
GOOD MORNING HOUSTON	Model	ABC Television
TWO KIDS COUNTRY	Singer	NBC Television
SESAME STREET	Guest	PBS Television

MUSIC VIDEOS:

TOMORROW	Guitarist	Propaganda
FOREVER YOUR GIRL	Featured	Propaganda
WE GOT A LOVE THANG	Featured	Dancer

THEATER:

HIP HOP GOES BROADWAY	Star	Hollywood Palladium
THE HARLEM GRILL	Quincy (Lead)	Midtown Art Center
GODSPELL	Multiple Roles	Hits Unicorn Theater

PUBLIC STAGE APPEARANCES:

DIONNE WARWICK'S AIDS BENEFIT	Singer	Universal Amphitheater
SAMMY AWARDS	Co-Host & Singer	Wortham Theater
PERFORMING KIDS INTERNATIONAL	Singer & Dancer	Westwood Mall
HOUSTON AUTO SHOW	Dancer	Astrodome

Recording Artist With "All God's Children" Int'l Recording Artist With L.A.X
NOMINATED FOR YOUTH IN FILM AWARD

===

NOTE: Confine your resume to one page, using smaller print as the resume grows. Delete less important items such as "Professional Training," "Special Skills," and Commercials.

Headshot

BLAKE McIVER EWING

3/4" Length Headshot

DANA DAUREY

Full Length Headshot

Carrie See Photography

Brad Hawkins

AMI-ANN

Composite

Hair: Chestnut
Eyes: Brown
Size: 5-6
D.O.B.: 8-17-87

Color Quik-Comp by Devron Tech., USA (212) 545-9380

80e

Chapter 6

PREPARING FOR AUDITIONS AND CALLBACKS

Desire is pure potentiality seeking fulfillment.
-Deepak Chopra, MD., author "Magical Mind, Magical Body"

ESSENTIAL ITEMS TO KEEP IN THE CAR FOR AUDITIONS

The following items should always remain in the car used for driving to auditions:

1. HEADSHOTS: There is nothing worse than getting to an audition only to discover that your pictures and resumes are at home. Showing up without the proper tools of the trade looks unprofessional. Casting directors have been known to lose their patience with parents who ran out of pictures or forgot to bring them. I remember witnessing a casting director tell a mother, in front of everyone, not to bother coming to her office again without headshots. This unfortunate parent fell victim to the last straw syndrome: too many parents showed up that day without pictures.

Always place your child's headshots and resumes in a separate attaché case, portfolio, notebook or folder to protect them from getting dog eared or wrinkled.

2. *THOMAS GUIDE MAP BOOK:* Even natives who think they know the city like the back of their hand can benefit from a *Thomas Guide Map Book.* Especially in a city the size of Los Angeles where quite a few auditions are held at off-the-beaten-path locations that even a native may not readily know of. Casting calls that take place on obscure side streets in the media district are troublesome because streets start, dead end, then pick up somewhere else in a different area of town.

At times the agent will give detailed directions; at other times, only the cross streets. Problems arise when the directions given assume that one already knows how to get from point "A" to point "B" in order to begin the journey at point "C." While one may think he or she knows the general area, it is easy to get turned around in Los Angeles where streets start out going North and South and end up East and West. Or where Freeway signs sometimes fail to note North, South, East or West. Rather, they assume, that the driver knows the geography of California by heart. For example, one has to know that the sign "405 Sacramento" will lead the driver North, or that 405 "Santa Ana" goes South. When running late for an audition, or experiencing anxiety about directions, one can easily forget which cities lie North and South of Los Angeles.

Parents must also remember to ask the name of the city (i.e., Santa Monica, Culver City, Beverly Hills, etc.) or area of Los Angeles where the audition is located (i.e., North Hollywood, West Hollywood, Mid-Wilshire etc.). Moreover, it helps to know the complete name of the street. For example, Lincoln Boulevard differs from Lincoln Street, and Twenty-Fifth (25th) Street is not the same as E. 25th Street. So, always obtain complete street names and addresses. Moreover, in Los Angeles, most major streets like Wilshire, Sunset, LaBrea, Washington, Lincoln, etc. extend all across Los Angeles into adjoining cities such as Santa Monica, Venice or Marina Del Rey. In the process, street numbers change abruptly after entering a new city. Once I drove all the way to Santa

Monica looking for an address on Lincoln Boulevard that was actually in the city of Venice. One can waste a lot of time, arrive late for the audition, or miss it completely by taking down only the address and assuming that you know which city you're going to. Never presume that you know unless you've already been there before and you're absolutely sure how to return.

3. HEALTHY SNACK PACKS: One must realize that young children live in the eternally present moment and cannot understand that "after the audition" does not mean tomorrow; or, forever for that matter. A responsible parent will, therefore, anticipate a child's hunger and prepare ahead of time for that need. I have heard exasperated parents tell a small child who complained of hunger at an audition: "But you just ate before we left home." Often parents fail to take into consideration their driving time to the audition. For example, even though I live in the Media District I try to give myself at least an hour of driving time to get from Burbank to West Hollywood (only a short distance in terms of miles) because of unpredictable traffic or road conditions.

Many times, when a child complains of hunger at an audition, a snack, such as fresh fruit or a handy little box of juice, will hold the youngster over. Moreover, having food available often acts as psychological security that keeps a child pacified. Since children run off of nervous energy at auditions a small snack will quickly revitalize them. Having fruit, juice and nuts on hand can give the child considerable comfort, not to mention adding to the parent's peace of mind. Besides, a hungry child is a cranky child. And a cranky child might as well have stayed at home because he or she cannot focus or concentrate on anything but hunger. Moreover, for unexpectedly long auditions, packing food to carry along can make the experience more like a picnic as opposed to a bad memory.

NOTE: Whatever you do, avoid refined sugar and processed foods (like donuts and pastries) which have artificial colors and flavors in them, i.e., canned soda. These foods can cause sugar rushes and crashes, unpredictable mood swings and hyperactive behavior. While candy can give a child an adrenaline rush, it lasts less than an hour, after which the child will need another candy fix. Meanwhile junk food eaters become cranky or sleepy which creates a vicious cycle of hyper energy and fatigue. Worst of all, too much processed sugar creates an inability to concentrate or sit still for very long in many children. Avoid the aggravation by providing fresh fruit or natural fruit juices that contain fructose, which the body assimilates naturally without adverse reactions. Far too many children end up labeled "behavior problems" when diet is the real culprit.

In Los Angeles, most parents who live way out in Orange County or deep in the San Fernanado Valley know to bring along healthy snack packs to prepare for delays in traffic or for auditions that go on for hours. Such parents also know how much time it can take to look for a fast food place to grab a bite to eat en route to the audition. Usually there isn't enough time or the line is too long.

Parents who do not take time to pack snacks often rationalize that they will take the child out to eat after the audition or assume that they will have time to stop for a snack on the way to the audition, overlooking the possibility that sometimes agents will page parents at one audition to have them go to another one right after they finish that one, thereby leaving no time to stop for food.

No matter how many times I have explained this simple point to parents, photo shoots or auditions run the risk of ruin because they end up lasting much longer than expected, causing the child to grow hungry and irritable. Even under the best of circumstances, it does not hurt to arrive with a packed lunch.

Remember, auditions can take anywhere from five minutes to several hours especially for open calls or dance auditions. Come prepared to stay for the duration. If your child has another audition scheduled that presents a conflict, tell the casting director and they will try to move your child's name up on the list. At other times, nothing can expedite moving the audition along because the casting director is waiting for a producer or director to show up. In that event, call the agency and let them advise you whether to go on to the next audition and come back later or stay and wait. Sometimes the auditions are too far apart to do a turn around like that, so let the agent make the decision.

4. PARKING MONEY: Keep a roll of quarters in your car to feed parking meters. Make sure you synchronize your watch with the meter because some meters only grant one hour, others two. But the most important reason to carry quarters is because ticket officers in Los Angeles take their jobs seriously, especially in the Media District. I have raced out of casting offices SIXTY SECONDS LATE, trying to catch the meter, only to find an officer in the process of writing a ticket, or one already on my windshield. Even if you catch officers writing your ticket, forget about trying to talk them out of it; they either go deaf on your plea, or respond with an insult or a sneer. Anyway you look at it their attitude clearly indicates that the ticket has your name on it. During such moments I'm reminded of those battery commercials that take a licking and just keep on writing that ticket. In a highly publicized news case, one ticket officer in Los Angeles wrote a parking ticket and placed it on the windshield in clear view of a dead body that was shot through the head at the driver's wheel. Trust me, the City of Los Angeles is dead serious about writing parking tickets.

If you have a child too small to leave in the waiting room while you run out to feed the parking meter, pay the extra money and park at a nearby parking lot or garage. In the long run it saves money. Even though initially it costs more than a meter, a parking lot is infinitely cheaper than a parking ticket, which starts at $30.00 for meter violations in Los Angeles. It goes up considerably for red zones and fire hydrants. Parents who go on a lot of auditions can easily accumulate parking tickets that add up to hundreds of dollars a month. And watch out for meters with tow away provisions after three or four o'clock p.m. which are designed to accommodate rush hour traffic. Even though the meter may not have expired they will tow your car away and write you a ticket (more than fifty dollars) for parking in a tow away zone. On top of that you will incur the expense of getting your car out of the pound (along with cab fare to get there). The whole process can cost you over $150.00.

ABOUT THOSE POLAROID PICTURES AT AUDITIONS

I took the time to address the issue of Polaroids because I have seen actors ruin their whole audition on account of one. They get "bummed-out" about how bad the picture looks.

Helpful hints for better Polaroids: (1) turn a little off-center from the camera and tilt the head slightly up or down; (2) try to avoid head-on shots even though the casting assistant will more than likely ask you to look directly into the camera.

For commercial auditions, most of the time casting directors will take their own Polaroid snapshots at the audition. They will then staple this snapshot to the *information sheet* (i.e., *size sheet*) that you fill out when you arrive, (the sheet asks for name, social security number, time of arrival and agent's name) then attach your headshot to the back of the sheet. At times the assistant may tell you to keep your headshot. It depends on the casting director.

Even though one can pretty much count on having a Polaroid taken for commercial or dance auditions, rarely will theatrical auditions require a Polaroid. A regular headshot will suffice since theatrical casting directors search more for acting ability than a look.

Since Polaroids are in color and more current than headshots, casting directors use them to match up commercial children with parents, groups or siblings. All too often a child arrives at the audition looking totally different from the headshot in hand after using the same headshot for a year or two. More importantly, Polaroids accurately reflect the child exactly as he or she appeared (hair style and all) on the day of the audition. That way, if the child did not give accurate information on the videotape, or did not speak clearly enough on tape, casting can go through the Polaroids and quickly match up the child's picture and information sheet to the videotape.

If one sits in any audition waiting room long enough he or she will hear parents, children and other adults complain about how unflattering these Polaroid shots look. Most of the time the shots do turn out bad, looking more like mug shots because the assistant takes a very close up view. Often these Polaroids come out over exposed with the color washed out. Or the nose looks distorted, like a reflection on a shiny door knob. But don't bother to complain to the assistant about how terrible your child looks on the picture. The assistant will only reshoot the Polaroid if the child's eyes were closed or the film defective. If you complain anyway, you will get a reminder that Polaroids merely serve as reference tools and have no actual bearing on the casting of the commercial.

If the Polaroid pictures consistently bother you buy your own Polaroid camera and take a picture of your child immediately before leaving home for the audition. Then you can substitute your picture for the one the casting director took. Use a white wall in the background and no one will know the difference since the child's outfit and hair is exactly the same as the Polaroid picture taken at the audition.

Also keep in mind that casting directors at commercial auditions videotape your child for the client's review. After the commercial is cast the Polaroids are passed on to wardrobe personnel so that they can have an idea of the talent's hair color and eyes when putting together outfits for the shoot.

SMOOTH RIDING TO AND FROM AUDITIONS

Make the drive to the audition as stress-free as possible for parent and child. One of the biggest causes of anxiety involves not allowing yourself enough time to get the child dressed, fed and out of the door with adequate time to reach your destination. Moreover, make sure the child went to bed early the night before and got enough sleep so that he or she has enough energy for the audition. If unavoidably tired before the audition, give the child something light and healthy to eat or drink, like fruit or natural fruit juice to boost energy. Then reassure the child that he or she can take a nap immediately afterwards.

Rides to auditions provide perfect opportunities to boost your child's self confidence and eliminate any particular concerns he or she may have about the audition; or to set aside problems from home and school that might interfere with the child doing his or her best at the audition. Lift or set aside any burdens the child may bear *before* walking into the audition room. Sometimes the child might leave home upset with a sibling, or a fight may ensue enroute to the audition. This diverts the child's energy into a negative, draining, or self-defeating thought pattern. Take time to clear the child's mind ahead of time, otherwise, the entire effort can turn into an exercise in futility.

HELP YOUR CHILD COPE WITH DISCORD IN THE FAMILY

Soothing lingering fears or frustrations may require a few extra minutes upon arrival at the audition. The extra effort on behalf of your child can make the difference between a successful audition and one that's a waste of time. Often a warm hug of reassurance and a vote of confidence will do the trick. As long as you're no more than fifteen minutes late for the audition, most casting directors will not penalize you. For callbacks, however, try your best to get there on time.

The same situation applies if parents have unresolved problems in the marriage. A case in point involves a client of mine from the East coast who was accustomed to taking her child to auditions on the train without assistance from her husband. The train gave her a sense of independence and self sufficiency about getting her child to auditions. When the family moved to California the mother found herself at a disadvantage not knowing how to drive; and on top of that, no driver's license or a car or her own. To complicate matters, the child's father complained often, in front of the child, about having to adjust his work schedule to drive them to auditions. This made the child feel like a burden to the family and responsible for her parents not getting along. In actuality, it was the financial pressure of the move and other problems in the relationship that had the parents fighting.

Eventually financial concerns, coupled with the husband's insensitivity, forced the mother to return to the East Coast without the father. Soon thereafter, whenever I spoke with this mother, she gave glowing reports about the change in her peace of mind and the child's happiness. Once again, the child now worked on a regular basis as opposed to sporadically in Los Angeles. And the mother's self-esteem returned by being able to get the child to auditions again on her own. She confided that the best part was not having to deal with her husband's constant complaints in front of the child, who was too young to understand that her parent's problems were much larger than a transportation issue.

The moral of this story is that parents would do well to remember that arguing in front of children may cause them to take on problems too heavy for adults, let alone children. Often parents erroneously assume that children understand the obvious (i.e., that the argument has nothing to do with him).

In reality, young children cannot distinguish gray areas or clearly discern cloudy issues. When unable to avoid such a situation, during and after unavoidable arguments in front of the children, reassure the child that the disagreement lies strictly between adults and has nothing to do with him or her. More importantly, let your children know that both parents will always love them unconditionally, no matter what happens between adults.

Moreover, children need to know that parental arguments or disagreements do not necessarily mean that a divorce waits in the wings. By using this approach children can learn that it's okay to agree to disagree. In fact, more often than not they may find amusement in their parents antics, or the things they bother to argue over; often laughing at something their parents say during an argument.

CALLBACKS

On a *callback*, wear the same outfit worn to the original audition, unless specifically instructed otherwise. Most of the time your agent will remind you to do so. At other times the casting director will stress that the child return in the same outfit. Even if no one reminds you, do so anyway.

Keep in mind that something about the way the child dressed during the first call caught everyone's attention. The outfit also helps the casting director readily identify the child. The old saying: "If it ain't broke, don't fix it," applies here.

Occasionally, due to changes in the character or script, the casting director will call the agent and ask that the child dress a little more "street," "conservative" or "trendy." In such a situation, they liked the child inspite of the attire.

PRACTICE YOUR LINES

As stated in a previous chapter, on the first audition, casting directors do not concern themselves too much with whether the actor has memorized his or her *sides*. Everyone pretty much goes inside and reads from the script. By the *screen test,* however, casting directors not only look for how well the actor memorizes and delivers lines, but use of facial expressions, hand and body movements, or *blocking* (i.e. movement in front of the camera).

Sometimes, after the first or second audition, casting will hand out new material to read for the producers. For instance, when my son got a call for a screen test at Universal he had just gone on the callback the day before. Afterwards he received new material to read for two different roles. The agent called me at work the next day and I had less than an hour to leave work, go home and get Salim's audition outfit, pick him up from school, and rush to the screen test.

On the way to pick up Salim I became alarmed because Salim had over fifteen pages of sides and I could not find them at home or in the car. (They later turned up in my husband's car). Usually we use the drive to the audition to go over sides. I grew worried because Salim will sometimes memorize material quickly, using short term memory, then dispose of the material entirely.

Enroute to the screen test I explained to Salim that he was going to have to deliver his lines by memory in front of a camera and I could not find the sides for him to go over. He instructed me to "chill" because he knew all the lines to both roles. I did just that and Salim went on to get the role.

SIDES

SAG Rules require that actors have sides available at least 24 hours before the audition. Trust me, they must have meant under ideal circumstances. Many times the agent will get the call too late in the day to contact the client in enough time for the parent to drive across town to pick up the script. Having a fax machine helps. Sometimes, however, with a large casting in progress the casting office will not have enough time to fax sides to the agent. When unable to obtain the sides ahead of time, arrive at the audition early enough to read over the lines and become familiar with them.

Reminder: When arriving early specifically to go over the material, do not write your name on the ***sign-in sheet*** or ***call sheet*** until ready to go inside and deliver your lines. Once you sign in, the casting director will call names from that list, usually in the order provided.

Also, since one has no way of knowing how long he or she will have to wait between callbacks, it's a good idea to keep up with your sides. Buy a special note book for them and review your lines periodically just to keep them fresh in your mind. Sometimes last minute callbacks occur three weeks later. Such situations happen more often with movies or new television series because they have long lead times between casting and the actual ***shoot date.***

I find it preferable to audition during the final week before shooting begins. By that time, casting directors are pretty clear on what they do not want. Moreover, they have already interviewed a number of people at that point and the last round of interviews tend to carry more weight.

POINTS TO PONDER:

1. *Keep headshots, a Thomas Guide Map Book, healthy snacks and drinks in your car.*

2. *(A) Never assume you know directions to an audition. Check your Thomas Guide. (B) Be sure of the part of town and get the correct city name.*

3. *If you don't like the Polaroid pictures taken at commercial auditions, shoot your own before leaving home for the audition.*

4. *Make the ride to auditions as stress free and relaxing as possible. Listen to soothing music. Allow extra time for traffic, getting lost, or to prepare for the audition upon arrival.*

5. *Leave family problems at home or solve them ahead of time.*

6. *(A) Unless told otherwise, always wear the same outfit to callbacks. (B) SAG rules require that actors receive their sides 24 hours in advance. (C) Keep up with your sides and memorize them.*

Chapter 7

POSITIVE GOAL SETTING AND AFFIRMATIONS

The law of suggestion leads the mind to do its creative work with affirmations. Repetition lends to belief. When this becomes a deep conviction then things happen. -Dr. Wayne W. Dyer, author REAL MAGIC (HarperCollins)

Negative belief patterns can limit a child's success in show business, or in life, for that matter. For those unaware of the power of the **subconscious** mind and how easily it responds to subtle impressions, commands or certain types of music, I recommend doing some research on the topic. Neuro-Linguistic Programming (NLP), used with amazingly rapid results by many therapists today, provides state of the art techniques for quickly reprogramming negative habits from childhood that block the path to peace of mind, contentment and fulfillment. Understanding and healing childhood traumas prevent children from repeating the parent's old patterns of self-defeating behavior.

Throughout the ages certain types of music proved calming to the nerves. Today, classical or subliminal music is used successfully to increase receptivity to learning in children, cut down on sibling arguments, or to decrease hyperactivity. When I taught school I sometimes used positive subliminal music to calm down elementary children. Since the subconscious mind responds unmistakably to soft music playing in the background, during the ride to auditions I often play subliminal, classical, new age, or soft jazz. This type of quiet, calm music can make time constraints and driving in traffic less stressful for both parent and child.

The only time we do not play soft music is on the way to a performing audition. At such times we will play the instrumental track in the car so that the child can sing along with it. The same thing goes for dance auditions. While the music is playing the child goes over the *choreography* in his or her mind by visualizing the steps. Studies have proven that the subconscious mind does not know the difference between an experience vividly imagined and one that actually occurred. This makes positive *Visualization* a powerful technique. Athletes use it as an aid for excelling in sports; salesmen use it to see themselves successfully closing a sale. So why not teach your child to use it to see himself or herself as an accomplished entertainer, student, etc.?

Since older children tend to resist any music other than the latest trend among peers, gradually exposing them to new artists, in between the music they usually listen to, opens their minds and ears to other possibilities. After playing enough different styles of alternative music children will quickly express their preference. Through this process my son discovered that he liked the Eastern euphony of Enigma and Yanni. Among the classics, he came to favor Mozart's "A Little Night Music" and Beethoven's "Fifth Symphony." My daughter loves the beauty of Kenny G's French horn, the soundtrack to "Phantom of The Opera" and the soothing music of Denis Waitley's "The Subliminal Winner." And all three of us enjoy the synthesized sounds of Japanese artist Kitaro; in particular, "Silk Road."

AVOID NEGATIVE COMMANDS

In order to understand how the subconscious mind works, one needs to understand that it basically has no concept of a negative command. The subconscious literally takes us at our word. For instance, if I say "Don't think about a nice a day at the beach," the first thing you will think of is a carefree day at the beach because the subconscious mind filters out the negative command.

Therefore, if you tell your child: "Don't worry about forgetting your lines." Your child will hear: "Worry about forgetting your lines." As a result, when stating a command to a child using a negative, nine times out of ten, the child will go in and do the very thing you specifically told him or her to avoid. The rare exception involves children who, on a subconscious level, innately or automatically reprocess all negative commands into positive ones.

Simply tell your child: "Relax and have a good time," rather than "Don't be nervous," because when he or she goes inside the child will act upon directives from the subconscious mind, which repeat: "Be nervous."

Parents should also become conscious of their choice of words, noting all negative expressions used on a daily basis, then make an effort to reverse the automatic habit of adding a negative to a positive expression.

What you say to your child immediately before going into the audition room or on stage to perform sticks in the back of his or her mind: *Remember: what you say to your child is just as important as what he or she wears, or how well the lines are memorized, because the subconscious mind never shuts down; it operates on automatic pilot 24 hours a day.*

I explained the concept of negative commands to the parent of a child that I work with. At the time, the concept was either too new or she forgot. On the night of the performance the mother went backstage and did the very thing I cautioned her against.

The last thing she said to her child before he went on stage was: "Don't let the wireless mike fall off of your head." In reality, the mike was only an ornament because the child was lip syncing to the song as he danced. The little boy is an incredible dancer with unusual ability; not a singer. Naturally, all during the performance the child fidgeted with the head mike, trying to insure that it wouldn't fall off, just as his Mommy commanded. As a result, the little boy did not execute his dance routine to the best of his abilities. And of course, he couldn't because his focus inadvertently shifted to the last thing his mother told him.

After the show the mother was really disappointed. The next day I reminded her that she did everything I advised her to avoid. (Maybe I unconsciously threw in some negative commands to her?) Only then did she realize the power of a negative command. All she needed to say to her son before he walked on stage was: "Have fun and dance from your soul, like you always do." Fortunately, this mother learns from her mistakes and the little boy has gone on to become an incredible dancer because the mother now keeps her focus where it needs to be -- on his dance. When the child sings or raps along with the vocals, she does not encumber him with a head microphone.

In show business, I have discovered basically three types of parents:

(1) those that learn from the mistakes of other parents
(2) those who only learn from their own mistakes, and
(3) those who never learn.

Parents who fall into categories two or three require a long learning curve and cannot expect their children to succeed by leaps and bounds. Not surprisingly, parents in categories two and three are the ones who waste other people's time asking questions or seeking advice they have no intention of following. Unfortunately, this type of parent usually ends up unintentionally blocking the child's path to progress.

LISTENING TO MOTIVATIONAL TAPES

Children allowed the freedom to be themselves in the presence of adults, or who somehow held on to their natural fearlessness, possess an innate curiosity about new people, places and things that fosters their ability to develop instant rapport with others. Other children pick up this trait naturally by mimicking a parent who does so with ease. Fortunately, for those without it, this ability can be developed. Moreover, classes, seminars, books and motivational cassette tapes are readily available on the subject.

When my youngest was five I began buying motivational and subliminal tapes to play in the car as we drove to auditions or to school. Instead of listening to the radio I inundated my children's subconscious with positive messages as we rode around town together. I found that playing motivational and subliminal tapes over the years helped prevent my son from falling prey to cynicism picked up from peers during adolescent and teen years. Even now, they enable my children to recapture their original belief in themselves whenever their confidence lags behind. The tapes provide a boost of reassurance and validation. Keep in mind that children pick up an inordinate amount of negative programming at school or from friends who quickly undermine anything they do not understand.

During that summer when my two children and I first came out to Los Angeles with The Dallas Television and Film Workshop, I remember the skepticism of some members of that group towards the tapes I played. It took my children's success during our first year here to make believers out of them. The following summer when The Dallas Television and Film Workshop returned, many children from that group asked my son for the names of those motivational tapes we listened to. And the director of the workshop sent me a congratulatory card commenting on how well the tapes had worked for us.

I even used Bryan Tracy's ***Psychology of Achievement*** tape series to encourage an underachieving, sixth grade English Composition class to produce some of the best essays their school had ever seen.

Understanding the art of motivation is similar to learning which keys perform what function on a keyboard in order to operate computer software efficiently. Similarly, motivating others involves knowing which buttons elicit the right response. Children learn early on that certain types of behavior create specific responses from parents. Unfortunately too many children end up hooked on pushing the wrong buttons. Motivational tapes provide exceptional tools for understanding human nature and finding out the correct buttons to push in order to get exactly what we want out of life.

POSITIVE GOAL SETTING AND AFFIRMATIONS

The moments prior to an audition or performance, as well as the drive to the audition, are perfectly suited for peaceful meditation, reflection, or positive affirmations. Silence, music, motivational tapes, or books are all great choices to use as preparational tools before the audition.

Better still, make positive thinking and quiet time a daily part of your life. During moments of silence teach your child to get in touch with the "still small voice" inside of him or her. This technique can have an incredibly calming effect that automatically boosts a child's self confidence and places him or her at peace with the world. Many call this practice **meditation.** Meditation provides quiet time for shutting off the negative "chatter box" we all carry around inside our heads: that loud, confusing voice so filled with fearful thoughts we have a hard time hearing anything else, let alone something that might benefit us. Too often we become so tuned into our "chatter box" and out of touch with our "still small voice" that we have no way of experiencing peace or bliss. Mythologist, Joseph Campbell says that we must all learn to follow our "bliss."

The process of meditation involves thinking of nothing at all. This provides respite from worry, anxiety or problems that prevent one from attaining peace of mind. It also refuels the psyche by giving the mind a break before it reaches a point of mental exhaustion. Some people meditate by simply sitting quietly in a hot bath or Jacuzzi, lying alone to catch a few rays of sun on the beach or at the swimming pool. Others listen to soothing music alone without thinking of anything else. The most beneficial aspect of meditation involves permitting yourself to get in touch with your own counsel. The process also allows quiet time to focus on a particular issue and to seek divine direction or intervention with problems. Often this guidance comes in flashes of intuition or insight.

Affirmations are a helpful tool for quieting that chatter box inside ones head when we become caught up in anxiety, fear or negativity. Major bookstores and all metaphysical bookstores carry a variety of books on affirmations. See the end of this chapter for a recommended list.

Keep in mind that affirmations should be worded without negatives and stated in the present tense. For example: *"I deliver my lines naturally, easily and effortlessly,"* rather than: *"I will not forget my lines."*

Here are a few of my favorite affirmations from Florence Scovel Shinn's book *"Your Word Is Your Wand"* (DeVorss & Company Publications):

I am poised and powerful. My greatest expectations are realized in a miraculous way.

The following is good for creating harmony in your child's mind when he or she comes across someone at an audition who unsettles that peace of mind. (Sometimes other children will do and say little things to their competition designed to undermine confidence and poise): *There is no competition on the Spiritual plane. What is mine is given me under grace.*

Right before your child walks into the casting office it's helpful to repeat: *I am identified in love with the Spirit of this person.*

God protects my interests and the Divine Idea now comes out of this situation.

When your child is feeling frustrated with his or her best efforts repeat: *I am in perfect harmony with the working of the law. I stand aside and let Infinite Intelligence make easy and successful my way.*

If your child is disappointed about not getting a part, or after going through several callbacks and losing out to someone else, this one is helpful: *There are no lost opportunities in the Kingdom. As one door shuts another door opens.* At such times I remind my children that there will always be another audition. No matter how slow the season, the industry always manages to flourish.

For a general boost in prosperity consciousness, the following is excellent: *My good now flows to me in a steady, unbroken, ever-increasing stream of success, happiness and abundance.*

If your child is feeling intimidated by the audition material or by the competition, try the following affirmation: *There are no obstacles in Divine Mind, therefore, my good is unobstructed.*

There are times when my two children have to learn a new song and dance routine at the last minute. This can involve learning an entirely new choreography in one day, (and on a school night, no less). When this happens, I use positive commands while addressing the parents of the children who dance with my son and daughter, such as: *"After rehearsal everyone will know the steps perfectly."* I always stress that each parent tell their child how much fun the show is going to be and to remind the child of how easily he or she catches on to new dance steps. In such situations children are naturally competitive and want to keep up with their peers. This helps them rise to their level of competence. All parents have to do is decide to release their children from limitation and let them reach their higher good. Children innately believe that they are invincible. All too often parents, teachers and friends instill beliefs that limit children even though they do so with good intentions, often without knowing that they are setting the children up for failure.

RECOMMENDED TAPES:

The Following Tapes are Available Through Nightingale Conant Corporation:

Les Brown: *Courage To Live Your Dreams*
Dr. Wayne W. Dyer:
 How To Be A No Limit Person
 Choosing Your Own Greatness
 You'll See It When You Believe It
Loeher and McLaughlin: *Mental Toughness Training*
Nightingale Conant: *NLP: The New Technology of Achievement*
Earl Nightingale: *The Essence of Success*
Anthony Robbins: *Personal Power*
DenisWaitley: *The Psychology of Winning*

BOOKS WITH AFFIRMATIONS:

Susan Ford: *WOW, AM I POWERFUL*
Og Mandingo: *THE GREATEST SALESMAN IN THE WORLD*
Catherine Ponder: *PROSPERITY SECRETS OF THE AGES*
Anthony Robbins:
 PERSONAL POWER
 AWAKEN THE GIANT WITHIN
Florence Scovel Shinn: (DeVorss & Company, Publishers)
 YOUR WORD IS YOUR WAND
 THE GAME OF LIFE AND HOW TO PLAY IT
Marianne Williamson: *A RETURN TO LOVE*

POINTS TO PONDER

1. *An outlook of positive expectancy is the most important asset an actor can own.*

2. *If one prepares ahead of time, studies his craft, and expects to do well on an audition, he will.*

3. *The focus should always be on the present moment, i.e., doing one's best. At the audition one should not fixate on getting the job; rather, on being relaxed and confident.*

4. *More importantly: enjoy the audition process. Have fun with it. Casting directors run into far too many over-anxious, uptight actors who trip all over themselves trying to impress others. If one focuses on the only variable he has control over -- i.e., himself -- then everything else will fall into place.*

5. *When we first moved to L.A. CED agent, Bob Preston told me: "Forget about the audition once it's over. Go on to other things."*

6. *Fear and anxiety is the opposite of faith. Faith releases our flow of good, assuring us that we may confidently expect things to manifest in their own perfect time.*

Chapter 8

COMMON FEARS ABOUT SHOW BUSINESS

One of the major issues that we as Americans have to address is our unbelievable lack of respect and concern for the way we care for our children, and how that is reflected in some of our school systems. --Marianne Williamson, Author of "A Return to Love" (quoted from "The BodhiTree Interview" by Mark Kenaston & Dana Alan LaFontaine, Issue No. 2, Spring 1992)

Many parents who approach me about getting their children into show business have various fears. Most worry about child exploitation. Many fear their child will end up uneducated or an arrogant, "Hollywood Brat" who thinks the world should cater to his every command. Some fears are fall-out from the old studio era when no laws protected children in the industry from exploitative studio bosses or producers.

Even with the public's growing social consciousness and sensitivity towards children, the potential for abuse always remains. Fortunately, the risks have been greatly minimized as a result of child labor laws introduced in the 70's and 80's nationally by the Screen Actors Guild and locally by the California Labor Board. Moreover, the predominance of children's casting directors and agents who are enlightened parents has reduced the potential risks for child actors. Parenthood tends to create natural empathy towards children's issues. Many agents and casting directors are also former stage moms. Some have children in show business while others are sympathetic former actors. This list amounts to people concerned with the welfare of child actors. Personally, I feel that the combined presence of so many women (who are also mothers) that hold high level positions in the kids entertainment market has helped create a positive impact on working conditions for children in the industry.

Agents, managers and casting directors are required to schedule auditions and callbacks AFTER SCHOOL. If the child is taken out of school, they must provide a studio teacher. They also make sure that *work permits* remain up to date. In California work permits are renewed every six months and not reissued if the child's grades fall below a "C" average.

STUDIO TEACHERS

The best and the brightest in America should be our school teachers. We need to wake up to the fact that our children are our most precious national resource. Shame on us that we would spend so much money on our Minutemen and so little on our children. --Marianne Williamson, Author of "A Return to Love" (quoted from "The BodhiTree Interview" by Mark Kenaston & Dana Alan LaFontaine, Issue No. 2, Spring 1992)

Children working in the entertainment field who live outside of California are not as well protected legally because California Child Labor Laws provide for a *studio teacher* on the set who is certified to teach all subjects the child would normally take at his or her regular school. (Most states do not have this mandate). For instance, a California child studying French or Calculus, must have a studio teacher capable of teaching those subjects. Moreover, the standards for becoming a studio teacher are tougher than those for a regular instructor because studio teachers must have multi-subject credentials to teach all grade levels.

When school is out, the studio teacher doubles as a *welfare worker* who enforces child labor laws by protecting the child's physical welfare and insuring that he or she does not work beyond hours specified by the state of California for each age group. *(See next chapter for work hours)* This rule applies to both union and non-union sets.

Elise Ganz, a California studio teacher says: *"We remind the director that they have to take a break or that the child's day is done at a certain time."* The presence of the studio teacher takes pressure off of the parent. Ganz, explains: *"A lot of times, parents aren't that assertive, so it's up to the studio teacher to step forward. The parent thinks that if they put up a fuss, it will hurt the kid's career."* (from Zoe F. Carter's article, "Baby, It's You.")

Anytime a child has to work more than an hour on post-production work such as wardrobe, makeup, looping or dubbing, a studio teacher is required to be present. Otherwise, whenever a child is taken out of school and has to work the child must have a studio teacher present. Record companies, music production companies and print work all must provide a studio teacher because they fall under the umbrella of the "entertainment industry." Once again, this applies whether they are union or non-union. Incidentally, some record labels attempt to take advantage of this rule by saying that the child will only be in the studio an hour or so when they know the session will last most of the day. If the parent goes along with companies not providing a studio teacher, the parent can be fined or found in violation of child labor laws and lose the child's work permit. Also note that a statute of limitations exists for reporting violations, therefore, reports must be filed in a timely manner.

Teachers I spoke with revealed that those who do get fired when they report violations to the union rarely fight the decision because it's such an involved process. And the production company or movie studio involved will usually cover up for the real reason they fired the teacher in order to protect themselves from penalties or bad press. Fortunately, this is the exception, and production companies rarely, if ever, defy a studio teacher's authority. Occasionally some studio teachers fall in awe or fear of the director and will not stand up for the rules. Most, however, do a wonderful job of protecting child actors.

In circumstances where a parent feels that the child is being pushed too hard or beyond safe boundaries he or she should tell the studio teacher first and let the teacher take care of it. Should the studio teacher: refuse to enforce labor laws, willfully disrespect or mistreat the child, or prove ineffective, the parent can request that the production company replace that studio teacher.

Further, if a studio teacher becomes overwhelmed by the child's school assignments or does not feel able to teach higher level subjects such as Chemistry or Calculus, the parent can request an additional teacher for that subject. Furthermore, a studio teacher must bring in an extra instructor if he or she has to teach ten or more children on the set.

In making requests on behalf of the child's education, the parent should forget what others may think of her and concentrate on having her child's educational requirements met.

Fortunately each state has its own provisions to prevent child actors from getting an unexcused absence when they miss school in order to work. When we lived in Texas (a non-union right to work state) I felt relieved that such a law was enacted since the Houston Independent School District has very strict attendance policies. A child can be held back a grade if he or she has more than five unexcused absences.

In contrast to California's work permits, Texas has a "no pass, no play" rule. If a student fails any subject, he or she cannot participate in extra-curricular activities. Even the school's star quarterback gets laid off the team until grades improve. The same thing applies for working in the entertainment field or for any activity outside of required classroom subjects.

In Texas, most of my children's teachers cooperated with me as long as I told them ahead of time that my child needed to miss school to shoot a commercial, film, or print job. They provided assignments to finish at home, allowing my children to make up any tests missed while absent.

Although Texas does not provide studio teachers on the set, my two children had no problem staying on the honor role while working. Both children understood clearly that they had to do their homework, otherwise they would lose the privilege of acting and going out on auditions.

If we had a particularly long day on the set, however, I would talk with the teachers and obtain an extension for the school work. As long as I kept the teachers informed and took the time to come up to the school and pick up assignments, they willingly worked with me. In fact, several teachers from Will Rogers Elementary in Houston still keep in touch with my children and follow their careers.

DEALING WITH DIFFICULT SCHOOL TEACHERS

There are, of course, those teachers who do not look favorably upon children in show business. I have run into my share of difficult teachers during the course of my children's careers. In the process I discovered that some teachers already have preconceived negative notions about child actors, stage parents, or the business in general. Some feel that child actors expect special consideration by nature of the work they do.

Needless to say, a fair amount of jealousy also exists. For instance, while attending a school for academically gifted children, my daughter had a teacher refuse to accept homework that the teacher had assigned herself, which Crystal **completed on the set** with a studio teacher. To add insult to injury, this teacher told my daughter, in front of the class, that she did not "approve" of child actors. Crystal explained to me that when the teacher made that comment in front of her classmates she felt as if she had been punched in the face by prize fighter, Evander Holyfield. She took it as a personal slight and put down.

In a different school district, my son had a teacher force him to take a test the day he returned from the set over material covered in the classroom while Salim was out. This reflected poorly on his test results. The teacher refused to drop the grade or to allow Salim to take the test over. In such situations **The Board of Education** for many school districts prevent teachers from testing a child actor the day after returning from work because every child needs equal access as well as time to study information missed while absent. Any fair-minded teacher will not deny a child reasonable opportunity to succeed as opposed to setting the student up for failure.

I ended up having to meet with the principal at my son's school for intervention in the matter. Eventually, after several meetings, my son got to make up the test. But only after I threatened to bring in higher authorities on the matter.

Based on that experience, I would advise parents to do their research and know the laws in order to determine what recourses are available. With the teacher and principal, establish up front your awareness of the law and that *you are only asking to be dealt with fairly,* making it clear that you do not expect special consideration; nor are you trying to get your child out of doing work. It also helps to remain calm, rational, firm and to stick to the point. Moreover, it will weaken any chance of getting what you want if you allow yourself to get pulled into a shouting match. Sometimes it helps to remind the faculty of who they are working for and of their obligation to uplift and promote the general welfare of students, not to hold them back or discourage them.

Admittedly, confrontations with teachers pose an unnecessary emotional drain. Keep in mind, however, that if stage parents do not go to battle for their children on important educational issues, the child actor will, by default, be unfairly barred from working, which is what the teacher may want anyway.

ENMITY FROM PEERS

At one point I was forced to take my child out of an academically gifted magnet program and enroll him in a small private school with other child actors because of threats to his life the day after he appeared on a popular television show. During this time he was enrolled in a program outside of the City of Los Angeles, which did not have any prominent child actors. Until that television show aired (where he was interviewed as a special guest regarding his upcoming movie role), no one knew that Salim was an actor. He was in junior high school at the time and a group of boys at this school, who were already envious of the way he dressed, became incensed over the attention he received over-night by the most popular girls at school after this television show aired. As a result, Salim's name ended up on a "hit list," and I received a call from my son to pick him up before lunch time when the hit was scheduled to take place.

Of course, circumstances for each child is unique. Even Ron Howard admitted in a magazine interview how he frequently got into fights at school over the fact that he was a child actor. With that in mind, most parents who have children in show business should set aside extra time to investigate the school's overall philosophy regarding child actors. If the student body is comprised of a significant number of child actors that is a good indicator that the school tolerates child actors and might not have a negative mind set against children in show business.

I make it a point each year to visit with new teachers to find out up front how they feel about my children missing school in order to work. If I detect any form of bias that cannot be worked out, I will immediately seek a transfer to another classroom.

It also helps to establish rapport with office assistants at your child's school. I have found that a good relationship with the principal's secretary can make all the difference in how well your child's school year goes, especially in elementary schools. For instance, when my children were in elementary school, I always went the extra mile for their school secretary. When possible, I saw to it that Francis got free passes to events that my children were involved in. She, in turn, kept an eye out for them, which gave me a measure of comfort that cannot be counted in terms of dollars.

PERFORMING ARTS SCHOOLS: PROCEED WITH CAUTION

While many magnet and performing arts programs in public schools across the country have developed reputations for producing plays and musicals which rival those of professional companies, parents of children that work in the business should consider: at what cost? Often the demands placed upon students who participate become so exhausting that no latitude remains to audition for or to take paying jobs that offer considerably more publicity and acclaim to the working child. In fact, children enrolled in performing arts programs who leave the school production to work on Broadway, television, or film, can expect their grade in that class to suffer, not to mention disapproval from the teacher or the magnet school coordinator.

One case in point is a talented teen dancer I know enrolled in a high school performing arts program. This school has a highly acclaimed performing arts program. The young lady in question received a prohibition from her teacher against going to a Saturday callback for a national commercial because of a dance rehearsal scheduled that day. The irrationality of this demand lay in the fact that this teen was the best dancer in the entire school and knew the choreography well enough to teach the class. Missing a few hours from an all day rehearsal would not in any way have affected this child's performance. More importantly, this teen missed out on an opportunity to pay for her college education had she gotten this national dance commercial. Ultimately the teen did not attend her callback out of fear the teacher would kick her out of the musical production and give her a failing grade to boot.

After personally witnessing this teenager being unduly harassed by the teacher during rehearsals, the mother asked that I speak with the magnet school coordinator on behalf of the teen. I agreed, curious to find out if, in fact, the teacher had such absolute power over the students in her production. If so, I wanted to know how something so contrary to what a performing arts school was designed to produce (i.e., professional students that go on to make a living off of their talents) could be condoned.

The magnet school coordinator indeed confirmed that the teacher had the power to lower a child's grade for missing rehearsals or for taking time away from the production to take a paying job. The teacher could also drop the teen from her production with a failing grade. The coordinator justified this practice by explaining that they felt that their production was just as important as a professional one. At that point I reminded him that the child was perfectly capable of missing weeks or even months out of that semester long rehearsal schedule and still out dance everyone on the day of the performance. This child had won Star Search and other dance awards which the coordinator was aware of. In no way were these exaggerated assertions. The coordinator cut me off with a reminder that those were the rules. When I went on to explain that this child's father had recently died, leaving the family with no insurance; (meaning that this child needed the extra income a commercial could have brought in for the family) he told me that he could not make exceptions.

Stunned that a performing arts school could refuse to make an exception for a gifted child who had exceptional circumstances, I left the school saddened and angered by such inflexible, insensitive and totally unreasonable people who felt a need to inflict such policies onto unsuspecting students.

That night I called a friend of mine in Texas who has two daughters enrolled in a private school with a well known dance program. Much to my surprise I discovered that her children suffer under the same type of policies with rehearsals every day after school until 7:00 p.m. during the week and each Saturday, all semester long. That school, too, discourages children from working professionally by leaving no room for it, while penalizing them for missing any rehearsals. Moreover, my friend's daughters are both in honors classes which require hours of homework and research each day. As a result, the demanding rehearsal schedule leaves little time to prepare for academic classes, let alone a social life.

In lieu of the foregoing, my feeling is that performing arts programs appear more ideally suited for children who have no professional work ties, no agent and who want to use the free training and experience as a foundation for a career in show business. From the two unrelated examples cited, one can see the incredible amount of stress, sacrifice and commitment demanded from students in performing arts programs.

Before enrolling your child actor in such a program, speak with the coordinator and the teacher to find out ahead of time the price your child has to pay if he or she misses rehearsal in order to work. If the price is too high, unfair or unreasonable, you might want to consider taking the child out of the program. See Chapter 11 titled: "Educational Alternatives."

THE HOLLYWOOD BRAT SYNDROME

Usually problems develop when parents begin to lose touch with who they really are and start identifying themselves through the child's success. To avoid the Hollywood Brat Syndrome, parents need to put "the big picture" into perspective without allowing guilt about being unable to work cloud relevant issues.

If bad behavior from a child actor remains unchecked at home it ends up spilling over into the professional life, often creating irreparable damage. For instance, one child actor I know who had recently landed a television series told me that whenever she could not get her lines right, she demanded a rewrite. As one might imagine, after only one season, this child was desperately looking for a new television series.

Many times children turn into tyrants when they know that their income helps support the family, especially if the parents do not take the time to explain why. Often the child does not understand that one of the parent's had to quit a job, deplete the family savings accounts or move out to Los Angeles in order to give the child a shot at stardom.

In order to help the child put the big picture in focus, parents might want to define the nature of the entire process while making the child aware that the whole family has to make sacrifices in order for the child to have the opportunity to act. The child should be informed, without making him or her feel guilty, that the family's support and involvement are necessary in order to get:

(1) an agent;
(2) headshots;
(3) proper wardrobe;
(4) transportation to auditions;
(5) someone to coach him or her;
(6) emotional support and encouragement; or
(7) a parent or guardian on the set

Moreover, the working child actor has to realize that while all of his or her needs are catered to, the needs of other family members may go unmet in the process. With that in mind, the child actor should understand that everyone in the family "chooses" to give their support out of love and dedication. This type of approach might prevent the child from "acting out" through inappropriate behavior because he or she feels burdened by the sacrifices everyone makes or because he or she fears not living up to the family's expectations. Letting the child know that everyone supports his or her aspirations out of a belief in the child's talent and abilities can alleviate many unspoken apprehensions. Moreover, reassure the child that he or she has the right to a change of mind and can quit the business without penalty. Family support should be given unconditionally. In that manner, the child will not feel pressured to succeed for the sake of the family, as opposed to succeeding for his or her own innate desire to do so.

Furthermore, keep one adult in the family employed so that the child can have a sense of security and not be made to carry the burden of being the sole support of the family. Both parents should not quit their jobs in order to manage the career of their child. Especially in the beginning. If the child becomes a mega-star the demands made on one parent can eventually become too great and the other parent may need to help.

The only other instance where both parents might need to give up their jobs is if more than one child is on a television series, or working regularly in film. Then both parents may eventually have to divide up their time between the children if the shows are a hit. In particular, for young children who need someone they trust to look after their emotional well-being on the set. Some projects are simply too long-term and demanding to pay someone else to handle that responsibility on a full time basis, especially for children under the age of 12. But again, everything depends on the maturity of the child and how supportive the crew is.

THE NON-SHOW BUSINESS SIBLING

Another problem involves the multiple-child, one-child-in-show business family. At times, the emotional needs of the non-working child can get unintentionally over looked. For instance, talking non-stop about the child actor, as if he or she is an only child, can make the other children feel slighted. Every family member has to have his or her own special place in order for the system to work.

There are times, however, when the child actor has legitimate special needs. Particularly when getting ready to audition for a big part or to film a job. Once those needs are met, however, the requirements of other family members must once again be taken into consideration and attended to. This way, one child does not form the mistaken impression that he or she is all that matters in the family.

It also creates problems within the family if the child in show business is placed on a different level from siblings. Especially if that child receives preferential treatment or is allowed to run the household. Moreover, I've seen parents react as if anything the child actor does is adorable, overlooking bad manners or obnoxious behavior while pretending that the child actor can do no wrong. Further, I have seen child actors scream at their parents on the set--literally curse them out--or make unreasonable demands in front of others. By the time these parents wake up and realize that no child can grow up without boundaries, it is usually too late. The child has already barred them out of their lives or filed a law suit against them for being irresponsible parents.

It helps to bear in mind that your child is only a star to those who do not know him or her. Children are quite capable of appreciating their own uniqueness without putting someone else down in the process. In fact, if a child feels good inside he or she will have no need to put anyone else down.

At home the child actor should not be set apart from siblings. This creates unnecessary animosity or sibling rivalry. I'm not saying that the child actor does not need to receive commendation for a job well done. The family should never pass up an opportunity to let the child know how lucky, unique and special he or she is.

Furthermore, child actors should receive praise and celebration every time they book a job, or if the child is on a television series, after every taping. A child's good works need constant praise and reward. At the same time, the working child needs to be taught common courtesy, respect for others and gratitude. On the other hand, bad or unacceptable behavior should immediately be put in check.

Child actors need to know that each of us is significant to everybody else in the broad scheme of things. We simply have different vocations or professions. Everyone's job is equally important in the sense that we are all a part of the whole that makes the entire system work. It is not healthy to encourage a child actor to believe that being an actor makes more of a difference, in the broad spectrum of things, than what other people do for a living. True enough, the child actor is a part of the web that weaves magic and makes it larger than life. Still the child should learn to seek happiness and joy in all of the many facets of life, not just acting, since success and fame often flee on fast feet. When the inevitable happens parents do not want to find themselves left with a child confused about who he or she is because of mistakenly attaching identity to what he or she does. The two should remain separate. Moreover, I have found little glitter and glamour on actual Hollywood sets. That comes in after the project is finished and on the big screen. It's a part of the mystique that Hollywood has woven, not reality. Keeping reality in the forefront will automatically put the ego in check.

POINTS TO PONDER

1. *New parents often fear their children will be exploited, end up uneducated or a Hollywood Brat. Fortunately, those situations are the exception rather than the rule as a result of California Labor Laws and rules by the Screen Actors Guild designed to protect child actors. In California, studio teachers, who also double as social workers, are required on the set to insure that the child receives three hours of school a day and that he or she works under safe conditions.*

2. *For a child who already works in the business, a performing arts school might interfere with the ability to audition for or to book paying jobs.*

3. *Be prepared to intervene if your child is not allowed to make up tests missed while out working or if forced to take a test the day he or she returns from work over material covered while out of school. Many school districts have provisions that protect child actors from such action.*

4. *Avoid the Hollywood Brat Syndrome by ensuring that: (a) the parent runs the household; (b) the child realizes that he or she could not be in show business without family sacrifices; (c) the child actor realizes that all children are special — he or she is no better or less than anyone else, he or she simply has a high profile career; and (d) that only good behavior gets rewarded.*

Chapter 9

CHILD LABOR LAWS

Just as the child becomes bankable, suddenly nature has its way they pube, and there you are. Nancy Carson New York Children's Agent (from "Baby, It's You." by Zoe F. Carter, Premiere Magazine, Nov. 1991)

Whenever possible, television shows that depict teens prefer to hire young adults who look like teenagers since they can work beyond the ten hour limit set for sixteen year olds. "Beverly Hills 90210" is only one high-profile example. Remember, *"It is economics, not ideology that drives the entertainment industry,"* says writer, Robert W. Welkos. (From *Special Report on Personalities*). In addition, it costs the production company more money to work with minors because of the added expense of hiring a studio teacher, not to mention the three hours set aside during the day for school.

As a result, some producers would rather avoid the extra expense and time by hiring young adults who can play 15 to 18 year old roles. Fortunately, the popularity and economic benefit of children working in television and film has prompted producers to willingly put up with the inconvenience. In effect, a positive return on the investment usually makes a difficult task worth the bother.

SAG RULES REGARDING WORK HOURS FOR MINORS

Please note that the following SAG rules apply nationally. If a state rule conflicts with a SAG Rule then the stricter of the two rules apply. *The AFTRA-SAG Young Performers Handbook* (Published by The Screen Actors Guild) specifies the following breakdown of hours each age group can work on a studio set. School time is understood to construe three hours of tutoring:

1. Minors at least two years old but less than six are permitted at the place of employment for six hours. Minors more than two years of age but less than (6) years of age are permitted at the place of employment for six (6) hours (excluding meal periods but including three hours of school time.)

   Lunch time is considered to be one half (1/2) hour. If it extends to 1 hour the extra half hour does not extend the work day for the minor but is included as part of rest and recreation).

2. Minors who have reached the age of six (6) years but who have not attained the age of nine (9) years may be permitted at the place of employment for eight (8) hours (excluding meal periods but including school time).

3. Minors who have attained the age of nine (9) years but who have not attained the age of sixteen (16) years may be permitted at the place of employment for nine (9) hours (excluding meal periods but including school time).

4. Minors who have attained the age of sixteen (16) years but who have not attained the age of eighteen (18) years may be permitted at the place of employment for

nine (10) hours (excluding meal periods but including school time).

(Note that at the age of sixteen (16) a child does not need a welfare worker when school is not in session. If the child has not completed his high school requirements he still needs a studio teacher when school is in session.)

5. The work day for a minor shall begin no earlier than 5 a.m. and shall end no later than 10 p.m. on evenings preceding school days. On evenings preceding non-school days, the minor's work shall end not later than 12:30 a.m. on the morning of a non-school day.

As stated in the previous chapter, a studio teacher also doubles as a social worker on the set. The studio teacher is helpful in finding ways for the company to adhere to the rules without too much inconvenience to the child or the company in an effort to avoid shutting down the set for violation of child labor laws.

MUSIC VIDEOS

Music videos have not yet fallen under the guidelines of SAG or AFTRA. As a result, no definitive pay scale exists for actors or crew members, which means that pay for these jobs can vary from $50.00 a day to $500.00, depending upon the production company's budget and the agent.

Since music videos require just as much work for agents, in terms of casting, many have a minimum standard for their talent and will not send clients out on videos that do not pay their minimum amount. Moreover, some of the biggest names in the music industry only pay talent $75.00 a day. And most videos are notorious for adults or *emancipated* youngsters working twenty hour shifts in order to accomplish incredible feats within a few days.

Usually no overtime provisions exist on music videos because talent is paid a flat rate and adults can work unlimited hours.

Dancers, however, are the ones who tend to really get over-worked on music videos because they have to dance over and over as the director shoots enough footage to fit in all of the scenes.

Many music videos, especially for independent labels, do not offer any pay at all. Dancers and actors take these jobs on the off chance the video will become a hit and provide lots of television exposure or publicity. This happened with a six year old client of mine who appeared gratis in a music video contest for MTV. That video won the contest and the child appeared on "Entertainment Tonight" and received favorable write ups in several trade magazines.

A similar circumstance happened to my daughter, who was recruited on the spot to appear in a music video that my son was hired to shoot for Quincy Jones. She happened to be there with me and the director put her in the scene with a group of other children who paid to do the video. Even though Crystal made her appearance without pay, the camera focused several close-ups on her. Later, as a direct result of this video, Crystal ended up booking several paying music videos.

The average music video is completed in a day or two. A few will take a week when more than one music video is filmed back to back. Music videos often try to cram too much into too little time. Take the following example: In one music video my daughter landed a principal role for a big rock star who had a week to film two videos for his album. The assistant director gave Crystal a 3:30 call time on a Sunday afternoon. We were there all evening waiting for them to finish a scene and shoot the one scheduled right before Crystal's.

By 10:00 the crew still had not set up the scenery for the scene ahead of Crystal's. The director called down and offered to bring in a bed for Crystal to take a nap until they were ready for her. Crystal was excited about working on the video and more than willing to stay past the mandatory cut-off time of 10:00 for children since it was summer and she had no school the next day. The social worker, however, would not agree to it, so we had to leave with Crystal quite upset about waiting there all day and all night and having to leave before they could shoot her scene. Later I found out that they had literally worked all night to complete the scene before Crystal's, and her particular scene had to be cut out completely.

With music videos the aforementioned story is not an isolated incident. All too often music videos run way over schedule because too many scenes are scheduled for one day.

POINTS TO PONDER

1. *If at all possible, directors would rather hire an 18 year old or older to play teen roles because adults can work unlimited hours and do not need a studio teacher on the set which saves considerable expense.*

2. *In the 6 to 10 age group, when possible, a director will hire an older child who looks younger because the older child can work longer hours. (See SAG-AFTRA rules in this chapter for the number of hours each age group can work).*

3. *Presently, music videos do not fall under the guidelines of any particular union. As a result, pay is often low and hours long. Actors like doing them because they build credits and can offer phenomenal exposure if the video is a hit.*

SPECIAL TEEN SECTION

WITH ADVICE WRITTEN BY TWO HOLLYWOOD TEENS

SALIM GRANT
Of NBC's "Saved By The Bell"

EBONIE SMITH
Of The "Lethal Weapon" movies

Carrie See Photography

ON BEING SHOW BIZ TEENS

Written By
Salim Grant and Ebonie Smith

Introduction: Salim and Ebonie are both teens who have been in show business well over a decade. Salim is a series regular on NBC's *Saved By The Bell* and has co-starred in movies such as *Ghost Dad, The Hitman,* and *Angus*. He was an original cast member of *Barney And The Backyard Gang;* is a current member of the international recording group *L.A.X;* a lead singer with *All God's Children;* and is presently producing songs for his solo R&B album as well as other major recording artists. Ebonie starred as a series regular on *The Jeffersons* and later as Webster's girlfriend on the popular television series *Webster*. Many remember Ebonie as young LaToya Jackson in the television mini-series: "The Jacksons: An American Dream," as well as the mini-series "Women of Brewester Place." She also co-starred in all three of the *Lethal Weapon* movies and starred as *T.J.* in the Hallmark educational series *Talking With T.J.*

WAS THERE LIFE BEFORE SHOW BUSINESS?

You've already heard Salim's story of how he got his start in Chapter 5 of this book titled "Getting Ready to Get An Agent" (p. 70). At this point, I think it's appropriate to share my story.

EBONIE: The truth is, I cannot remember a time when I was not an actress. I got my start at the ripe old age of three when I was enrolled in my first dance class.

One of the mothers at my dance school had a child on a television series and four other children working in commercials and print. This lady commented to my mother that I "ought to be in pictures." My Mom took her seriously since this lady was a professional stage mom. Of course it also helped that this mother was willing to answer all of my Mom's questions. Upon following this lady's advice, Mom sent my pictures to five of the agents that she recommended. Four of them called wanting to sign me. Since I was just three at the time I only did modeling and print work the first few years, appearing in department store and baby doll ads long before I even knew I was in show business.

By the age of six I landed my first television series as Jessica on *The Jeffersons* (i.e., George Jefferson's granddaughter). I find it amazing that a decade later people still recognize me from this role; no doubt because I remained short and petite, weighing in at barely a hundred pounds.

THE AUDITION

"Riiiiiing! Riiiiiing!" It's your agent and she has a call for you at 3:00 sharp! For elementary kids this is immediately after class while high school kids are barely pulling out of the parking lot. (Do these people think we can fly?). For mothers this is right around the time when *Oprah, Geraldo, Jenny,* or one of those talk shows is on. (Mom will have to tape that episode). For Dads, a game might be on. (He'll have to catch the highlights on the radio). Sacrifices! These are but one of many sacrifices that one must make for show business.

After following the directions your agent gave, often you pull up in front of a funny looking little office building thinking to yourself: "This can't be it!" Then you walk into a crowded room full of people matching your description. Immediately you try to dream up a means to make yourself stand out from the crowd. As you scrawl your name and social security number on the "sign in" sheet you recognize a few names of fellow acting buddies. We call them "The Regulars," because you see them at almost every audition. This group can include people who don't like you or that you don't like. Some look so unsuited to the character that they make you wonder what they're doing here at your interview (of course everybody is thinking the same thing). At that point you either psychologically concede and give the role over to the competition, or you decide that you're not going to walk out without your best effort. If the competition looks stiff you go off to yourself and practice your lines to make sure that you get called back even if no one else in the room does.

The main thing to remember is to give the audition everything you've got. That way if you don't get a callback you know that it's because you weren't right for the role; not because you did a lousy acting job. So don't get your heart set on any one job. Just because you don't get this one doesn't mean that you're a terrible actor. You could have been too tall, too thin, too heavy, too pretty, not pretty enough, not tough enough, not sassy enough -- who knows? There will always be another audition and there is always another job out there with your name on it. As one door closes, another one opens. Which brings us to:

DEALING WITH DISAPPOINTMENT

In the real world a person is usually hired based on skills, competence, experience and/or education. Often an actor or actress lands a role primarily on a "look." At other times it's because he or she happens to be signed with an agency who represents the writer, director or producer of the script and that agency presents the talent as part of a package deal. In addition, other factors out of your control, determine whether or not you get to land and/or keep the role you got. At any point, during or after the production, a director can change his or her mind about whether you stay in the scene, or if the project even makes it to the screen.

SALIM: When I was younger, each time casting directors came out and told my Mom and me what a great job I had done I always knew that I had booked the job; especially when they inquired about my availability. Nine times out of ten I got the part. It's that one time you're wrong that really bugs you.

Case in point: I landed a national Pepsi commercial with several other teens directed by the same guy who did Michael Jackson's Pepsi commercials. We had a great time filming for two days at Big Sky Movie Ranch. I told everybody to look for me on Super Bowl Sunday. Well, the commercial did air that day, but with younger kids instead of the teens I filmed with. Good thing I hadn't counted on those residual checks.

EBONIE: I landed a role in an hour long *pilot* for a drama series that filmed in Baltimore. Upon returning home my agent told me that the pilot had not been picked up and would not air. Six months later I looked through the t.v. guide and saw the show listed so I called my family and friends and told them to look for me. Well, the episode was just as I remembered, that is, up until my scene. It had been reshot with another actress. That's when I learned that the job isn't yours even though you've done the work and gotten paid for it. Fortunately for Salim and me, both jobs were not successful projects. Salim's Pepsi commercial was only for a limited run and that pilot didn't even make it through one season. Now we don't call anyone unless we've seen the final cut ourselves. But more importantly, the roles we have ended up in were ones that complimented our careers and sharpened our skills.

THE COMPETITION

After years of working in the industry we have become familiar with our competitors and their personalities. Some have turned into friends. Others have such an overly competitive spirit that they are unpleasant to be around. We believe that negative competitive traits result when kids feel unduly influenced or pressured by their parents. This can lead to unkind or unhealthy behavior toward other kids in the business. Some parents will not even allow their kids to associate with the competition out of fear that it will threaten their child's chances of getting the role. We do not feel that other actors have anything to do with our ability to win over the casting director and client to get the part.

We believe in being prepared ahead of time, dressing the part, getting into character, and then having fun with the role. If you have a good time at the audition you are more likely to get the part, if you're right for it. That's where preparation comes in. If you know your lines before you get there, you're less likely to become stressed and anxious when you arrive. That's why you should always have your agent fax the sides to you in advance. That way you can arrive at the audition relaxed. When you're at ease it shows and the casting director will feed off of your confidence. With that in mind, if you cannot get the sides in advance, be sure to arrive at the audition ahead of time so that you can memorize your lines before going in.

THE BALANCING ACT: SCHOOL AND WORK

Since Child Labor Laws require that young actors maintain a "C" average or above in school it is important to put school first. If your grades suffer, so will your ability to work. So no matter what, we learned to put parties, telephone calls and movies on the schedule behind school work. It also helps to study ahead in your classes so that when you are working a demanding job and you're tired some evenings, you won't fall behind if you miss a homework assignment.

We had to give up extra curricular activities such as sports, the drama club, or debate team in order to pursue our careers because all of these activities take place after school which is when auditions take place. Plus, we never know when we're going to be out of school for days, weeks, or even months at a time, so there's no point in taking a lead in the school play unless the school can work around your schedule and is flexible with rehearsals.

SURVIVING PUBERTY: WHAT HAPPENS WHEN YOU'RE NOT CUTE ANYMORE?

When we were young all we had to do was remember a few lines and look cute. As we got older acting ability became more important once we had out grown our cuteness. Talk about a rude awakening! As a singer Salim could not believe the difference in how audiences reacted to him before the age of ten compared to thirteen.

SALIM: It was like night and day! I remember bringing the house down with my song and dance routines when I was seven and eight. Adults and children would stand up and cheer! At almost every live performance the audience demanded an encore. Naturally I came to take all of this for granted. I was thirteen when I really noticed the difference. It was at a competition judged by music industry people. The audience was mostly high school students and so were the majority of the competitors. I, on the other hand, was still in Jr. High, but I had a dynamic song with great female back-up dancers. When a group of high school girls from the front row began to cheer during my performance, a sizable group of guys got up en mass and walked out of the auditorium right in the middle of my song! Believe me, if I had not been performing professionally for half of my life I would have walked off the stage, but I kept on singing and dancing as if nothing had happened. The audience barely applauded my performance. I was so out done that I told my Mom I wanted to leave before the judges made their decision. She insisted on staying for the sake of the dancers who had not paid attention to the insult. I didn't see any point. Of course it did not help my wounded pride one bit when I won first place. From then on I began to notice how much harder I had to work to get an enthusastic response out of my audience. In retrospect, however, those experiences only made me work harder to be the best. Ebonie noticed the difference in how casting directors reacted to her once she was older.

EBONIE: Before, I did not have to worry about studying the character because I "was" the character. It had not occurred to me that casting directors prefer to cast little kids "to type" which means that they choose a child who "is" the character they are looking for as opposed to trying to teach a child how to "become" someone they are not. Via this process the director does not have to teach the child to act because all the child has to do is be himself or herself. Which is exactly what I had to do when I was younger. When I entered puberty I was thrown off guard to find myself suddenly having to work hard to figure out how to fine tune my skills to fit the different types of roles I was going out on. I also had to invest a considerable more time and energy into studying the character and coming up with creative ideas to get an angle on it. When I was younger all I had to do was recite my lines or read the script well.

Looking back, however, I realize it was to our advantage that our careers slowed down a bit when we hit puberty because it gave us time to switch gears and learn how to stretch ourselves as actor and actress. I learned to try out different characters and roles, becoming surprised at how much depth and potential I had inside of me as an actress, just as Salim had to figure out how to pull something unique out of his voice as it changed. We are both better for our experiences. Not everyone weathers puberty well. And we have to give our mothers credit for supporting our bruised egos and for believing in us when we were having trouble believing in ourselves. It certainly helped us make it through the transition.

STAYING GROUNDED

We realize that as teen actors we also serve as role models. Therefore, we strive to be nice to everyone, within reason. Having people recognize you in public can be flattering. It's one thing, however, to acknowledge an actor or actress in passing and quite another to invite yourself to the dinner table at a restaurant.

Because we grew up in the business we are not overly impressed with other actors or with ourselves. But more importantly we have been raised to have a strong sense of self and family which has nothing to do with how much money we earn or how many credits we accumulate. We also have friends and associates whom we value that are not in the entertainment field. Even though we happen to love what we do in front of the camera, we are also pursuing degrees in film which will eventually place us behind the camera as directors, producers and writers. This collaborative writing effort gave us confidence in our abilities to work together on a project and see it through to completion while juggling our work schedules.

We've seen some of our peers go on to fame and fortune and have taken note of how it changed many of them. We simply plod steadily along never losing sight of what's real in Tinsel Town. Even though we realize that money and power can cause one to question the motives of people who come into your life, it should not affect your relationships with old friends, unless merited. We've lost some friends along the way who got the "big head," which was pretty difficult for us to relate to since we don't understand the concept. We've also seen some of those same people after their show got canceled, and wondered what they were going to use to inflate their heads with now.

ASSOCIATION BREEDS ASSIMILATION

We make it a point not to choose our friends and associates based on superficiality, status, popularity or economics. What's most important to us is common sense, educational and career goals, a good sense of humor, and strong values.

We've learned that our choice of friends can make or break our career. Association really does breed assimilation. Hanging out with kids who have no goals or aspirations can cause us to lose sight of our own goals or to fall short of reaching ours because friends who have nothing but time on their hands cannot understand or appreciate that your time has to be balanced between school, work and play.

It became clear to us, through trial and error, especially after entering puberty, that when we hung out with struggling, failing or complaining actors that we too struggled, failed or began to complain. The same thing goes for "kicking it" with friends who party till late on school or work nights, or who drink and do drugs. Oftentimes, being in show business means that we have to make adult decisions regarding our social life since the wrong decision could affect us for life.

Of course none of this means that we haven't made our share of mistakes along the way, or that we're immune from making the wrong choices in the future. We simply strive to learn from our mistakes so that we won't turn them into bad habits that we can't break.

THE COLLEGE YEARS

Because one never knows when a work opportunity will arise, the college years can be a challenge. For example, after a teen completes his or her high school requirements there is no further provision to permit those three hours from each work day for school with a tutor the way they did before we finished high school. Ebonie and I both enrolled in college early. I was fifteen and a half when I entered Los Angeles Valley College (Valley) part time and Ebonie was sixteen when she entered The University of Southern California (USC) film school full time.

EBONIE: Shortly after my second semester at USC I auditioned for a series regular role on a popular television series only to realize that getting the part would mean putting school on hold for the term of the television contract. Before college I did not have to worry about that. Now I had to take into consideration the following: USC is an expensive private school and my scholarship only paid for half of the tuition. Therefore, dropping out for even one semester was a costly decision any way that I looked at it. But more importantly, a television series would mean forfeiting my scholarship, which was an even harder decision.

After talking it over with my mom, we made a decision. I would hold off on any series regular roles until I graduated (unless someone made me an offer I couldn't refuse, like starring in my own television show) and continue to do what I did the first semester at USC: guest spots on television shows and commercials. These jobs only require one day to one week away from school, which is easy to make up. Longer periods are more difficult. Moreover, with the summers off I can also do cameos or supporting roles in film. Salim was faced with the same situation during his first year as a full time student. The previous year he had only taken one or two classes each semester in order to have an easier time juggling acting, school and private music lessons.

SALIM: My first semester as a full time student at Valley I was taking 12 hours of journalism, broadcasting, and music classes -- all of which I enjoyed. I even had all A's and B's going into mid-term (which was a tremendous improvement over my first year when I was taking classes like Algebra, Geometry and French). Right before mid-term I landed a role in a feature film that required five weeks away in Minnesota, along with two weeks here in Los Angeles. Because of mandatory classroom participation I had to drop the music classes. Since my journalism teacher also taught my broadcasting class I asked if I could call each week, get the assignments and mail them to him. He agreed. With the time difference and the demands of my shooting schedule I never caught the professor in his office, and he did not return my calls, so I had to drop those classes.

The next semester I landed a regular role on a television series after mid-term. That semester I was only taking two classes and was able to switch over to evening class with one, but had to drop the other, which would have worked if I had not gotten a recording deal that required me to be in the studio after work. So I took an incomplete in that class. This semester I'm catching up by taking 17 hours, which include two television classes, one class before work and two evening classes. I record in the studio on weekends.

My decisions in the above instances had to do with the fact that I'm attending a junior college, not an expensive private school, like Ebonie. After I finish Valley, however, I plan on transferring to USC's Film School. Once there, trust me, I will not be dropping classes in the middle of the semester. In particular, not after paying private tuition fees. Besides, I enrolled in college young, which put me ahead of most kids my age, therefore, the odds are in favor of me finishing school with my peers even though I work two jobs.

In conclusion, even though it is not always easy being a show biz kid, we feel blessed to be able to make a living doing what we love.

Chapter 10

TEENAGERS

MODELING FOR TEENS

Children over the age of ten often fall in the "risk" category. In Kyle Counts' article, Los Angeles agent Judy Savage, explains that, *"every year after six becomes more difficult. There may only be ten incredible six-year-olds, but later the competition is much more fierce."* Exceptions include: really small and precocious children, those with a track record of booking jobs on their own; and youngsters bubbling over with untapped talent such as singing, dancing, or specialty skills such as gymnastics or martial arts. The cuteness, innocence and naiveté that children six and under tend to have begins to fade as they age, forcing older children to rely more on ability, skill, and personality as opposed to a "look" alone.

Moreover, after the age of ten, most children begin to enter puberty. Some adolescents experience rapid growth or sudden weight gains. Others begin to look awkward, feel uncomfortable in their new bodies, or become shy and introverted. Unless the child is already small for his or her age, these factors can make representing a child about to enter puberty a risk. In such cases, the agent does not know how much time he or she has before puberty kicks into high gear.

As a result, one should take time to find out in advance the demand for and availability of work for adolescents and teens (trends do change) before investing money. Ignorance can unknowingly inflict unnecessary damage to a parent's pocket book as well as the child's fledgling self-esteem. Teenagers are already going through enough adjustments just trying to grow up in a confusing, fast paced world without unnecessary disappointments.

Colleen Cler of The Colleen Cler Modeling and Talent Agency explained that *"often adolescents or teenagers take rejection personally, thinking that something is wrong with him or her when the problem resides with the fact that they simply are not a marketable size or height anymore. During this time, parents and teens are easy prey, and often fall victim, to expensive modeling school scams or unreputable casting services that pose as agencies and charge unreasonably high fees for pictures and classes."*

Colleen Cler added that after a girl grows out of a *"children's size 10, and a boy out of sizes 12-14"* their modeling career is pretty much over or put on hold until girls reach a height of 5'8" or 5'9" (with a 5'7" minimum) and guys grow to a minimum of 5'11." Modeling is the one area in the children's entertainment field where a considerable growth spurt does not put a teenager at a disadvantage.

TEEN MALE MODELS

Even before boys become teenagers, a steady influx of calls come in for young male models, which makes print work a strong area for boys. Naturally, since fewer males choose modeling, this lessens the competition in that area. Moreover, as boys grow older, peer pressure from friends will cause many to discontinue modeling at that age. Ultimately this situation creates a vacuum waiting to be filled by new talent, and generates more work for those who do continue to model as teens.

Colleen Cler explained that *"even after boys grow out of a size 14, those who have reached at least 5'11" continue to work. In particular males who work-out or lift weights to develop muscles."* Colleen adds that height alone is not enough; teenage boys need to be *"built."* At that age many boys tend to be under-developed in the shoulder and muscle areas. When clients call Colleen looking for teen male models they ask for the *"teenager's height first and a size 32" waist second."*

Unlike theatrical work for 17 year olds, the good news, explains Colleen Clere, is that there is *"quite a bit of work for 16 to 18 year old male models"* because they fall under the heading *"young men's division."* This type of modeling usually involves *"casual wear such as jogging suits, jeans or related sports wear.* There is very little high fashion work for boys in the 16 to 18 year old category.

TEENS, IT'S NOT HOW OLD YOU ARE IT'S HOW YOUNG YOU LOOK

By the age of seventeen, teens new to the business find it difficult, at best, to find a theatrical or commercial agent willing to represent them. The age of seventeen can put a teenager who has never worked before in "No Man's Land;" in particular if the teen looks his or her age or older. For example: a 17 year old who looks too old to play 14 to 16 year old roles (and work the longer hours for the adult age grouup) would not be as desirable as someone who is legal age and looks younger which gives an 18 to 21 year old who looks young a distinct advantage over a 17 year old who looks his age or older. Overall, it is economically more feasible in many situations for a producer to hire an adult who can play younger as opposed to a 17 year old who would require the additional expense of a studio teacher, limited work hours, and an extra three hours during the day for school work. The exception, (mentioned earlier in this book) involves tall male models or someone who already has a name or exceptional credits.

Moreover, teens who have not worked before find themselves competing against children with ten years or more work experience behind them, not to mention a SAG card in hand. Los Angeles agent, Judy Savage made a cogent comment on the situation: *"at eighteen or nineteen, suddenly you're competing with kids from all over the world."* (from Zoe F. Carter's article, "Baby, It's You" *Premiere Magazine*, Nov. 1991) There's an old saying, in this business: "In by six, out by ten." *Ages 6 to 10 are peak work years for children.*

ENTERING THAT AWKWARD STAGE

During the onset of puberty, many teens tend to lose their natural spontaneity in front of the camera, gain weight or grow awkward and self-conscious. Tarquin Gotch, senior vice president of Hughes Entertainment says that, *"The very characteristics that make them bankable are so short-lived. Often what you like about them is their childishness and charm. That all changes when they grow a beard and start hanging out on street corners and smoking cigarettes."* (from Zoe F. Carter's article, "Baby, It's You," *Premiere Magazine*, Nov. 1991)

Of course, not all children become awkward looking or shy as a teenager. Many teens weather the transition smoothly, explaining why one should find out the particular mind set his or her agent has about this matter. If an agent believes that work stops for children after the age of twelve, that agent will not work hard for someone in that age group. As a result, make it a point to inquire about your agent's belief system regarding teens. People tend to act according to their beliefs. If your child's agent is stuck in a pattern that does not fit your particular situation, then find another agent.

Corky Nemec, who starred in the Fox television sitcom "Parker Lewis Can't Lose" somehow managed to hold on to his natural awe of the world as a teenager. Light, his agent, says, *"When someone is Corky's age [18], they either have it, or they don't. When he first came to us, he had charm, sweetness, intelligence and a little bit of naiveté. You could still see the wonder of the world in his eyes."* (See Kyle Counts "Hollywood Reporter" article).

Remember: every business has its requirements. For the real world, education and experience counts. For show business, talent, personality and a *look* are critical factors. Experience helps, but may not be an absolute necessity. And I do not mean that one has to be drop dead beautiful to act or model. Colleen Cler points out that their agency is known for *"a certain editorial look that includes cookie cutter cute, appealing, healthy looking kids."* As a result, even the character types they have are *"cute."* For theatrical or commercial work, however, if a child is too attractive it can work against the youngster because so many roles call for average girl or boy next door looks, character types, or for ethnics. With ethnics, however, usually the Hollywood standard is stereotypical, rigid or narrow, failing to take into account the diversity of skin tones and facial features within every race. All too often the stereotype for ethnics in commercials, television and film depicts a negative extreme that may not necessarily be attractive.

EARLY MATURITY

Just as sudden growth spurts can interfer with a child's career, the onset of early puberty can also have an adverse effect. While some television shows can rewrite the script to include the child's early maturation, other formats cannot. For example, a show like "Head of The Class" was not conceptualized to include the sudden maturation of youngsters in the script. As a result, it could only run so many seasons with the same cast members intact since youngsters do grow. Another example was "21 Jump Street" which limited itself to youthful looking undercover police officers who played high school students. Again, the story line could only go so many seasons before stretching its premise while the lead actors grew to look more mature than high school students.

As mentioned before, rapid physical maturity can prevent a younger child from working in an older age category since he or she cannot work the additional hours of the older age group.

One youngster that I know from a popular television show developed physically beyond her years too quickly for the show to maintain its premise. There was nothing the producers could do to keep the child from growing out of the little kid role they originally hired her for. After cancellation of the show this young girl had a difficult time finding work in her age group.

For the most part there are certain basic features that constitute a plus in all areas of the entertainment business: good skin, even teeth, a healthy head of hair, correct posture, and good grooming.

Moreover, a charming or winning personality, strong acting skills, dance or vocal ability, self-confidence, humility, good work ethic and an attitude of gratitude will add to any actor's success in this business.

During adolesence make it a point to keep acting skills and abillities polished because one never knows when an opportunity might come along; at what point a child is going to grow into his or her body; or when the child's original self-confidence will reappear. To mitigate damage while teens are going through the awkward age, encourage good eating habits, drinking plenty of water (as opposed to soft drinks) regular exercise, active hobbies such as roller blading, tennis, jogging, etc. and never forget to tell them how cute, wonderful and talented they still are. Even though teens may put on an aire of self-sufficiency, they miss all the attention, affection and adoration they received as little kids. Which is why parents have to make it a point to give as much positive feedback as possible, keeping in mind that teens need it just as much now as they did when children. It is all too easy for parents to get caught up in criticizing the way teens choose to exercise their new found options as oppposed to praising all that they are in the process of tying to become.

POINTS TO PONDER

1. *Parents interested in modeling for their children should start as early as possible (i.e., from infancy) because fashion and editorial work pretty much stops for girls after they outgrow a size 10 and for boys after they no longer fit a size 12 or 14. At that point the child has to wait until a girl reaches a minimum height of 5'7" and boys 5'11." Although some product work remains available for kids who grow out of standard model sizes, it is not enough to keep them busy.*

2. *Teen male models who reach an acceptable height, along with a body build to match (i.e., broad shoulders and muscles) can find steady work in the "Young Men's Division" for major department stores, newspapers, magazines, etc.*

3. *During puberty rapid physical maturity or growth can restrict the amount of work available for such a teen unless he or she has a specialty talent such as singing, dancing, figure skating, martial arts, etc.*

Chapter 11

EDUCATIONAL ALTERNATIVES

Production companies and movie studios often notify agents that they will only see ages 18 or over for certain teen roles. In the alternative they might audition a younger *emancipated* teenager who has taken the appropriate test to complete his or her high school educational requirements.

The *California High School Proficiency Exam* (CHSP) allows teens to meet educational requirements for early high school graduation. Upon successful completion, a teen can then work the three extra hours set aside for school, which eliminates the need for a studio teacher, provided, of course, the teen is at least 16 years of age at the time of the exam. The exam can be taken at an earlier age with permission of the child's teacher or school. From an industry standpoint the CHSP is a practical alternative for tall or physically developed teens who might not be able to work commercially or theatrically because they look older than they really are. The CHSP exam provides a safer, more viable laternative for teen actors because emancipation along does not meet state educational requirements and can leave a child open to exploitation (more on that later). Moreover, taking the CHSP exam does not preclude the student from contining to study with a teacher under an

Independent Study Program (ISP) in order to complete regular high school credits for college entrance or from attending a regular high school to obtain a diploma..

EMANCIPATION AND EARLY HIGH SCHOOL COMPLETION

Many parents of children who develop early will opt for *emancipation*. This process involves petitioning the court to grant a minor the right to represent himself or herself as an adult in business affairs, normally around the age of 14. If the child is emancipated before high school educational requirements are met, however, he or she still has to have a tutor on the set until the age of 16, which will adversely affect the casting director's decision to hire such a teen when the director could have an 18 year old instead who can work the unlimited hours without the added expense of a studio teacher. Once emancipated, the child will no longer need an adult to sign contracts, which leaves the child open for exploitation through lack of experience and ignorance. Moreover, as outlined, emancipation serves little purpose without also taking the CHSP test for early high school completion.

THE STUDIO ACADEMY

In response to the special needs of child actors, studio teachers in Los Angeles opened a private school to serve the needs of children in the entertainment industry. The school is called *NORTH HILLS PREP* and is located at 9433 Sepulveda Boulevard, North Hills, California 91343. Call 818-894-8388 for more information.

INDEPENDENT STUDY PROGRAMS

As stated above, for those children planning on attending college, taking the CHSP exam does not preclude a child from continuing to take required classes through an *Independent Study Program (ISP),* or a regular school in order to meet graduation requirements for college programs. ISP allows children to work at home under the guidance of an independent study teacher whom the child meets with once a week to turn in homework, receive new assignments and take tests.

Many child actors find ISP programs the most viable of all educational alternatives because of the flexibility for accommodating the child actor's unpredictable work schedule. Moreover, the ISP teacher follows standard educational guidelines regulated by the state for required graduation courses. The child also receives credit for enrolling in classes at local colleges that the ISP teacher cannot teach, such as higher level math or certain foreign languages. Keep in mind that not every child is mature enough, has enough self discipline or inner motivation to excell in an independent study program.

SUPPLEMENTING YOUR CHILD'S EDUCATION WITH A COMPUTER

In order for the child enrolled in an ISP program to excell while working independently, he or she should have a personal computer with state of the art software that includes an SAT program, typing tutor, higher level math, and foreign languages. A personal computer with a CD rom and voice module is ideal since these computer programs talk to the child, providing important feedback for wrong answers as well as correct pronunciation for foreign languages.

Studies have shown that, as a result of the sophistication and advanced technology inherent in today's computer programs (not to mention the national information highway), educational computer programs provide a vast array of personalized knowledge that a private tutor would find difficulty matching or competing with since the best corporate minds come together to create each software program. The greatest incentive of all is that children love the challenge of working with computers. Schools that have changed over to computers have higher test scores, lower drop out rates and higher daily attendance.

POINTS TO PONDER

1. *For older teens who have out grown their age group, emancipation is a legal option that enables teens to work the longer hours of an older age group or category.*

2. *Remember that an emancipated teen will also need to take the California High School Proficiency Exam (CHSP) in order to dispense with the necessity of having a studio teacher on the set. As a result, the CHSP is a better option than Emancipation. The latter can open the child up for exploitation since he or she can legally sign contracts.*

3. *Independent Study Programs (ISP) offer the best alternative for accommodating a child actor's unpredictable work schedule. Supplement your child's education with a personal computer.*

EARTHA ROBINSON
DISCUSSES DANCERS
AND THE STATE OF DANCE

Eartha is Chief Choreographer for the recording group *All God's Children*. She has worked as Assistant Choreographer to Debbie Allen, Michael Peters, and Otis Salid, helping choreograph *Polly, Sister Act II, Sarafina, School Daze, Emmy Awards, Academy Awards, Image Awards, Comic Relief,* and *The Jackson Family Honors,* to name a few. Eartha was an original *Fame* dancer on the long running television series. She also choreographed a few episodes for *Fame* as well as *A Different World*. As an actress, Eartha was featured in the critically acclaimed PBS movie *Daughters Of The Dust,* on stage in *The Wiz* and *Arms too Short To Box With God*.

Q: WHAT DO YOU THINK ABOUT THE STATE OF DANCE TODAY? Answer: Under my training with Alvin Ailey in New York we were taught discipline. We came to class with a love and respect for the craft. I think that the art form needs to be taken back to a deeper place than it resides now. We've lost a lot of the inner discipline, focus and feeling for dance.

Some of this loss has to do with the medium of television. Film, in particular, is done out of sequence and then edited down to a bare minimum. This detached process can cause a wonderful dance piece to lose its power. But more importantly, when I came from the stage in New York to Hollywood I found that a lot of the dance numbers for television and film were just not as demanding as the type of training I received in New York. Such a situation can make a dancer complacent, which in turn generates a loss of drive to strive for higher levels through practice and rehearsal every day. When it's too easy there's no need to push. That's why periodically I have to go back to New York to remember my roots and sharpen that edge I need as a dancer and choreographer.

Q: WOULD YOU ELABORATE ON WHAT ELSE HAS CHANGED? Answer: In addition to the disappearance of discipline, dancers at auditions have not only lost respect for the choreographer but their craft as well. At auditions, instead of standing quietly on the sidelines paying attention to the choreographer while someone else is auditioning, dancers will talk among themselves, or practice their routine. Another thing I've noticed is that at many auditions, dancers don't watch the choreographer closely enough or listen attentively to the counts. They just jump into the steps blindly. But most important of all, common courtesy has practically disappeared. In fact, I was once cursed out by a dancer who did not make my final cut at an audition.

Q: WHAT AUDITION ADVICE WOULD YOU GIVE TO DANCERS? Answer: Dancers should try to make themselves look a little different from everybody else so that they can stand out. Besides, if dancers don't feel good about how they look or what they're wearing, it's easy to become distracted at an audition by what everybody else has on or how well they dance. All of this creates a drain of energy that can cause dancers to lose focus when it's their turn to go up before the choreographer. Dancers need to work on building up strength and security within themselves. Those who stay in the back row at auditions rarely get seen and their self-confidence remains low as a dancer. The minute dancers place themselves on the front row they instantly challenge themselves to keep up and do their very best. Dancers should not be afraid to put pressure on themselves.

Q: WHAT ABOUT YOUNGER CHILDREN AND DANCE?
Answer: I think that kids should be old enough to let you know that they want to dance. It's not a decision a parent can make for a child because dance involves a lot of hard work and practice.

Chapter 12

DANCERS: REACHING A POINT OF READINESS

For everything there is an appointed time. Even a time for every affair under the heavens... -Ecc. 3:1

That first major audition requiring dance skills can be intimidating even for experienced dancers, but especially for a child. In particular if that child has natural ability but no training or experience in front of an audience. Moreover, much of the competition may have years of training behind them.

Depending on the age of the child, some newcomers mistakenly think that the audition IS the job. Especially younger children who do not realize that other children at the audition are competing for the same spot. Avoid confusion by telling the child what to expect BEFORE the audition. This may not be easy for new parents who do not know what to tell the child other than the brief stats that the agent gives consisting of what, when and where as provided by **The Beakdown Service** (i.e., a computerized daily listings of castings grouped into commercial, theatrical and print categories, broken down according to ethnicity, age and gender). For dance auditions, the information agents receive often tends to be scanty. Whereas theatrical breakdowns usually have a more detailed description of the character since television and film projects are based on a screenplay that's already written.

Careers are like pyramids. You have to build a very solid base.
-Tim Angle/TRIAD (from "The L.A. Agent Book")

In any case, parents should do their best to reassure children that they won't be asked to do anything different from the other talent at the audition. As a last resort, seize the opportune moment at the audition to ask the casting assistant what will be expected of the children. Sometimes casting directors or assistants at commercial and dance auditions will explain to everyone waiting in the lobby the requirements of that particular audition. Even if they do not, at all dance auditions have the child come prepared to create improvisational steps on the spot, to follow a choreographer's instructions, or to dance to a song other than the one the child came prepared with.

When a parent is unable to give a child details about the audition, use common sense and simply remind the youngster to keep a friendly, open mind and follow instructions. This will prevent the child from expecting one thing ahead of time then getting confused, disappointed or thrown off guard if required to do something else. Sometimes just reassuring the child that all you expect as a parent is the best job the child can do will provide immeasurable comfort for the child.

AN INSIDE LOOK AT THOSE DYNAMIC DANCE AUDITIONS

Just as no one would expect a runner to enter a marathon race and actually finish it without having trained for the event, no child should expect to go into a dance audition without the necessary preparation. Therefore, when child actors are not working, keep them enrolled in dance classes, vocal lessons, or acting workshops. These classes give the child's muscles, vocal chords and mind the necessary preparation to compete well when the opportunity presents itself.

Since competition can be fierce, unless your child is truly resilient or has good basic self esteem, he or she might not bounce back quickly from a dance audition for a film, television movie or Broadway show. In these auditions only winners remain standing in the end. Further, these auditions tend to be long and drawn out and can take anywhere from two to six hours. Bob Roth, Director of "Plane Crazy", a live dance show at Disneyland, said that *"These auditions attract everyone, from seasoned pros to beginners. And even though we're ruthless, it's really for their own good. Some of these people just need to find new professions."* (From "Special Report on Personalities").

At dance auditions a choreographer teaches the entire room a set of dance combinations. The child either keeps up or is automatically out of the game in the first round. Those who do keep up get a few minutes to practice, at which point, the process of elimination begins.

Rarely can a dancer earn a living off of dance alone; I, therefore, encourage children to do it for fun. Since the children's dance market fluctuates greatly, kids who dance should develop other abilities like singing, gymnastics or acting in order to expand their options. Moreover, jobs for dancers tend to pay dancer's scale, which is lower than actor's scale. Dancers in commercials, however, do manage to earn the same rate as actors. Teresa Taylor-Campbell, Director of The Dance Department at BBA or The Bobby Ball Agency.

At unusually large dance auditions, the choreographer divides the room into groups. Often these groups have a dozen or more dancers who take turns in front of a panel of judges. After the group performs an assistant points to, or calls out the names of those who made it to the next round. The rest are told good-bye. At large auditions, it can take a while before all the groups in the room get a chance to go before the panel of judges. During this time the fortunate few asked to remain get to watch the choreographer audition each group and learn from the mistakes of others.

Those that remain are taught an additional set of dance combinations to add to the first set already learned. The process of teaching new steps, adding them to the old, and eliminating those who can't keep up or execute the steps skillfully is repeated until the entire routine has been taught.

Hours later, out of several hundred people that may have auditioned, only a few remain behind, tired, exhilarated and proud of their efforts. The dancers left standing know that, most likely, they made the show as a **regular** or **alternate**. Before the group leaves, the choreographer will either announce who got the job, or tell the group to expect a call later. Having made it to the final round is an accomplishment in and of itself so if your child was among those left standing congratulate him or her, praising the fact that practice and hard work pays off, then move on to the next project or class without anxiously awaiting that confirmation call.

LEARNING TO VIEW SETBACKS AS OPPORTUNITIES

For those who did not even make it to the first round of eliminations, the experience might become downright discouraging which can lead to the child giving up on dance altogether. Without the ability to see each setback as an opportunity for growth, a child will not survive show business. During the elimination process I have seen children cry or leave the room angry and upset. As a part of the decision making process, before a child decides to pursue dance professionally, a parent would do well to rent a copy of the movie *A Chorus Line* and watch it with the child. This movie is pretty representative of how demanding, detached and callous dance auditions can be.

Keep in mind also that there may be times when a child arrives at a dance audition and notices that the competition is too advanced for him or her to compete fairly. A realistic parent knows when it's lack of confidence (which can be boosted) or lack of talent (that can only be worked on) and will encourage the child to make the right decision.

For the child that got discouraged by the dance audition (which is understandable since dancers are eliminated in front of their friends, family and peers) that child will need encouragement and a new perspective in order to internalize the experience positively. The parent may want to point out that the dance audition gave the child a valuable opportunity to see where he or she stands against the competition. Without this gauge, dancers cannot accurately determine how far they need to go in order to catch up with their peer group, or how much practice will be required to do so. On the other hand, if the child is above average, he or she needs the competition to grow and get better.

AUDITIONS ADD TO EXPERIENCE

Before and after the audition, as a parent, avoid acting desperate or anxious about the child getting the job. This will place undue pressure on the young performer or create disappointment if the job does not materialize. Encourage your child to enjoy the audition process for the sake of itself. Explain that each audition contains a built in opportunity to enhance audition skills, which means that no actor or dancer loses out because he or she learns and grows from every audition. Besides, with the exception of open calls, the child has already made it through an initial selection process by being chosen from the many headshots submitted by agents and managers for each casting call.

Kids who want to work as dancers should absolutely love to dance. Because of the large number of competitors at each dance audition, the child needs to possess something unique. Ability always comes first, but just as important is a clean, natural "singular look" that connotes conceptual thought; a "sparkle" in the eye and enthusiasm; as opposed to an inappropriately dressed, unappealing child with a stressed out, anxious demeanor. Teresa Taylor-Campbell, Director of The Dance Department at BBA or The Bobby Ball Agency.

Since auditions are only *OPPORTUNITIES*, not *PROMISES*, reserve a certain amount of gratitude and excitement for each and every one in accordance with the advice of Rickey Barr of the Rickey Barr Talent Agency: *"an actor should work on his energy. A lot of times, when actors go in to meet producers and directors, they get so nervous. Don't be desperate. Be happy that you have the interview. If you're right for the part, you'll get it."* (from "The L.A. Agent Book" by K Callan)

Wise King Solomon reminded us that *"The race does not belong to the swift, nor to the mighty the battle. For accidents and unforeseen occurrences befall us all."* In its broadest sense, this quote means that even under ideal circumstances no one can accurately predict the actual outcome of a situation. We deal primarily in probability, chance, and favorable odds. Although odds might favor the most experienced singer or the best dancer for the job, sometimes other factors weigh more heavily in the decision making process, such as plain old good luck.

At other times, being in the right place at the right time has its advantages. The child may have that perfect something a casting director or their client is looking for. Casting director Mali Finn says that *"children don't usually know how to develop a character, so you're looking for a child who is the character."* (from "Baby, It's You" by Zoe F. Carter, *Premiere* magazine). Casting directors have to sift through a lot of children before finding one who embodies exactly what they are looking for. For example, in the movie, "Flashdance," Jennifer Beals had a dance double who performed many of the most difficult dance moves for her. Obviously, Jennifer had enough basic dance training to render her a strong enough candidate to make the screen test. In the end, however, it was Jennifer's exotic looks and acting ability that tipped the scales in her favor.

POINTS TO PONDER

1. There's an old saying that "a quitter never wins and a winner never quits." Any child who becomes devastated over every audition he or she loses, will not fare well because there will be times when the child makes it to the last round of auditions and won't get the part. Well, "That's the breaks."

2. A child actor has to be able to view setbacks as opportunities. Instead of feeling that he or she lost the job the child should commend himself or herself for getting to the final callback, and be proud of making it through all of the other children in the earlier rounds of competition.

3. Someone once said that success is failure turned inside out. By necessity a child must learn how to deal with defeat in a constructive manner.

4. Although children need to know that they have the option to quit the business at any time they choose, the child must also understand that once he or she has accepted a job there is an obligation to honor the commitment unless to do so would cause physical or emotional harm.

INTERVIEW WITH
LOU ADLER
A MUSIC LEGEND

Lou Adler and his partner Herb Albert, started out writing songs for Sam Cooke. Later, Lou went on to produce the longest running movie in history, "The Rocky Horror Picture Show." Among his many accomplishments, Lou produced Carol King, The Mamas & The Papas and directed the Cheech and Chong movie, "Up In Smoke." Lou is also co-owner of the Roxy and the Whisky on Sunset Boulevard in Los Angeles.

Q: COULD YOU TELL US ABOUT "THE ROCKY HORROR PICTURE SHOW" AND WHAT MADE YOU DECIDE TO BRING IT TO TELEVISION AFTER MORE THAN TWO DECADES? Answer: I saw Rocky Horror for the first time in London at a 100 seat theater and got excited about it, so I went after the rights from Michael White. We agreed to share interchangeable credits of Executive Producer and Producer in London and America.

I ran the play at the Roxy for a year. It was a huge success. So I decided to take it to Broadway where it failed. In New York the house was too big and the critics gave it bad reviews. The venue in Los Angeles, with its rock 'n roll setting, was perfect for the play. Plus, the size of the Roxy, which seats about 450 people, was ideal.

And I think that a lot of the negative reaction from New York critics had to do with the play coming from a successful run in Los Angeles to New York. The excitement that the play generated in Los Angeles, however, created enough interest to land a movie deal.

As far as the decision to bring it to television, Rocky Horror tells you what to do with it next. The timing was right and there was a Fox Network, which was also the perfect venue for Rocky Horror. And Fox allowed me to incorporate the live theater audience with movie footage, which kept the television version from being flat and one dimensional.

Right now Rocky Horror plays in 200 theaters every week and is passed down from parent to child. When audience participation begins to fluctuate, as Producer, you have to ask yourself what you can do with it next to get a new or larger audience.

Q: CAN YOU GIVE THE READERS A COMPARISON CONTRAST BETWEEN THE DUTIES OF A PRODUCER AND THAT OF AN EXECUTIVE PRODUCER? Answer: The titles Executive Producer and Producer differ in film and music. In the music business a Producer of an album is equivalent to a movie director. Whereas an executive producer on an album is the equivalent of a movie producer.

Many times, Executive Producer is a token title for someone who has a hands off, part-time involvement with the project. The producer is on-line with the film and on the set everyday. He usually gets involved with the project very early on and sets it up at a studio. Often he has a hand in casting, rewriting the screenplay, etc.

At times a person may come in very early on in the project, but can't make a deal, so he passes it on to a producer who may have a little more clout, or to a director. At other times someone can come in late and end up placing the deal at a studio. Or he could be the one to bring key people to the film, like a star or a sought after director, who would make the project more desirable or bankable. For his contribution to the project this person could receive a percentage of film profits (the percentages tend to fluctuate depending upon who utimately ends up getting the film deal made) and the title Executive Producer.

Q: YOU STARTED OUT WRITING SONGS FOR SAM COOKE. CAN YOU TELL US ABOUT THAT? WHAT SONGS DID YOU WRITE FOR HIM? *Answer:* I started out with Herb Albert as his song writing partner. The biggest hit we wrote for Sam Cooke was "What A Wonderful World."

At the time, Bumps Blackwell was producing Sam Cooke on Keen Records. Bumps owned the distinction of discovering Quincy Jones, Little Richard, Lou Rawls and Bessie Smith, among others. He was a phenomenal catalyst and motivator.

At the time I got started, Sam's first record "You Send Me" was out and doing well on the charts. Herb and I had already tried to play our demos for the major labels without success so we decided to try the independents.

Bumps Blackwell thought our demos showed promise and decided to take the two of us under his wings and teach us what he knew about songwriting, producing, etc. Bumps was always a little ahead of himself. As a result, Herb and I spent our first two months at Keen Records trying to find Bumps. He always spread himself so thin it was hard for him to keep appointments he had scheduled. But he was the greatest!

Q: DO YOU COME FROM A MUSICAL BACKGROUND? *Answer:* No. I had no musical background. Just an interest and a gift for writing. In high school I wrote lyrics for school songs and dialogue for school plays. So I decided to try my hand at writing pop songs. Herb and I met through girlfriends. He played the horn and knew enough piano for us to write songs. I tried to play the trumpet but gave it up when it made my nose bleed.

Q: I ALWAYS STRESS THE IMPORTANCE OF SINGERS LEARNING TO PLAY THE PIANO. *Answer:* Absolutely. No matter what area of the music industry you want to go into, knowing the piano is going to help you somewhere along the line. It fits into all categories.

Q: DID YOU EVER HAVE ASPIRATIONS ABOUT BEING AN ARTIST, OR HAVE YOU ALWAYS BEEN DRAWN TO WORK BEHIND THE SCENES? <u>**Answer:**</u> I learned early on that I could not sing. In school I acted in plays, but at some point I felt more comfortable behind the scenes as opposed to out front.

Q: DID YOU EVER DO ANY DIRECTING? <u>**Answer:**</u> I only directed two movies: "Up in Smoke" with Cheech and Chong, and one movie for television called "Ladies and Gentlemen, The Fabulous Stains" with Diane Lane. I loved directing. It's just that during the 80's I went into semi-retirement to spend time with my two young sons, coaching sports and enjoying being a father.

Q: I'VE NOTICED THAT YOU SERVE AS A MENTOR FOR YOUNGER PEOPLE. WOULD YOU COMMENT ON THAT? <u>**Answer:**</u> I think it's important especially since Bumps took so much time with me and Herb teaching us everything he knew. Bumps would put us in a room and have us listen to records and tapes for hours on end. He taught us songwriting techniques and pointed out what worked in a song and what did not. He took a lot of time teaching us about the music business. The industry has grown so much since I got started. Now it's difficult for a young person to get through the door by himself. That's why mentors are important, mentorship can give young people the break they need to launch a career.

My son Nic chose not to go to college because he loves the music business. That's his chosen career path. You might say that his vocation is his college. As a result, Nic takes his work in the studio as seriously as a good college student takes his classes. Personally, I feel that there's nothing like practical street learning, especially in music where that fresh street edge is so important.

Whenever I can impart to young people some of the knowledge I've accumulated over the years, it makes me feel that I'm doing something worthwhile, and that I'm passing on the legacy that Bumps gave me.

Q: WHAT ADVICE WOULD YOU GIVE TO YOUNGSTERS WHO WANT TO PRODUCE OR DIRECT? **Answer:** It is important for young people to practice and utilize what they have available to them. If they come up with an idea for a story that they want to produce or direct, they should write the story down from start to finish, then go back and polish that piece until it's the very best writing they are capable of at the time. One must practice and become skilled at his craft so that when it's time to present the material, the creator has something he is proud to show; something that's worth seeing or hearing.

This is a "do it" type of job. You can't just think about becoming a writer or producer because it's too easy to stay where you start if you don't take action. Once you put an idea into final written form then you've got a tangible commodity to sell, not an unwritten idea.

Q: WOULD YOU DISCUSS ODE RECORDS AND YOUR YOUNG GOSPEL GROUP, "ALL GOD'S CHILDREN." **Answer:** When I came out of retirement I started the children's label, Ode Records. At that time the music industry had become more corporate and most of the independents had been bought up. I felt that the best way to gain footing as an independent was to do alternative music such as gospel, children's music or things the majors don't concentrate on.

My love for gospel goes back to my days with Sam Cooke and Lou Rawls. I always felt that gospel should be more mainstream and should have gained more popularity than it enjoys. I had the idea to do a children's gospel album because I wanted to introduce children to gospel at an early age so that they could carry it on to adulthood.

I called Merry Clayton to work with me on the children's gospel project since she's such a gifted gospel singer. She recommended Terry Young and Maxi Anderson to write and produce the album. Right now Terry is in the middle of writing an album for Merry who is a tremendous talent that somehow, never became successful. She was in a couple of television series and does a lot of background singing but never got that big break.

Maxi and Terry are very experienced in the studio, easy to work with and are open to input. As Executive Producer, I felt good being able to leave two competent and experienced producers in the studio. They are self starters and capable of working well independently. Plus the two of them have a diversified musical background as recording artists, background vocalists, musicians, arrangers and writers. This helped cut the learning curve for the children, who received a wonderful education from Maxi and Terry in terms of vocal arrangements, mike techniques, etc.

The most delightful thing about *All God's Children* is that we did not know in the beginning that we would end up with so much talent in one group or that so many lead vocalists would emerge.

Q: WHAT IS IT LIKE OUT THERE AS AN INDEPENDENT GOING AGAINST THE MAJORS? *Answer:* The sheer volume and buying power of the majors equates to clout, which controls the music business. This means that an independent has to fight for space, and that makes it difficult to be an independent record company. Of course, I could have taken my children's project to one of the majors, but I would not have been able to get the kind of attention I wanted for *All God's Children* if I had taken it to a large label. As an independent you have control over the project and can follow your own vision.

Incidentally, I had the first independent label ever to be bought by a major, Dunhill, which became ABC Paramount-Dunhill. I had The Mama's and The Papas on that label.

Chapter 13

SINGERS: IN PURSUIT OF A RECORD DEAL

Good just isn't good enough. A new artist needs an edge in order to be better than what's already out there.

Every year the National Music Seminar (NMS) holds a conference attended by a virtual "Who's Who" of the industry: artists, record executives, managers, agents, bookers, video, radio and retail elements of the music business. In 1993, for the first time, NMS added a Kids' Music Seminar to its already impressive symposium. A few years ago one would have been hard pressed to find even a hand full of labels willing to sign a child or teen vocalist. Now, virtually every major record label either has a children's division, plans to open one, or have a hot young act already on the roster.

Once the "Hundredth Monkey Principle" kicked in, record labels began to cash in on the tremendous buying power of kids, ultimately giving them what they wanted: music by and for young ears only. In Hollywood everyone knows how to follow trends, and record labels are no exception. Following the lead of Lou Adler and his label, Ode Records, which features children's albums by Shelly Duval, Cheech, Waylan Jennings young group, All God's Children, independent labels are on the rise and looking for young talent which creates exciting opportunities for young singers.

BUT CAN THE CHILD SING?

Singing requires an innate talent that nevertheless necessitates training and development to mold it into something marketable. If your child cannot hold a note, all the training and wishing in the world will not turn such a child into a song bird. The parent might as well settle for helping the young hopeful become the best dancer or actor possible.

Admittedly, some successful artists on the radio are a long way from vocal acrobatics, singing easy songs that have limited range. In fact, one often hears fault-finding of many popular singers who are accused of not being able to sing at all. Upon closer examination, however, one will find that all gold, platinum or award winning recording artists have something unique, innovative or different about their style. Granted, they may have a raspy, hoarse sounding voice, or may sing in a monotone. Still, such artists CAN hold a tune, DO stay on pitch, and sing their songs IN key. More often than not, many such artists are great writers and musicians who possess a unique "vibe" that distinguishes them. Some artists also possess strong songwriting skills, incredible musical ability, or a special something in their voice or act that sets them apart from the crowd.

FOR CHILDREN WITH MORE DESIRE THAN TALENT...

If a child is: *(1) TONE DEAF*
(2) HAS TROUBLE SUSTAINING PITCH
(3) OR, HAS DIFFICULTY STAYING ON KEY

do not waste your time and money pushing that child to become a lead vocalist or solo recording artist. Such a child may still find an outlet for the desire to sing by joining a church or school choir, or at best, as a recording group in need of a back-up singer. Keep in mind, however, that many back-up singers are phenomenal lead vocalists who are simply passing the time or making money in the interim until their big break comes along.

Many children are great dancers, have a wonderful look and stage presence, but will never have what it takes to sing lead. If the child truly wants to sing, encourage him or her to join a group and sing background vocals or learn an instrument and perform as a member of the band. Many singers do quite well as back-up vocalists or musicians.

Of course there are parents who argue that a vocal coach can teach a child techniques to help the young singer stay on pitch or in key. This is true to a certain extent. A vocal coach can train the child to overcome weak lines in a song through PRACTICE, PRACTICE and MORE PRACTICE. And with enough work, a child with one or more of the three problems mentioned above, might even record rather impressive vocal tracks in a studio, provided a vocal coach or producer feeds the child's lines one by one. Even with the most impressive training money can buy and under the best of circumstances, a child who does not have a natural ear or perfect pitch will inevitably go off key while singing a song live all the way through. Often this happens because the singer relies on practice and memory rather than a natural ear or an intuitive inner voice that sings THROUGH the child. Nervous energy can also block everything a child has learned, causing him or her to revert back to innate limitations or bad habits. Which is why people in the industry look for natural talent, i.e., a child with perfect pitch who can stay on key without much effort.

Even though record labels go through a rigorous screening process, if an artist ends up costing the label too much time in the studio, or cannot consistently give the producer what is expected or desired, the label will end up canning the project, shelving the child or both. Which explains why, when a record label listens to a demo that strikes their ears, they want to hear the artist sing the songs live to instrumental tracks. In such performances record labels look for:

(1) charisma
(2) stage presence
(3) ability to emote

(3) vocal range
(4) perfect pitch and tone
(5) an eye pleasing, marketable look

A tone deaf child may learn considerable technique, develop incredible range and sound wonderful in certain parts of a song; he or she cannot, however, manage to maintain proper pitch or stay on key throughout a song. Usually the problem resides in the fact that the singer cannot hear the bad note, nor can he or she easily mimic sounds. The best singers have an amazing aptitude for listening to what they hear and then singing it back identically, note for note. Great singers also have strong improvisational ability and intuitively know how to create ad libs that make a song sound distinctively their own.

PREPARING TO GO PRO

Parents of children who have demonstrated exceptional vocal ability in talent shows, competitions or live performances should ask themselves the following questions before spending money on a *demo tape*: the parent should determine if the child has (1) a burning desire to become a recording artist? or, (2) enough vocal range, a unique style, stage presence, and an eye catching "look" to stand out from other artists in that age range?

Remember, average talent requires considerable money of one's own to enable such an artist to rise from the deep heap of mediocrity. This investment involves buying outstanding songwriters, producers, arrangers, choreographers and a good publicist to promote the artist. Given enough advertising dollars, one can pretty much sell anything. Otherwise, a singer will have to jump through a lot of hoops before impressing a record label enough to invest in an "average" artist who does not own the blatant potential to "blow" his or her competition out of the water. Record labels want certain intangible collateral to insure a return on their investment.

Parents should keep in mind also that many producers have no problem taking demo money for a child who cannot sing. This type of producer figures the parent should have some clue that their child has no talent, which makes it easy for the producer to rationalize that the parent obviously has money to burn on a no singing child. In the end this type of producer decides that he or she is doing the parent a favor by fulfilling a wish.

SESSION WORK AS A BACKGROUND VOCALIST

Before spending the money, time and energy to record a demo, the parent should go into the venture willing to lose the money graciously, or decide that it is a good investment towards buying the child experience working in a recording studio. This investment might pay off later in session work for the child as a background vocalist on an album, film or television show. That's assuming the child has "some" talent or at least "average" talent for the producer to work with.

Those interested in background work (which can be steady and create credits on the resume) should have the child audition for other adults who make their living as session singers. Background singers usually receive calls directly from producers to work on an album or television show. Usually an experienced singer, who has worked with that particular producer before, gets the call, and that singer gathers up other singers for the producer. Most of the time the background singers chosen are people that the caller has worked with before or has heard sing somewhere. Once the child has done a few jobs with the singer who calls, that person will keep the child in mind and call again when there's more work.

GETTING READY TO AUDITION FOR A RECORD LABEL

Have the child establish a track record of winning trophies, accolades and the admiration of fans at live shows. These shows generate excellent opportunities for a child to polish up on stage presence while picking up pointers from other performers. They also allow time for the young performer to develop a particular vocal style and to come up with a *look* for presentation before a record label.

The child may need a little more training, experience in the studio, or work with live audiences before he or she is ready or will feel comfortable going before a record company. Each child is different. Some are born trying to sing and dance before they talk or walk; others have to grow, mature and develop their talent with time. One thing for sure, practice at home, study with a vocal coach or vocal tape, and performance in front of live audiences will only enhance the child's chances of success.

A young performer with a parent who knows how to sing; who has a natural ear for music; or, someone in the family with musical training has a built in advantage. Such children have the convenience of free voice or music lessons at their disposal. Those who do not, have to find the money or teacher and time outside of the home, which requires an additional investment of money, time and dedication.

THE IMPORTANCE OF LEARNING TO HARMONIZE

R&B groups such as In Vogue, Jodeci, and Boyz 2 Men have the distinctive ability to harmonize and blend notes beautifully. Moreover, there was a time, particularly during the heyday of Motown, when everyone took for granted that a group could sing in perfect harmony. Now groups with the ability to harmonize are the exception rather than the rule.

Granted, in order to create harmony, one has to sing along with someone else, which makes it impossible to learn harmony solo. And, in order for an instructor to teach harmony to a student the instructor must innately possess an ear for creating notes slightly different from the melody that blend in perfectly with the melody line.

For an artist to sing harmony, he or she also has to be able to hear the melody note while singing a higher or lower note without becoming distracted by the other notes. Until a child figures out how to sustain the right key while singing harmony, he or she will start out on the correct note then automatically slip back into the key of the melody. Harmony requires the ability to hear yourself and hold the note while listening to others sing in a higher or lower note simultaneously.

Solo artists who think they will never need to learn how to harmonize should keep in mind that the ability to harmonize on a recording saves money in the studio by not having to hire and teach background vocalists. Many accomplished solo singers can sing three part harmony with themselves on lead and background vocal tracks.

HELPFUL HINTS FOR LEARNING TO HARMONIZE:

While learning harmony, it helps to place a finger over one ear to hear yourself while listening to members of the group with the other ear. Even though harmony demands patience to teach and practice to learn, mastery creates sheer magic for listening audiences. It can also mean box office dollars, as Hollywood learned with the phenomenal success of "Sister Act." In fact, Whoopi Goldberg's character in the movie enchanted millions of audiences by teaching the choir incredible vocal arrangements in expert harmony.

Keep in mind that learning harmony comes easier to a child than an adult, so start early. Research reveals that the ability to acquire music and a foreign language diminishes sharply after puberty. Of course this does not mean that one cannot learn music or a foreign language after that age; it simply requires more effort for mastery. So give your child that all important edge, spoken of so often in this book, by putting the child in a choir or group that sings harmony or finding someone to teach harmony.

The same goes for piano and guitar lessons. Start as early as the child demonstrates maturity, ability or interest. Learning an instrument will not only sharpen the child's ear, but can mean self-sufficiency as an artist because a youngster who can play keyboard or guitar will not have to depend on another musician for live performances. Musical ability will also expand the child's options later should he or she decide to move into producing songs for a demo or album.

VOCAL COACHES AND PRACTICE TAPES

Non-singing parents who are unable to coach their child vocally should enroll the young performer in voice lessons, a musical theater class, or purchase video and audio tapes to learn by. In Los Angeles, Vocal Power offers audio and videotapes for practice.

Vocal coach, Roger Love, who is Seth Riggs trained, has an excellent videotape titled *Get Out of the Shower And Sing* that's available for $20.00 (Call 213-876-3989 or write 3151 Cahuenga Blvd. West, Suite 107, Los Angeles, Ca 90068.)

Of course a personal vocal coach is always best, but video and audio tapes are convenient and practical when one cannot afford to pay for private lessons, or if the singer's schedule does not permit going to a vocal coach.

Because Hollywood is so visual; stage presence, personality and an appealing "look" make the top of the list. Musicality is next, combined with an instinct for choosing the right music for auditions. A fabulous singer can lessen his or her chance of booking a job by choosing a song unsuitable to vocal style or range. More importantly, during an audition have your tape cued, or sheet music in hand, then cut to the chase in showing off vocal range because most auditions do not allow much time to stretch vocally." Susan Salgado, Director of The Music Department at Bobby Ball Agency (BBA)

PUTTING TOGETHER PERFORMANCE ROUTINES

Parental involvement in choosing and putting together a couple of performance songs for a child can take up a considerable amount of time. Moreover, children need an audience during rehearsals and the parent can serve as champion and critic, helping the child to correct wrong notes, create natural and believable facial expressions and to stick with a difficult dance step until it's mastered. In the process, adults can encourage and inspire the child. Never browbeat, put-down or intimidate. Otherwise, children will rebel and resort to self-defeating behavior in retaliation.

Keep in mind also that a child can become overwhelmed by the amount of effort that goes into learning a single song and dance. The good news is that it gets easier with each new song. In the meantime, pacing the rehearsal and permitting breaks when necessary can prevent a child from feeling stressed. If a child has reached his or her limits of endurance, end the session, regardless of whether you've completed the full rehearsal time. Moreover, schedule time for homework first, not afterwards, because the child is often too tired following a rehearsal to concentrate on homework. If the parent leaves school work last, this can create needless frustration for a child who wants nothing but a hot bath and bed after practice.

Learning one up tempo song and one ballad, preferably from Top 40 tunes, can take a child a long way through the audition process for talent shows, competitions, musical theater or theatrical auditions. Depending on the child, it can take from a few days to a few months to master one song. The most effective process involves breaking the song down line by line, making sure that no note goes unnoticed for its chance at excellence. After vocal mastery and learning the choreography, move on to stage presence, such as projection, eye contact with the audience, emotional expression and proper use of the microphone. This includes how to hold the mike steady, pulling it in closer for low notes, and further away for loud notes.

SINGING WITH CHOREOGRAPHY

Singing and dancing at the same time requires stamina and practice along with practice and more practice in order to build up endurance. Weeks or months of rehearsal can go into just one song. Further, many live concerts, television shows and films allow the artist to sing along with their vocal track when strenuous dance movements come into play because doing both requires a great deal of breath and control. One method of mastery involves having the choreographer stage the singer in and out of the dance routine. For example, on lines involving full lung capacity, choreography for the lead singer is simplified. If dancers do knee bends, floor work or gymnastics, then the singer can do a smooth spin or a half bend, saving all of the difficult or breath taking moves for the chorus (at which time the singer has support from background vocals). The chorus gives singers a break, allowing them to weave in and out of the flow of the choreography and to dance full capacity with the other dancers during that time. After the chorus, the singer can step forward and sing the verses, utilizing full vocal power in conjunction with limited dance movements.

Singing while jogging helps build breath control, smoothness and perseverance for strenuous choreography. Dance several times a week in hip-hop, funk or street classes, also provide powerful workouts. In most of these classes the teacher takes no captives.

HANGING OUT AT THE HOTTEST DANCE STUDIOS

I encourage all new clients to take hip hop classes from the most popular dance studios in the Hollywood area under choreographers who work with the biggest stars in the business. In these classes children and adults dance together, which compels newcomers to keep up with more advanced students. This process creates a sink or swim situation. Most swim, however, easily getting caught up in the energy of rising to the occasion. After a few classes newcomers learn an entirely new routine in an hour and a half.

Real singers know not to underestimate the importance of dance to the success of their recording career. True enough, if one has a good look and a great voice, record companies can surround your act with professional dancers. If the singer cannot dance at all, however, the dance entourage will only highlight that inadequacy.

INDUSTRY PROFESSIONALS SPOT TALENT AT DANCE STUDIOS

Dance studios serve as a convenient way station for parents, agents and producers in search of a dance agent or for talent to work in musicals, music videos or the record industry. Producers need children who can dance which makes dance studios a logical place to look. Moreover, dance studios post flyers everywhere, detailing auditions. Even those who do not attend dance classes know to drop in at dance studios and read the bulletin board. More importantly, for newcomers, agents make their rounds at all the hottest dance studios in search of new talent. Usually, the director of the dance school hand-picks those students who are ready for representation by an agent.

Typically, when a producer or record company auditions through a dance studio or dance agent, they already have a concept, complete with budget, producers, and songs just waiting for the right talent to fill the slot. Auditioning for a record deal directly through a dance studio, agent or referral can save money, time and effort in putting together a demo and shopping that demo to record labels.

For example, when my daughter was 11 years old she received a group recording offer from a major label. At the time I had not even begun to think about putting together a demo for Crystal. What helped Crystal get the offer was the fact that she had four days notice to learn a new song and dance routine (which is a lot of time from industry standards). We practiced that weekend, choosing a difficult song that combined rap and vocal ability because the girls needed to be able to rap. By Monday, the day of the audition, Crystal was super confident. Ultimately, circumstances would not permit us to go through with that deal, but at 13 Crystal landed a better solo deal when her brother produced a song for an artist with a label looking for a singer Crystal's age. It was an easy sell since Crystal had just recorded a song on Michael Jackson's album (with a group) as well as an international dance demo with her brother and three other show biz teens for a European producer. In both situations the producers involved were looking for a specific act.

SEIZE EVERY OPPORTUNITY

In readiness for impromptu or unscheduled auditions, one should always have in the car your child's portfolio and an instrumental track with at least two songs. Teach young performers to "seize the day" if someone asks them to audition on the spot. If the instrumental track is not available, have the child sing without music. For example, my son ended up booking several jobs through a songwriter-producer because he did not hesitate to sing on the spot for that producer while on the set filming a show. I gave the producer my business card and months later got a call for a job that Salim did not have to audition for because he came highly recommended by that songwriter-producer.

For children who dance but cannot sing, give them an edge by encouraging the child to rap since many commercials use rap (including Barbie). Moreover, many popular songs have raps incorporated in the middle of them. The best thing about rap is anyone can do it since rapping does not require singing ability.

BACK-UP DANCERS

For a solo act it really adds impact to have a group of dancers accompany the singer. Four dancers would be ideal, with two on either side. But the more the merrier. Look at MC Hammer's entourage. Dancers fill up the stage and share the responsibility of keeping all segments of the audience entertained at once. When adding dancers to perform behind your child, as parent, you assume the responsibility of finding and paying for the choreographer, rehearsal space, and supervision during rehearsals. Naturally this process entails time and patience, in particular, if one wants to create a piece that impresses.

Participation in talent shows or benefit concerts can create name recognition. A&R people at record labels prefer to sign individuals they have seen perform or who come highly recommended to the label.

Once a child has done the grunt work of learning a couple of songs, mastering the choreography, microphone techniques, stage presence, vocal style, and a unique look, it's time to start presenting the child professionally at community benefits, galas, charity concerts, or opening acts for well known groups. As mentioned earlier, in Los Angeles, Vocal Power offers **showcases** for their students and invites industry personnel to these performances. Other viable options include: **ASCAP and BMI** showcases (the music publishing end of the business), school talent shows, local and national talent competitions judged by professionals in the industry, or simply performing before family friends and relatives who automatically brag to others. Word gets around fast. By staying in the mix, your child might receive a referral that can add a boost to his or her career. Word of mouth always has and will continue to be the best form of advertisement.

By performing regularly in front of live audiences, especially in talent shows or competitions, the child quickly discovers how he or she measures up against peers. In the process a young artist can also get a feel for how much harder he or she needs to work to equal or surpass the competition. But best of all, a child can pat his or her own back for being the best of that particular crowd on a given day.

In addition, live performances give a child the opportunity to iron out kinks and imperfections in an act before going in front of a record label where the stakes are much higher. Even with children who are naturally and incredibly talented, if one puts such an act up against an experienced stage performer (who might not even have as much talent), the experienced child will win out every time because he or she has learned stage presence and the art of wooing and captivating an audience.

More importantly, by being visible in public, especially highly publicized benefits or fund-raisers, one never knows if an *Artist and Repertoire (ie., A&R)* person from a record label will approach the parent and child after the show. Moreover, an A&R person will remember an act that impresses him or her, even if no current opening exists within that label. Often, getting a deal hinges on whom a record label already has on its roster. If a company has an act too similar to your child's style, you may have to wait until the competition has run its popularity course, or find a competing label who wants someone just like your child to go up against that other artist.

CREATING A LOOK

After the young artist has learned two strong songs it is important to create an eye-catching look. Music videos made personal appearance (along with dance ability) almost as important as the artist's vocal talent. Therefore, encourage healthy eating habits and exercise *before* the onset of puberty in order to easily shed those excess pounds that can creep up during that time. Always present the best image possible.

Consulting with a hair and make-up person and a wardrobe stylist can be helpful at this point. It does not have to cost a lot of money either. A new haircut, hair color, or hair style can work wonders on an otherwise plain appearance. For the cost of a cut and blow dry, one can come up with a new look that might be just the thing the child needed for a boost in confidence and career.

As parents we tend to dress our children the way our parents dressed us or the way we wanted them to dress us, without always paying attention to whether that style works on our child or not. When in doubt, seek out someone who has a flare for dressing themselves and their child with class and style. Explain that you're trying to come up with an eye-catching stage look that suits your child, then let this person know what your budget is and ask if they would help you come up with something within that range. Let this person know that you will give them referrals and that you're willing to pay a small fee. For someone interested in becoming a stylist, they might do it for free just to get their name out there. Also, refer to some of the suggestions on dress mentioned in the next chapter titled: "Wardrobe, Investing In Tools Of The Trade."

GROUPS VS. GOING SOLO

Groups require a lot more work than a solo act because of all the different personalities and other parents to contend with. Each member also has his or her own individual learning curve. Not everyone will master the songs or choreography at the same pace. On the other hand, groups tend to be easier to market because their combined presence appeals to a wider range of people in the audience, which can generate more album sales.

Unless talent is distributed pretty much evenly among group members, enmity and strife may result. In particular, the nature of a group requires that members spend countless hours together, which makes the ability to blend and get along crucial. More importantly, the manager of a group sets the tone for how members will interact with each other. If the manager treats each child as equally important to the success of the group, then no external reason will exist for rivalry or insecurities. Finding such a manager can prove difficult at best.

Look for a music producer who allows the artist to develop a unique style rather than one who attempts to model the singer after himself, or who limits the child's vocal range.

In a group situation, fearful, insecure or pushy parents who are easily intimidated by other members of the group pose the biggest problem. Secure parents, however, concentrate at home on rehearsing and preparing the child's songs and choreography in order that the young performer can put forth his or her best effort during rehearsals or shows. Such a parent knows that cream has a way of rising to the top while the rest eventually fall by the wayside. That's why groups composed of family members or relatives tend to outlast others since family bonds tend not to break as easily.

One may have to go through a few groups before finding a compatible situation that suits the child's talent or personality, therefore, a parent should take time and work with a group BEFORE signing a contract. If a parent signs too soon, the child might end up miserable for years, especially since a contract ratified by the court requires court approval for dissolution. I made the difficult decision to pass up on several recording offers for both of my children either because: (1) problems presented themselves too soon, (2) the situation did not feel like a healthy environment for children, (3) or the contract offered unfavorable terms that were non-negotiable.

A parent has to make such decisions based upon what feels right inside. That's where advice from a good entertainment attorney who is not intimidated or in awe of stars, executives or powerful music producers is invaluable. Remember that opportunity does knock more than once if you decide not to settle for less than the very best situation you can come up with for your child as opposed to the first thing that comes along.

FINDING THE RIGHT PRODUCER

For those not fortunate enough to land a record deal through a dance studio, agent, or a contact, the most direct route involves a music producer who currently works with acts signed to different record labels, or a manager who does the same thing. Successful producers and managers have their fingers on the pulse of the industry and know just what type of artists each record label currently needs. At times, requests tie directly into who won at the Grammy's the year before. Right before the Grammy's speculation runs rampant on favored artists, based on record sales which prompt labels to rush and sign new acts capable of following in the winner's footsteps.

MASTER - APPRENTICE FRUSTRATIONS

Children are 'diamonds in the rough' which means that parents need to be extremely careful in choosing professionals to work with them. Along with the right qualifications, producers need to have patience and a love for children in order to bring out the best in every child they work with. Maxi Anderson, Producer "All God's Children"

I have heard children who are powerful belters captivate everyone in the audience with their incredible vocal range. Later, after listening to their demos, I wondered how the producer could NOT allow such children to fully utilize their vocal range on the demo. After all, record labels look for that ability in a singer's voice. In fact, vocal range and style sets a singer apart from the crowd of performers who simply sing well. Sometimes the problem lies in the fact that some producers want to play it safe by settling for a _good track_ when they could put in a little more work to get a _great_ track filled with ear tingling notes. And there are those producers who simply do not know how to pull a command performance out of the artist.

A more serious and insidious problem, however, involves producers with unfulfilled aspirations as an artist. An unwitting singer can find himself or herself caught up in subtle forms of sabotage arising out of the producer's deep subconscious desires gone unmet for too long. Moreover, no producer would willingly admit that deep inside he or she would rather hold the competition back until he or she has made it himself as an artist, in particular if the producer feels that the artist has more talent, stage presence, credits, or a better look.

Beware of producers who are frustrated artists and want nothing more than to mold your child into a clone of what they themselves would like to have become. -Maxi Anderson, Producer, "All God's Children"

The same thing goes for vocal coaches struggling to get their singing careers off the ground, or musicians who cannot be effective teachers to students that show great promise or potential. One of my son's guitar teachers admitted, after we had dropped him as a teacher, that he only felt able to give more of himself as a teacher AFTER his own group finally got a record deal. Before that time Salim felt let down on many occasions when this instructor either refused or would not make himself available to teach him a song for an audition or a job.

A red signal flashes when I hear a producer announce that getting a recording contract lies in the future somewhere, in particular, if this person has passed his or her prime. That fact, alone, indicates that either a serious character flaw or lack of talent has gotten in the way of achieving the goal earlier. Besides, very few singers break into the record industry after the age of thirty. Willie Nelson has the distinction of being one of the few who made it big after forty. Furthermore, one can rest assured that a frustrated artist-producer will keep the best songs for his or her album, leaving only rejects for the artist. If possible, try to find a producer satisfied with producing; one who has willingly given up plans to become an artist, or a producer who already has an established recording career. This type of producer usually has fewer subconscious blocks about a new artist because he or she has already made a mark in the business and no one can take that away.

Regardless of how hot a producer USED to be, the business banks on who is happening TODAY. As a result, producers either keep up with trends or get lost along the side of the road. Keep in mind the following when dealing with a producer not currently working with any major record labels: Even though that person may have wonderful songs, desperation to break into the business or to get back into it (for "has been's") somehow gets in the way of success. Remember, no one wants to work with frantic people, they tend to offend. Besides, that hungry look in their eyes scares others away.

Moreover, such producers may attempt to control the submission process of the demo after you've already paid for it. Use a producer to shop your demo only if he or she has current contacts in the record industry because record company executives tend to job hop. Furthermore, unestablished, unsuccessful or "has been" producers may attempt to piggy back on your child's project by pushing themselves as an artist, or by promoting other artists that they are also currently producing right along with your child's demo. In particular, look out for producers who feel that your child has more talent or potential to succeed than he or she does.

A qualified producer is one who takes a young singer's raw talent, then nurtures and expands upon it. The end result is a powerful and polished reflection of the child's natural abilities. -Maxi Anderson, Producer "All God's Children."

Similarly, avoid egocentric producers obsessed with control. They will allow the artist no say-so or input in interpreting the song. Such producers act territorial about their material, demanding that your child sing the song EXACTLY as they do. It won't matter if the child's voice does not lend itself to that style; this type of producer will not want even the slightest ad lib or improvisation added; thus, stifling the originality of your child as a budding artist. Ultimately, working with an egocentric producer ends up an exercise in futility because the parent will never come out of the studio with anything that even vaguely represents the child well. You might get a GOOD demo on your child, but not one that gets record labels excited about signing your child to a record contract.

Always follow your gut instincts; they send off warning signals when there's potential trouble, danger or problems ahead. It's up to you as a parent to listen and get your child out of harm's way. A wise person once said that to be forewarned is to be forearmed.

PUBERTY AND MALE VOCALISTS

During adolescence, some male vocalists never recover fully from their voice cracking at a live performance. They end up phobic about it happening again or fearful that they have lost their range. Many fears carry over into adulthood and can end what might have become a promising career before it really began.

One has to take into account, when dealing with an adolescent male artist, that his voice will change. Usually without much warning. With that in mind, you can either hurry up and get a recording contract BEFORE the voice changes or, by necessity, wait until the voice has stabilized and stopped cracking, which can take a year or two.

As mentioned in the chapter on *"Teenagers,"* becoming taller or looking older than your age group poses a disadvantage for young actors. My son's sudden growth spurt necessitated that we turn our attention to his music where issues of height do not come into play as hard or fast.

As Salim's voice began to deepen the producer we worked with on his first demo would not allow him to sing in his natural voice. The producer confined Salim to a high falsetto to make him sound like a young Michael Jackson. Unwittingly, I deferred to the producer's judgment since he had several hits in his history. In retrospect, since this man had not worked with an artist as young as Salim, I think he thought he was doing the right thing. In the process, however, he limited Salim as a vocalist.

The great are only great because we are on our knees: Let Us Arise. -Pierre J. Proudhon

During the year it took the producer to finish four songs for the ***demo***, (an unreasonably long time by any standard) Salim's voice developed more bass, losing much of his falsetto range. Even though Salim's voice dropped almost a full octave during that year, the producer kept all the songs in a higher key than Salim's natural voice, making the recording process much more tedious than necessary.

As it turned out, Salim's first full demo became an exercise in futility because by the time the producer mixed the tracks, Salim's voice had changed completely. In the end, Salim could not even sing live to the original instrumental tracks because they were no longer in his key.

This producer failed to take into account that a young male teen who looks and sounds older than his age can create cross-over buying potential. In effect, a mature voice stands to capture the early 20's age category while automatically pulling in adolescents and teens by virtue of the child's actual age. Moreover, it can create a mystique or enigma. It is a good idea not to lay ones common sense aside in favor of the opinion of a professional who may know his or her job, but lack vision.

I was forced to start all over with a new demo that not only reflected the maturity in Salim's voice but his range as well. In the meantime Salim's voice was still changing and began to crack on the high notes. To ease him through the transition, I allowed Salim to sing in his natural and chest voice, using his head or falsetto voice only minimally on stage. The problem with Salim's voice cracking occurred when he moved vocally from natural to false, creating fear that he had lost his falsetto ability completely. I assured him that this was only temporary. We continued to practice, using Roger Love's voice tape (mentioned earlier in this chapter) and experimenting with new ways to hit the high notes without cracking.

We discovered that certain movements of the lips, neck and head make notes come out with a distinctly smooth quality. It did not take long for Salim to create and incorporate new sounds that worked for his voice. Further, I would not allow my son to attach himself to the fear that he could no longer sing the high notes. I exercised patience with him and explained that he would have to find, on his own, another way to bring the high notes out in his new voice without forcing the notes; they were still there.

Since my son liked to sing R & B, I encouraged him to imitate the masters in his genre--great male vocalists with tremendous range in their voices like Jackie Wilson; the lead singer for Earth, Wind & Fire; Eddy Kendricks of the Temptations; James Ingram; and Al Green--who has his own special way of crooning high notes. At the same time, I continued to have Salim do live appearances, singing songs that he felt comfortable with--trying out the rich texture of his new voice, while sprinkling in a few high notes as confidence boosters. These live performances created immense belief and reliance on his own innate ability to overcome temporary obstacles that can get in the way on the road to success. As usual, practice provides the greatest assurance.

GETTING MUSIC IN THE RIGHT KEY

With many songs, a singer will have to utilize more than one octave, going in and out of chest voice, middle voice and head voice. If the instrumental track is not recorded in the singer's natural key he has to strain unnecessarily to reach the top notes. As a result, even the natural voice will not sound as smooth and the bottom notes will come out too low. Worst of all, it will frustrate the child to no end and make the young artist feel that something is wrong within. Avoid this aggravation by transposing the music into the right key for the singer's voice. Besides, with music in the right key, the song will flow easily and effortlessly as the singer transitions from one octave to another, utilizing all three voices while singing. With computerized and automated recording studios, it does not take much effort to transpose a song's key.

PAYING UP FRONT VS. DEMO SPEC AGREEMENTS

I have paid to have demos done and I've had them recorded under **Demo Spec Agreements**. Both have their pros and cons. Depending on what type of ego the producer has, paying for a demo should buy more control and creative input. The operative word is "usually." I have paid for demos that turned out to be a waste of money because I could not get the producer to exercise or listen to common sense. In such instances, no matter how diplomatically or eloquently I stated my case, a male producer ignored me simply because of my gender. These experiences have taught me to stand my ground and remind the producer who's paying for what. If that does not work I simply tell the producer that I will not pay for something

I know does not serve my child's or my client's abilities. Usually that will do the trick. It helps to find a music manager or entertainment attorney who can introduce you to producers currently working with record labels. They can also intervene for you if the producer becomes a problem.

Depending on how many tracks the studio has, the price for recording a song varies considerably. One can record a decent demo anywhere from $300 to $1,200.00 with the median price around $500.00. Before learning the in's and out's of demos, I ended up paying more than I should have because I did not know to ask for a flat rate per song. If one pays by the hour, the producer can take as long as he or she wants to get the song done. Depending on the experience of the producer it might take anywhere from twelve hours (if the producer is extremely fast and working with a seasoned sound engineer) to forty eight hours. Recording studios charge from $35.00 per hour all the way up to $400.00 and above per hour. The median rate falls somewhere around $60.00 per hour. (It is also cheaper to buy blocks of time in the studio, usually in four hour increments). Studio time includes laying down the instrumental tracks, lead vocals, background vocals, and mixing. Anything can and does happen in a studio, so allow for variables or unforeseen occurrences (i.e., mechanical problems) that inevitably crop up. If that happens, the client should not receive a bill for down time or engineering incompetence.

Always be prepared and make each audition a learning experience. Expect the unexpected. Susan Salgado, Director of The Music Department at Bobby Ball Agency (BBA)

I would caution that one avoid paying more than $500 for a single song, since demos are a gamble, with no assurance of quality in the end. For best results, listen to someone else's demo that impresses you then find out who produced it and get that producer to record yours. Moreover, listen to a producer's song catalog first and try to select a song that's already completed. Otherwise, allowing the producer to write a song specifically for the artist can hold unpleasant surprises since you don't know what you'll end up with.

Of course the producer will try to convince you that this is the best thing for your artist, once he or she has taken the trouble to write and compose for your child. Nine times out of ten you won't get anything as good as a song that is already complete. Besides, by choosing a song from the producer's catalog, the instrumental track and background vocals are already done. This can save untold time and money, especially if you're paying by the hour. In addition, a child who has been in the studio before can go in and lay down lead vocals in less than two hours when working with an experienced producer and engineer.

While the suggestions in this chapter do not guarantee your child a record deal, they should increase the odds in favor of success. As with anything else, talent, persistence and perseverance always prevail.

POINTS TO PONDER:

1. *To shop a deal to a record label a singer needs four original songs--two up tempo, and two ballads that showcase the artist's vocal range.*

2. *It is important to present songs to a record label that have hit potential because record companies now release singles while the album is under completion. Record labels prefer acts that walk in the door polished and ready for air play on the radio. It saves time and money.*

3. *An artist is more valuable to a record label if he or she is self-contained: can write, play an instrument, produce and arrange vocals. This type of artist has longevity in the business.*

4. *Try to find a producer who will record your demo under the terms of a Demo Spec Agreement.*

5. *Avoid producers, teachers or vocal coaches who are also frustrated artists.*

6. *Due to the power of music videos, learning to dance is almost as important as singing ability in terms of selling a song. The advent of music videos made it important to look good on T.V. Artists must, therefore, watch their weight and personal appearance-- in particular female acts.*

7. *Agents, producers and record labels often look for talent at dance studios.*

Chapter 14

WARDROBE: INVESTING IN TOOLS OF THE TRADE

Work on your appearance. Another responsibility you have is to be the best-looking that you can be, given what you came with ... If you are not pretty, be clever. -K Callan, author "The L.A. Agent Book"

CREATING A "LOOK" FOR YOUR CHILD

Parents who do not possess an innate flair for fashion which highlights the child's best assets and minimizes the youngster's worst, can learn by studying fashion trends and picking out what works with "traditional wear" (i.e. clothes that never go out of style, like Oxford shirts or plaid pleated skirts). Current ideas and insights are available everywhere you look. Observe what other children wear on television shows. Pay attention to the way school children dress. Stay abreast of fashion at the malls, on the street or in fashion magazines.

In the process, remember to take into account your child's personality and include the child in the selection process. Within reason, allow your child to make his or her own individual fashion statement. Yes, this requires letting go of our parental ego since there will be times when the latest fashion trend that children come up with will look like something the dog just brought in. In such situations it helps to combine the trend with good old common sense along with a few guidelines thrown in for good measure to ensure that the child does not come off looking ridiculous.

For example, just because the cool guys are wearing pants three times their size belted half way down their hips, it might not be in your child's best interest if he or she has heavy hips or the wrong physique to pull off that particular look. As a compromise, one might adjust the waist line a little higher and gather the oversized pants onto the waist rather than letting them sag on or below the hips. The sad reality that people with big bones or heavy hips have to face is that most fashions were meant for bone thin models with no hips. If your child has difficulty grasping that concept, point out examples of unflattering fashion statements and make comparisons or ask for comments on how that person could dress to minimize problem areas. For example, an overweight person in tight, brightly colored biker shorts with the midriff hanging somewhere between the cut off sports top and the elastic waist band might look smaller in dark colored, loose fitting clothing that flows. Exaggerated images can quickly get the child's attention and help the youngster visualize the importance of dressing in clothes that suit the individual body type.

SET ASIDE SPECIFIC OUTFITS FOR AUDITIONS ONLY:

BOYS: Little boys tend to be easier to dress than girls because their wardrobe is simpler. Basically, their audition attire is complete with a pair of Levi's jeans (plain), shorts, a couple of brightly colored tee-shirts (with no logo) a nice sweater, oxford shirt, sneakers, loafers, and a baseball cap. These items will pretty much dress him for any audition. The reason for no logos is because the production company has to obtain permission from the manufacturer to use logos, which may entail paying a fee. Otherwise, why give free advertising?

As my children grew older, choosing audition outfits turned into a nightmare because both of them sought total independence and autonomy in that area. It served no purpose for me to rationalize with them that I must know something about fashion since the outfits I had selected over the years kept them employed in show business along with compliments from directors and wardrobe people on their choice of attire. Reality carried no weight with them as they grew older. It reminded me of the poet Judith Voist who said that "It's hard to be hip and over thirty."

For everyone's peace of mind, I came up with a compromise: two separate sets of clothing. One for auditions only, and the other for school and play. For the latter, my two children were allowed to pretty much do their own thing as long as the clothes were clean, relatively wrinkle free and not likely to slide completely off of their bodies. Audition outfits became a joint shopping venture, with me holding final veto power.

More important than personal appearance, is naturalness and ease of comfort while waiting to be called in to audition. Once inside, the child needs to be genuine and honest in his or her emotions and reactions to the material.

GIRLS: At one point my daughter refused to buy anything but boy's designer high top basketball sneakers that in no way flatter long, thin legs. Not to mention the fact that they cost twice as much as the cute little penny loafers, adorable Victorian boots, or black patent leather dress shoes she needed for many of her auditions. Moreover, since Crystal wore sneakers most of the time, I ended up giving away practically brand new audition shoes every year. I felt blessed when her taste began shifting. Now she buys Doc Martin boots, cowboy boots and other shoes in addition to sneakers, which work well with different audition outfits. Now, I no longer cringe at the thought of spending a lot of money on shoes that I know my daughter can wear with outfits other than jeans.

Naturally, any little girl in love with high top tennis shoes would not be caught dead in a dress. Until she turned eleven, the only way I could get Crystal in a dress was for an audition.

Needless to say it was a waste of money for me to buy the dresses I loved to see her in. I was also quite grateful when her taste in clothes expanded to include skirts and dresses again.

Strive to be creative with your children's wardrobe, especially little girls. For example, on some auditions I dress-up Crystal's jeans with cotton lace around the pockets. At other times I put an interesting appliqué on the back of her jean jacket, or a unique pin on the lapel. When Crystal has outgrown her overalls, I cut them off and let her wear leggings or plaid boxer shorts that show underneat along with Victorian or Doc Martin boots. At other times I take one of my solid colored silk, cotton, or linen blouses, (which are over-sized on her) coordinate them with a print or plaid vest, a pair of leggings and three quarter length boots. A variation on the theme includes Levi's jeans, jean shorts, pleated short skirts with sweaters or collegiate sweat shirts. Ked's type tennis shoes and plain white socks, or three quarter length boots and socks to match the color of the boots work well with most outfits.

Some kids have heads and faces that are well suited for hats. Remember, when shopping for hats or caps to take the child along because hats have to fit the child's face, head, personality and a particular outfit otherwise they become an eyesore that looks out of place. Try to choose hats with small brims or brims that can be pinned or turned back in order to accent the face and eyes. For that same reason, wear baseball caps turned to the side or flipped back to keep from concealing the child's face.

Regardless of how cute the hat is, some commercial casting directors will ask the child to take the hat off for the camera. In this case "hat hair" can be a distraction for the child. Comb hair underneath the hat in such a manner that the child can run fingers through it to quickly make the hair presentable.

The key to good taste entails understatement. Each child needs their own style, in keeping with tradition, yet a look that's fresh or current. The most important thing is to choose a style that suits the child's personality. Moreover, dressing radically different from other children at auditions can work against the child, particularly, if the outfit is unsuited for that call. For example, if the commercial requires regular school attire and your daughter shows up in a party dress or your son in a suit, the child will feel over dressed and uncomfortable.

For parents who have trouble creating outfits that work, as stated earlier, simply imitate the way that other children dress at auditions, while adding a slightly different touch or angle to the outfit. Also, pay attention to outfits that everyone compliments, especially casting directors, then copy those. That is, provided the child can pull the look off. And study carefully the proper use of accessories. For instance, the wrong socks or belt can totally destroy a perfect outfit, whereas, just the right belt, scarf or pin can also make or break an outfit. With accessories, avoid wearing more than one at a time unless bought as a set. They can compete with each other and end up looking gaudy.

Do not forget the power of color. Having a color analysis done for your child will enable the parent to determine just which hues bring out the best in that child's skin tone, hair and eye color. A color analysis is not expensive. However, if one cannot have it done, good old common sense will come to the rescue. A stunning outfit in the wrong color will go totally unnoticed or make the child look drab.

While one does not want to break the budget on expensive clothes, avoid buying clothing made from cheap material that will break down after a few washings or outfits that fall apart the first time worn. And stay away from fabric that beads up into little round balls of fur on the surface. Instead, buy clothing made from natural fibers like cotton, linen or wool. Even at discount stores, if one knows what to look for, it's easy to find inexpensive outfits made from good quality natural fabric that makes the outfit *LOOK* expensive. Moreover, a study of expensive designer clothes reveals that good fabric, simple classic cuts and fine workmanship are distinguishing features. Many inexpensive labels sold at outlets or discount houses adhere to high standards of design, workmanship and fabric.

For girls, keep an accessory bag with combs, brushes, styling gel, hair spray, hair bows, ribbons, headbands, ponytail holders, belts, socks, a pair of low cut, white, canvas Ked-type tennis shoes and a basic pair of black, patent leather, round toed Mary Jane shoes. This accessory bag is a necessity for photo shoots. On other calls the bag comes in handy upon arrival at an audition when the casting director requests a change in the child's hair style. Some casting director will ask that you release the child's ponytail or take off the child's bow or headband. This involves restyling hair on the spot.

CONSULT YOUR AGENT ON APPROPRIATE AUDITION ATTIRE

Usually, when your agent or manager calls they will tell you how to dress your child for the audition. If not be sure to ask. There is nothing worse than fighting the traffic to get to an audition on the other side of town only to discover that everyone else is in dance shoes and togs, and there you are in clothes you can't possibly dance in. I have had that happen on a couple of occasions. We might as well have stayed at home. Something as simple as an outfit can enhance or erode a child's confidence, making him or her feel at a distinct disadvantage against the competition.

GETTING TO THE AUDITION ON TIME

The same concept applies to your child showing up for an audition without enough time to prepare for the dialogue. For example, if your child's competition has had all day or several days to prepare for a scene and you arrive at the audition with only ten minutes to go over the sides, your child will not be equipped to put his or her best foot forward.

It makes good sense to give a child every conceivable edge in terms of appearance and preparation. For that matter, parents are also well advised to go out of their way to do what they can to increase a child's confidence, including allowing outfits that the child feels good about wearing on auditions. Children who feel confident about the way they look and who are adequately prepared possess ease of comfort during the audition. These minor details can enhance a child's ability to focus on the audition material.

In Zoe F. Carter's article, "Baby, It's You," Casting Director, Mali Finn feels that *"the saddest thing in the world is to have a child come in with a big, fake, impersonal smile plastered on their face."* Finn also feels *"embarrassed by children who come on too strong"* or who are too stagy. The flip side of that coin is not being able to smile at all, or going through the audition with absolutely no show of emotion on the face. Instilling balance and confidence in all areas of the preparation process will dispel nervousness, allowing the child to relax and be at ease.

POINTS TO PONDER:

1. *While audition wardrobe does not have to be expensive, it does need to be appropriate to the type of casting call. For example, if the audition calls for play clothes, do not bring the child in Sunday best.*

2. *If uncertain how to dress for an audition, ask your agent or manager; otherwise, use your best judgment. When in doubt, clothes that the child would normally wear to school or that the child feels comfortable in are a safe bet.*

3. *Observe what other children wear at auditions, and if you like an outfit, ask where they bought it. Try to look current without being too "trendy."*

4. *Avoid wearing more than one accessory at a time to prevent looking cluttered.*

5. *For girls, stay away from big hair bows, ribbons or hats that hide, overwhelm, or draw attention away from the face.*

6. *As for hats, try to avoid them for commercial auditions. If not, make sure the hat does not shade the face. Casting directors may ask the child to take the hat off for the camera.*

7. *For auditions, children should always be neat and clean with their hair combed.*

Chapter 15

NOW THAT YOU'VE BOOKED A JOB

When you walk in a room, you have about four seconds while people decide to hire or not hire you. It's your vibes. They may call it your nose, but it's your vibes. You have to go in with the qualities that are the most assessable to you. You've got to get those people to buy you. -Martin Gage THE GAGE GROUP (from "The L.A. Agent Book")

SHARING YOUR GOOD NEWS...

Even though it's pretty exciting news for the family ANYTIME a child books a job, NOTHING compares to the thrill of that first assignment. Feeling honored beyond belief, parents usually rush to tell everyone they know that their child got picked for the part over all the other kids who competed for the spot. Nine times out of ten this turns out to be a bad move. Unless you are ready to find out who your true friends and supporters are, resist the urge to get on the phone and share that wonderful news indiscriminately. Sometimes those you least expect will not be happy for your child. Face it: human nature lends itself toward wishing someone else's good fortune was their own.

Moreover, through example, teach your child to show good taste and sound judgment in sharing good news about booking a job. In particular, calling someone who auditioned for the same role and telling them that you got the job. That falls in the poor taste category. Moreover, that child who lost out or the child's family might feel that you're lording the win over their child just to make the child feel bad or inadequate. Keep in mind that the other person's disappointment does not automatically imply jealousy or ill will. Some people simply need time to get over the loss.

Further, examine your motive for telling the other person: Is it simply: (1) to brag, (2) to exalt yourself or your child at the other person's expense, or (3) to have a friend share your joy with you? Before dialing that number be sure that your motive is right. And above all, make sure the person on the other end of the line genuinely wishes you and yours well. Allow those who do not to hear your good news through the grapevine. It operates 24 hours a day on open channels in Hollywood. Furthermore, if your gut feeling or previous experience indicates someone is not in your corner, why rain on your own parade? On the other hand, if a real friend wishes you well and shares your joy as if it was his or her own, such a person might feel a bit hurt should you not call and share the good news. So take the time to evaluate ahead of time, the type of person you are dealing with before opening your heart and door.

PROTECT YOUR CHILD FROM VICIOUS COMPETITORS

Keep in mind that children pick up negative or poor attitudes at home. In the wrong environment or under the wrong influence they easily learn subversive tactics designed to undermine their competition's confidence. One incident that immediately comes to mind involves a young friend of my son's. This child called and informed Salim that he had booked a movie role that they had both recently auditioned for. Thinking nothing of it, Salim extended his congratulations. A couple of weeks later, however, Salim received a callback for the same role that this friend said he had booked, prompting Salim to ask the casting director if they were recasting the part. The casting director told him that the role had never been

Now That You've Booked A Job

cast. Salim quickly realized that his friend had made up the story as a form of one-upmanship since Salim booked more jobs than this child. On a different occasion, this same boy rushed over to our house after he and Salim had both auditioned for a recurring role on a new television series. Again, he informed my son that he was offered the role, leading Salim to think that he had lost out. The next day, however, the agent called my son with the news that my son had gotten the part. That incident finally taught this young man a lesson in lying and convinced Salim not to believe anything this guy said.

Another story I found amusing was related to Salim by a classmate of his who starred in a successful television series. During this young girl's final callback at network another young girl walked out of the audition room ahead of Salim's friend and remarked: "I got the part, so you might as well go home." The mother of Salim's friend was ready to gather up her daughter and leave. Salims friend, however, insisted on having her turn. Guess what? Salim's friend got the starring role. The other girl was simply trying to undermine her competition's chance at getting the part. Moreover, if Salim's friend had not followed her own heart, she would have lost out on the role of her life time.

Always look beneath the surface and seek the motive behind questionable or self-gratifying acts that others volunteer out of the clear blue. Remember that some children and parents are so insecure and viciously competitive that they will do anything to get the job. In fact, in the boys room at an audition, one little boy sprayed hair spray into the eyes of his competition who had beat him out on several roles. In another incident, my son was hit in the eye with a stick by a younger cousin the day before an audition for a national Pepsi commercial. Salim's eyelid was cut and too swollen for him to go. As a result, we learned to keep quiet about auditions.

Moreover, some children and parents, who are doing poorly in the business, may send out negative vibes that drain energy and dissipate enthusiasm. Avoid such individuals at all costs. Also, stay focused and avoid distractions by reminding your child that everyone at the audition wants the job or they would not have bothered to come to the audition.

In situations where auditions require pairing up children or putting together groups to audition together, teach your child to search for a child with self-confidence who appears to enjoy what he or she is doing. When my son got his first recurring television role, casting was looking for three boys to play running buddies. Salim paired himself up with two other boys who were creative, energetic and talented. They had fun rehearsing the scene in the waiting room and collectively came up with ideas to make the characters more appealing. The three of them were cast together because they came across as real friends.

At commercial auditions, where there are no lines to go over, bring a book, note pad or Gameboy to entertain your child with. If the audition requires lines focus on your sides while waiting. I remember Bob Preston of the CED agency telling me when we first arrived in L.A., to remember that other mothers at the audition were not my friend because everyone is there with the same purpose in mind to get the job. So be friendly yet detached. That's my advice.

PLAYING IT SAFE TO AVOID ACCIDENTS

Remember that some children may allow nervous energy to develop into recklessness or carelessness right before shooting a job. Often children feel so good about themselves or so excited they mistakenly decide that they are invincible, especially boys, who throw safety and precaution to the wind.

I have had more accidents happen to my son the day before a shoot or important callback than at any other time. I finally got to the point where I insist that my children not tell their friends about a job until after the shoot. As an additional safety measure, I no longer allow my child to spend the weekend at someone else's house or to go out the night before a work day. This precaution prevents accidents, unnecessary fatigue, and promotes my children's well being for the shoot next day. Anytime I have broken this rule, my kids have come home either exhausted, sick or injured.

A case in point is the night before Salim appeared on "Good Morning Houston." A friend of mine came over with her two children. Salim was seven at the time. My friend's youngest daughter, who had been chasing Salim around the house in a circle, came running around the corner full speed ahead and collided in a direct head-on with Salim. Wouldn't you know that the top of the little girl's forehead was the exact height of Salim's eye, which immediately discolored and began to swell. I grabbed an ice pack and had Salim hold it over his eye. As a last resort I called my mother, desperate for one of her home remedies that I used to ignore. She recommended that I sprinkle meat tenderizer on a small steak and place it over the eye with an ice pack on top. As I followed her directive, all the while I dreaded the call to the agent canceling Salim's appearance the following morning. I kept ice on top of the steak throughout the night. By morning I was delighted to find absolutely no swelling and only mild redness, which was easily covered by makeup. Boy was I relieved!

Not every accident turns out so well. Remember that for any type of camera work, especially print work, scratches on the face, pimples, cuts, swelling and bruises that cannot be concealed by makeup can severely cripple your child's chance of getting the job. Fortunately, cuts and scratches on knees and elbows are easily covered by long sleeves or pants.

PACKING BASIC ITEMS TO TAKE ON THE SET

After protecting your child from recklessness the night before a job, concentrate on packing for the upcoming shoot. Usually a *wardrobe fitting* is scheduled prior to the date. In the very least, a wardrobe person will call to get exact sizes or to tell you what to bring. For actual wardrobe fittings, unless the fitting runs for more than a couple of hours, do not expect to get paid for this time.

When the *wardrobe person or costumer* calls and tells you what to bring, more often than not, they won't use a single thing of yours except maybe the shoes. That is, unless the costumer happens to like your taste in clothes. Much depends on the size of the budget, the reputation of the studio or production company, or whether the wardrobe person likes the way your child dresses. Some studios have a reputation for skimping on everything. In such case, they will definitely select items from your personal wardrobe. The same thing applies for non-union or low budget shoots: they will expect you to bring your own clothes.

As mentioned in Chapter 14 titled "Wardrobe, Investing In Tools Of The Trade," certain basic items of clothing should be set aside specifically for auditions: *White Keds-type tennis shoes, plain white tee shirts, blue denim Levi's type jeans (no stone washed or tattered ones) a pair of penny loafers or jazz shoes, oxford shirts and pleated skirts for girls.* Try to buy clothes with bright colors. Casting directors always ask for that. Avoid black, white, gray or earth tones. Pastels are a good alternative if no bright colors are available. The wardrobe person will usually request that you bring three different outfits in addition to the one the child wears to the set.

Again, for *GIRLS*, *keep an accessory bag already packed with bows, belts, shoe laces, white socks, hair ribbons, hair combs and brushes, curlers, hair spray, mousse, etc. Guys also need an accessory bag for belts, shoes, ties, hair brushes and hair spray.* Those see-through fishing tackle boxes make great accessory bags. They have neat little compartments of different sizes that hold everything. Just be sure to open the tackle box from the right side so that everything doesn't come tumbling out.

Note: Do not bring an outfit on the set that you or your child does not particularly like; the wardrobe person may fall in love with it. Moreover, do not get an attitude if the costumer selects the outfit that you brought on the set, which your child detests; or if she chooses clothing provided in the budget that the child hates. Whatever the studio or production company decides regarding wardrobe, (whether provided by you or not), bear in mind that the outfit is often chosen to suit the time period of the piece, the theme or *special effects* that may require shooting against a *blue screen.*

Controlling parents who simply must have the final say over every item of clothing their child wears can expect to find themselves butting heads with the wardrobe person who will complain to the director. Guess who will win? By the same token, if your child throws a fit about the outfit the wardrobe person chooses, or refuses to wear the clothing selected, expect escort service from the set with an alternate child immediately called in to take your child's place, or count on your child's scene ending up on the cutting room floor if a fight ensues over wardrobe changes.

The same situation applies to hair and make up. For example, my son did an episode of "The Wonder Years," which was a period piece. The hair dresser cut off his long, stylish pig tail at the nape of his neck. Mind you, it had taken Salim a year to grow this pig tail. No questions were asked, Salim's hair was cut off to conform to the style of the times for that television show. As a seasoned, professional actor, Salim did not make a scene or throw a tantrum with the hair and make up person. When he walked out of the hair and make up trailer, no one would have been able to spot his disappointment except me. At the age of eleven he was old enough to understand that sometimes one has to do what it takes to get the part. It did make him feel better, however, that I sympathized with him and validated his loss, along with a reminder that he was getting paid for losing that pig tail, which would certainly grow back.

CREATE A CHECK LIST THE NIGHT BEFORE

The night before your shoot make a check list of things needed, then go over the list right before walking out the door. Take note of the following:

(1) *AN ORIGINAL WORK PERMIT.* The studio teacher will ask for your work permit the moment you walk on the set. So have it handy. The child will be sent home and not allowed to work if his work permit is not current or if he does not have one. *(Please refer to Chapter 28 in the back of this book for information on how to obtain a work permit).*

(2) *AN ORIGINAL BIRTH CERTIFICATE OR PASSPORT:* Usually these documents are given to the assistant director or stage manager to verify U.S. citizenship, or to determine if the individual has a green card permitting him to work in this country. A copy will be made and the original returned to you.

(3) *AN ORIGINAL SOCIAL SECURITY CARD*: The production company uses this card to make sure your money gets credited to the correct social security account. The assistant director will make a copy and return the original.

(4) *HOMEWORK AND SCHOOL BOOKS:* Your child should bring his book bag with enough school work to last for three hours. The studio teacher will not be happy if the child fails to bring school work with him. She may require that the guardian go home or to the school and pick up the books or assignments. If you have your books and no assignments, the teacher may request that the parent call the school to obtain homework for the duration of the shoot.

(5) *WARDROBE BAG* should include at least three complete outfits and shoes, specified by the wardrobe person.

(6) *ACCESSORY BAG* filled with all your personal items such as hair brush, comb, hair spray, etc.

(7) *HEALTHY SNACKS* just in case it's an early shoot and they take a while to set up the snack table once you get there.

(8) *LUNCH MONEY* in the event that you are filming at the movie studio, instead of on location. Hot lunches are catered on location, not at the studio. Only a snack table is provided. So bring lunch money with you or pack a lunch. If the shoot runs into overtime there is a meal penalty and a hot meal is provided even if you are not at the studio. Overtime past a certain hour also requires that the production company provide either a hot catered meal or send out to a restaurant for food.

(9) *LOCATION MAP OR WRITTEN DIRECTIONS.* It's a good idea to ask for a mobile phone number at the location or studio where you will be shooting, just in case of an emergency with your vehicle, or in the event that you get lost in spite of directions. It is important that you phone in and let them know your status. If not, they will call your agent quite upset. Then your agent will call you equally as upset.

(10) PARKING. If no one explains ahead of time, be sure to ask where to park. In Los Angeles parking is always a problem. Sometimes the parking provided will be a nice little walk from the actual shoot, so add extra time for this inconvenience. Also, at some locations parking will be at a remote lot with a van to shuttle cast and crew. In that event, find out the van's schedule. This is an important consideration. For example, if you are told that your call time on the set is 7:00 you will need to arrive at the remote parking spot by 6:30 or 6:45 to get there on time, depending on how far the location is.

ON THE SET: WHAT TO EXPECT

The person to ask for when you arrive on the set is the First Assistant Director (A.D.), for film or commercials, or Stage Manager, for television episodes. Check in with that person, unless instructed otherwise. Remember that if you are more than five minutes late the A.D. will be pacing around waiting for you. Then, the A.D. will be that person with an agitated look. If more than fifteen minutes late they will place an all points bulletin with your agent. Whatever you do, get to your shoot early. If something happens, stop and call.

Depending on how early your scene will be shot, the A.D., or Stage Manager will either have the parent fill out paper work upon arrival or send the child immediately to hair and makeup. If the latter is the case, make sure that you remind the A.D. that you need to sign your contract or W2 form. For that purpose, have the agent's address and telephone number handy in case you have not already memorized it, or in case you do not have a headshot with the logo printed on it. Checks are customarily mailed directly to the child's agent.

If it is a school day, ask where the school room is so that you can drop off your child's books and work permit. Sometimes the child will be taken directly to the school room because his or her first scene will not be shot for a while.

Instruct your child that on the set the A.D. or Stage Manager needs to know where he or she is at all times. Even if the child is going to the restroom. If your child has finished three hours of school and wants to hang around on the set, instead of the school room, be sure to let the school teacher and A.D. know this. It is best to be within sight or sound of the A.D. at all times because they go into a panic if the child's scene is called and they have to scramble around looking for the youngster. Keep in mind also that scenes shot inside a large movie studio can grow hectic because the walls are usually painted black and everything is dark except for the stage where they are shooting. In the dark it is easy to melt into the background even when you are right there on the set. If the A.D. does not see the child, then the child is considered missing even thought the child might be right there in the studio. It can happen. Some studios are so large that when you are on the opposite side from where the scene is being shot, it can be difficult to spot a person from behind a piece of scenery or a partition.

Lunch is usually from 1:00 to 2:00. And they mean be back by 2:00 sharp. If possible, come back from lunch a few minutes early. Never late. Again, report to the A.D. or Stage Manager. Do not simply return to your dressing room and assume that they know you are there. The least little thing can send everyone into a panic because each minute of overtime can cause the production to run thousands of dollars over budget.

It goes without saying that you are to keep your child QUIET ON THE SET with a capital "Q." A red light will come on above the door exits to let you know that the cameras are rolling, so even if you are on the other side of the studio and do not hear the A.D.'s shout "Quiet on the Set!" or "Rolling!," all you have to do is look up over the door and see if the red light is on. That means it is time to shut up or whisper if you must speak. The scene has to be reshot if there is too much background noise. And that costs money.

No running on the set, either. Children love to run, rather than walk. There are so many wires and cables on the floor of sets one can easily trip and fall on to equipment or props. For a small child, hold on to one hand at all times to keep them from wandering off in search of adventure.

Unless your child is in the scene being shot, keep a respectful distance away from the actual set. There are so many crew members who need to be at the director's beck and call that additional people only get underfoot and in the way. If you want to watch other scenes shot, get a director's chair and watch it away from the movement of cameras and crew.

AVOIDING CELEBRITY HOUNDS AND GROUPIES

Bring absolutely no one on the set with you. One parent and one child is allowed. If you want someone else to visit the set for a brief time, get permission from the production office. Especially if it is a closed set. They will allow family members to visit on occasion. As a general rule, bringing other people along is frowned upon.

I had an unforgettable experience with someone following me to the set of a music video my daughter was shooting with a famous rock star. This lady lived in my apartment complex and I hardly knew her. She saw us leaving out and my daughter was all dressed up which prompted her to ask us where we were going. Thinking nothing of it, I told her who we were going to shoot the music video with. Since this lady was already in her car in the parking lot, she followed us to the location.

Once we arrived at the location parking lot, nothing that I said to this lady could dissuade her from walking on the set with me. She ended up being escorted off the premises by security when she tried to get to the star in his heavily guarded dressing room.

Bear in mind that perfectly normal people can turn into "Loony Tunes" or the most pathetic groupies you have ever seen when it comes to meeting their favorite star face to face. Let that be a warning.

POINTS TO PONDER

1. The day or weekend before a shoot make sure that your child avoids playing with hyperactive children who are accidents looking for a place to happen.

2. Make a check list the night before a shoot and be sure to include the following: work permit, birth certificate, social security card, wardrobe bag, accessory bag, school books, homework, snacks, lunch money, location map or directions to the set.

3. Upon arrival, find the Stage Manager or First Assistant Director (A.D.) immediately and check in. Have your work permit ready to show to the studio teacher.

4. Always return from lunch early -- never late.

5. Let the Stage Manager, A.D., or Studio Teacher know where you are at all times.

6. Be quiet on the set. Absolutely no running.

7. Never bring anyone extra on the set. And tell no one the location where you will be shooting. They may decide to surprise you and show up uninvited.

Chapter 16

RULES WERE MEANT TO MAKE LIFE EASIER AND MORE ORDERLY, NOT MORE DIFFICULT

Rules were designed to protect, to serve, and to create order out of chaos. In their enforcement, however, there must be room for flexibility. Otherwise, literal interpretations applied blindly to every circumstance can become an encumbrance to personal liberty, happiness and peace of mind.

Every business has its own set of rules. Since it is each individual's responsibility to learn the rules or inquire about them, even if one does not know the rules, others will automatically assume that you do and then penalize you when you don't. The most vital aspect of learning ones rights and knowing the rules is that such insight enables one to make informed, intelligent decisions. In addition, learning the rules can spare a parent and child unpleasant surprises and penalties.

The first time on a Hollywood set parents may sense a conspiracy of silence regarding protocol. The old saying "ignorance of the law is no excuse" seems to apply. Those who do not make it a point to ask questions and learn the rules will inevitably run into an over worked assistant director who takes self-righteous delight in beating the unsuspecting parent over the head with a rule book.

The *"AFTRA-SAG Young Performer's Handbook,"* published by The Screen Actors Guild, mentioned in a previous chapter, should remain in one's possession at all times on the set. Unfortunately, most parents have never even heard of this book, and even fewer have heard of *"The Blue Book."* The former is only given out after the child meets eligibility requirements to join SAG or AFTRA; the latter is published by The Studio Teachers Union and is available in bookstores like Samuel French that specialize in books for the entertainment industry. Non-union members may obtain the Young Performer's Handbook for a small fee through The Screen Actors Guild.

Parents who have not read either books end up under the misguided assumption that rules on the set are handed down out of nowhere. For some children, months or even years go by before landing a union job that makes them eligible to join the union, while others book a union commercial, television show, or film the first time out. As a result many children work non-union jobs for quite sometime before the parent discovers that two handbooks exist. Others join the union without bothering to attend the free orientation sessions or to read the wealth of material mailed out after joining SAG or AFTRA.

Upon working a union job, a child falls under the *"Taft-Hartley Law"* which allows the child to continue to work non-union and union jobs for thirty days before federal statute requires joining the union. After such time the child must pay union dues in the amount of approximately $1,000.00 via cash or cashier's check only. This one time fee is adjusted yearly according to the actor's earnings. Upon joining the union actors are prohibited from working non-union jobs after the thirty day period expires.

The Taft Hartley Law may also come into effect, for example, when a child is hired as an *"extra"* or *"atmosphere"* then *upgraded*, by the producer or director to perform *principal* work. A principal actor is anyone with speaking lines or someone who performs special business that advances the story line. If a parent does not know what the rules are, he or she will have no way of knowing whether the child has become SAG eligible, or more importantly, if the child's rights are being violated on the set.

Sixty three nations worldwide provide a family allowance to workers and their children; America does not. - Marian Wright Edelman (THE MEASURE OF OUR SUCCESS-Beacon Press)

SAG-AFTRA RULES REGARDING SIBLINGS ON THE SET

One SAG-AFTRA rule than often acts as a thorn in the side for families with more than one child states: *"Parents will not bring other minors not engaged by the Producer to the studio or location."* Since the average American family has more than one child, this rule falls under the burdensome category. Bear in mind that show business caters to "only" children; that is, only the child currently working. For all intents and purposes they do not acknowledge the existence of other sibling. Of course, the production company can make exceptions with the producer's or director's discretion.

When a child is working on location and the family has to be separated for long periods of time, this rule can pose an undue hardship. On the other hand, it is perfectly understandable why the rule had to be created. Younger siblings (under the age of six) running all over the set can be disruptive, especially if the parent does not or cannot keep the child under control. For those children, however, who are not hyperactive, disruptive or do not misbehave, the rule seems a bit unfair. My point is, flexibility should be used in applying this rule, especially for families with only two children.

Often people in authority forget that rules were made for the *benefit* of those they regulate, not their *detriment.* Those that pose an undue burden upon families are simply another reflection of America's lack of regard for children. Nowhere is this more apparent than on Hollywood sets. Unfortunately, this attitude trickles down from society in general. One has only to listen to the news and see what happens to adults or parents who abuse children. Nothing. Or, at best, a slap on the wrist. Not enforcing legislation that protects our most valuable national resource sends out a powerful message to children who are being abused: There's no point in confiding in or looking to the system for protection, because nothing is going to happen to those who harm them. The same situation applies on the set, which is a microcosm of society. If a parent or guardian does not remain aware and ask the right questions, the child may not complain until the damage has already been done, making it difficult to do anything about the problem in a timely fashion.

Parents who work outside the home do not need more guilt trips. They need help and real choices. Marion Wright Edelman, author of "The Measure of Our Success" (Beacon Press)

Our willingness to speak out seems a small price to pay for the well being of our children. Too often, on the set, parental control is readily relinquished to those in power out of fear that the child will be penalized, fired or not hired again.

For the most part, one can forget about asking for time off from work to be on the set with a child actor. Usually the parent has to quit his or her job to be with the child who works. California Labor Laws make it mandatory for a parent or guardian to be on the set with their child yet does not make allowance for the fact that the parent has to miss work or pay someone else to be on the set if that parent wants to keep his or her job. When one takes into consideration how much less children are paid than adults, along with the fact that most of them work less frequently, these statistics alone make it a hardship for poor families or single parent households to make a go of keeping their child in show business.

All of the major studios in Hollywood could easily subsidize child care facilities for their employees. Only a couple of studios have taken the initiative to do so. With all the excess spent on films and television shows, a child care facility would be a small investment in a large amount of goodwill towards the future of our children.

TOO MANY RIGID
NON-THINKERS IN CHARGE

Inflexible, non-thinking rule followers who are entirely literal in the execution of their duties are mindful of those Nazi war criminals who felt exonerated of any wrong doing in the murder of millions because they were simply "doing their job" or "following the rules".

Instead of passing the buck or denying responsibility for our actions, Marion Wright Edelman, founder of the Children's Defense Fund says: *"Don't give anyone the proxy for your conscience. And don't confuse legality with fairness. The policies that took tens of billions of dollars from the poor and middle class and gave them to the very rich in the 1980s as tax loopholes and capital gains were legal. But they were not just." (from "The Measure of Our Success" Beacon Press)*

Half the harm that is done in this world is due to people who want to feel important. T. S. Eliot from THE COCKTAIL PARTY

The circumstances of each family deserve to be dealt with on its own merit in conjunction with a sincere effort to examine whether or not the problem actually justifies applying the rule. Or in the alternative, to determine whether application of the rule will add to the well-being, safety or peace of mind of all concerned.

DEALING WITH THE
ASSISTANT DIRECTOR FROM HELL

It's unfortunate that far too many assistant directors are rule thumpers who take advantage of their positions because it makes them feel important or powerful. Sometimes parents and children will find themselves caught up in politics on the set that have nothing to do directly with them. For example, on one set, my son had a six o'clock call time one morning, which forced me to bring my daughter with us until her school opened. While my son was filming in front of the camera, my daughter and I were standing quietly in the back of the studio when the assistant director came up to me (she was upset about something else) and ordered my daughter off the set. At the same time she told me I could not leave Salim on the set to take Crystal to school. This prohibition would have effectively tied both my hands. I was stunned, since Crystal had already accompanied me each morning when my son had an early call time, after which I dropped her off at school once the playground was open. What added insult to injury was that I had cleared the situation with this assistant director before my son took the job. I simply could not believe her about-face.

When I reminded the A.D. of our agreement, she politely waved the rule book at me, feeling absolutely no qualms about backing out of an arrangement we had made earlier. I could have been like many parents I know who are too afraid of criticism or of being labeled a "stage mom" to do anything. Fortunately I believe in the advice of a wise person who once said: "If you don't want to be criticized, don't say anything, do anything, or be anything." I wasn't about to sit back and say or do nothing.

Don't wait for everybody else before you do something. It's always a few people who get things done and keep things going. This country needs more wise and courageous shepherds and fewer sheep. Marion Wright Edelman, author of "The Measure of Our Success" (Beacon Press)

Feeling setup by this A.D., who knew that my daughter's school was only five minutes away from the set, I was left with no choice but to go to the *producer* of the show for intervention. He assigned a driver to drop my daughter off at school and pick her up in the evenings, where she was given permission to hang-out in my son's dressing room. Further, after I apprised a co-producer of the incident, he personally went to Salim's dressing room and escorted her inside the studio, assuring my daughter that she could watch her brother film anytime she wanted.

Because I went over her head, the A.D. ended up turning into a nightmare. (I never said it would be easy to stand up for yourself). She began to set my son up for problems by not giving us the call time the night before. My husband put an end to the problem of no call time by phoning the A.D. at home in the middle of the night to get our call time. She then retaliated by giving me the wrong call time, thereby causing problems with the director when we were a half hour late one morning because of the wrong call time. On top of that, when I showed up an hour early the following morning (trying to beat her at her own game) I got a lecture from the studio teacher about liability issues surrounding showing up early. Realizing that I could not win for losing with this woman, I had no choice but to go to the unit production manager and inform him that this A.D.'s tactics were affecting my son's ability to do the job he was paid to do. The Unit Production Manager assigned a different A.D. for me to deal with (there were four A.D.'s on this particular set) which finally took care of that nightmare.

There also comes a time when circumstances dictate that one be willing to leave the situation if no reasonable solution is forthcoming. For example, we received an invitation to a wrap party addressed to "Salim Grant and One Parent." As a family we discussed it and decided that if the four of us were not invited, then none of us would go. I called the production company and informed them that Salim would not be able to attend because he did not want to exclude his sister and father. Fortunately, the lady handling the event understood and accommodated the entire family.

Every parent has to deal with rule related problems in their own way. The important thing is to come up with a viable alternative that will meet the needs of the entire family. Usually, if one deals with production companies from a standpoint of your priorities attempting to serve theirs, they are more willing to compromise. The important point to remember is that sometimes those in charge take advantage of their position simply because they have the power to confine others within oppressive guidelines that were never intended as such.

POINTS TO PONDER

1. *Show business caters to "only" children and excludes siblings who are not working on the set. In order to deal with this AFTRA-SAG rule, one must obtain clearance ahead of time to allow another child on the set (sometimes this is difficult if the other child is under the age of ten).*

2. *Be willing to stand up for your child and demand that he or she be treated fairly. If the matter cannot be settled amicably between you and the person causing the problem, do not hesitate to go over that person's head. The most important thing is your child's well being and peace of mind. If that is disturbed he cannot do his job as an actor. The production company will take action if their money is at stake or if the show is in jeopardy.*

Chapter 17

DEVELOPING COPING SKILLS ON THE SET

Trust in the miracle that you are...you create your own prosperity through your own efforts. Avoid the trap of expecting your prosperity to arrive in your life through the efforts of others. -Dr. Wayne Dyer, author of REAL MAGIC (HarperCollins)

The destructive forces in show business come in when children are left without coping skills or a support system to guide them through turbulent waters. Children need someone to fall back upon who love and accept them unconditionally, whether a teacher, family friend or relative. One strong parental or adult figure is essential to a child's self-worth since it is through the eyes of an adult role model or mentor that a child's individuality and sense of self is developed, nurtured and protected.

THERE IS NO SUBSTITUTE FOR SELF-ESTEEM

Self esteem is the most valuable commodity anyone can own. Once a person has it, the vicissitudes of life may still have an effect, but they will not take over or destroy a child's life. Allowing compromise of a child's self-worth creates a breeding ground for larger problems to manifest early on in small ways, and then to take on menacing proportions later on during teen and adult years. Whether on the set, or in real life not many adults, let alone small children, can distinguish between an attack upon one's "behavior" and one's "self." A child must be taught the difference.

For example, a situation may arise during a shoot when a parent has to let the child know that reshooting the scene as many times as the director likes does not necessarily mean that the child's performance is inadequate. Most directors film a scene over and over again until they think they've gotten enough footage from all different angles and perspectives to insure not having to reshoot the same scene at a later date (a prohibitively expensive approach since the cast, crew, and set would have to be reassembled for a reshoot caused by poor lighting, for example). If, as a matter of course, the child originally had to do a number of takes on this same scene, the child may assume one of two things: that the director is incompetent, or he is. Unfortunately, most children naturally conclude that they are at fault because we teach them that adults know more than children do. This instinctive reaction automatically creates feelings of inadequacy which may affect the child's performance.

Most directors are good at explaining retakes to a child. Some get too wrapped up in what they are doing, however, to bother. A communicative parent can easily clear up this issue for the child by reminding him or her ahead of time that situations may occur where the child will be unable to perform a scene to the director's satisfaction on the first few takes. Sometimes this happens because of a breakdown in communication. The child may not understand exactly what the director wants. In that situation, encourage the child to speak up, ask for clarification or a demonstration to quickly solve the problem. Other times, the child may simply need a short break to gain a fresh perspective on the situation. Provided the parent remains confident (assuring the child that he or she can give the director exactly what that director wants), the child returns to the scene fresh.

Encouraging a child to approach every difficult situation as an opportunity for growth is a valuable life coping tool. Children need to understand that just because someone else has a problem, he or she does not have to take it personally. A tall order one might say, even for an adult. True, but one that children can easily acclimate to.

Remember that some of the people that children have to deal with in this industry are dysfunctional adults or adult children who have yet to begin working through their own childhood traumas. (Of course, the same can be said about many of our children's teachers and the parents of their friends). Others are frustrated actors working behind the scenes because they could not make it (for whatever reasons) in front of the camera. Some are still waiting on an opportunity to get in front of the camera.

The most intimidating personalities children encounter on the set are those who enjoy wielding power over others because they were made to feel powerless at some point in their lives. These types grow up and take the hostility (held subconsciously) out on those presently under their authority. Help your child to recognize the power hungry-type and not allow their loud voices to intimidate him or her.

I once had a casting director admit to me that she enjoyed the power she held over mothers. Her diminutive stature, and the fact that she looked ten years younger than her age, was a contributing factor that made her bark much worse than her bite. I dealt with her by acknowledging her position and showing appreciation for the job she did.

Inevitably one will have to deal with difficult people in business and for that matter, in life. Some will be almost impossible to handle, others beyond hope. Fortunately, most simply need acknowledgment and appreciation for the job they do.

Both parent and child constantly need to monitor their self-esteem levels, which fluctuate and require periodic adjustments. The highs and lows can be mind-altering. Every time your child books a job he or she experiences tremendous elation along with "great expectations." Treasure and enjoy those times while preparing for the unexpected. Never allow one event to alter the entire course of your child's career.

When working with a stressed-out director, a crew that feels brow-beaten, a temperamental star or insecure cast members, intimidated by a child they fear might outshine them in the final cut, the following strategies can help your child cope with the situation and keep his or her balance.

POSITIVE PROBLEM SOLVING ON THE SET

Whenever there is a personality clash or conflict on the set, (in school or at home) use the following steps to help solve the problem:

1. First of all, teach your child to admit and accept responsibility for whatever part, if any, he or she played in the problem. If it is determined that the problem rests primarily with the other person, then:

2. Attempt to figure out how this problem can be avoided in the future based on modifying the child's reaction to irrational or unpredictable behavior and help the child accept the fact that he or she cannot change or exercise control over anyone but himself. Then:

3. Determine what lesson needs to be learned from the situation because once the lesson is truly learned, the child does not have to worry about running into or repeating that scenario again.

4. In those instances where the child has done nothing to provoke the situation (other than being in the wrong place at the wrong time), or has inadvertently become the object of someone else's misplaced frustrations, remind the child to detach himself or herself emotionally from the situation. People often act or react from a position of fear, uncertainty or insecurity with a tendency to attack the least powerful person who happens to get in their way at that time.

5. Explain to your child that there are a lot of fearful, frustrated adults who are afraid to lash back at their bosses, spouses, or other adults who make them feel ineffectual. Instead, they take power away from those who are weaker or smaller than themselves, thus making children easy targets.

6. When a defenseless child becomes the object of a senseless attack from an adult the child develops a natural need to vent. Otherwise, the child will act out this rage through mimicking the same type of behavior he or she was subjected to. We call it "the pecking order" or "big bank takes over little bank." In essence, the older, or bigger child takes advantage of the younger or smaller child by virtue of the fact that he or she cannot appropriately take those frustrations with a parent or adult out on the older or more powerful person. This creates a sad cycle of abuse that takes a tremendous toll on our society.

EMPOWERING YOUR CHILD BY SETTING BOUNDARIES

The real tragedy is that this whole cycle of abuse could be eliminated in one generation if we empowered our children by teaching them effective coping skills to channel negative energy. Moreover, helping a child fine-tune his or her sensitivities to the emotions of others will enable the child to detect (by reading body language and tone of voice) when a person is about to explode from pent-up anger, frustration or stress. By becoming aware, the child can get out of the way because the average person gives warning signals via tense facial expressions, tightness in the muscles of his or her body or terse, cold and biting remarks. Others will simply ignore you when spoken to. The child should learn to read these signals and get out of harm's way. If, for example, the child witnesses another person publicly embarrassed by someone in authority over him or her, common sense dictates not bothering that person with a request or demand at that particular time. Timing is everything.

THE BEST DEFENSE IS NO DEFENSE

If your child becomes the brunt of a verbal or physical attack on the set let the child know that he or she has a choice. Psychologists have established that violent personalities feed-off of their victim's fear. It incites and entices them to do further harm. If, however, the child knows to remain calm, emotionally detached and understands that the other person's rage is coming from feelings of pain and betrayal inflicted by someone else in the past, the attacker is left without the necessary fear, anger or antagonism to fuel his fire. Moreover, Proverbs 15:1 states that "An answer, when mild, turns away rage, but a word causing pain makes anger to come up." Let the child know that his or her power lies in choosing not to react verbally or emotionally.

On the set, some directors frustrate easily. Fortunately, most directors who work with children know that they can get more out of a child by using honey instead of vinegar. Furthermore, the studio teacher will intervene should a situation grow tense.

It can unnerve a child to witness a director speaking in a demeaning manner to an adult actor because the child will naturally anticipate that the director will do the same to him or her. Luckily, for the most part, children do not have to worry about directors yelling at them because most Assistant Directors take that as their privilege. In such instances, caution the child to listen, and not to bother trying to reason with the A.D. nor to react hastily in defense of himself or herself. All too often this amounts to taking the bait, and getting trapped. Dr. Deepak Chopra says that *"the perfect defense is defenselessness."* Encourage your child to pick his or her fights carefully. Very few issues are worth fighting over. Moreover, when we no longer have the need to defend our feelings, opinions, or self against attack, nothing is there for the other person to attack which prompts the attacker to move on to easier prey.

If a child understands that he or she can dislike what a person does but still like that person, forgiveness and its resulting peace of mind can take place. Children must first, however, separate a person's behavior from the person. Who a person is and what that person does are often at odds. We all rub each other the wrong way on occasion, but that does not mean we are fundamentally unacceptable. Human behavior changes.

Further, to prevent your child from storing any rage or frustration about the attack or attacker, validate the youngster's feelings. Let the child know that he or she has a right to feel angry, upset, betrayed, let down, or whatever. Then assure the child that he or she can (when the other person is calm and no longer in an attack mode) talk to the person who attacked him or her and let that person know how he or she feels. If it is not safe or prudent to talk directly to that person, have the child write out his or her feelings about the situation on paper and mail it to that person. Should you decide not to mail the letter, have the child burn the letter in a symbolic ceremony designed to release the anger along with the smoke. In so doing, the cycle of anger, rage and violence becomes broken because the child has validated his or her feelings. In addition, the youngster comes to understand the psychology behind what happened through the process of writing or talking about it. In effect, the child embraces his or her feelings as opposed to denying or suppressing them, thus owning power instead of becoming a helpless pawn in an adult chess game.

Ultimately, if a parent is willing to listen to the child, the two can come up with ways to deal with any problem in a positive manner, whether arising on the set, or in life. It is essential to allow your child to have a voice in the things that matter; to have permission to tell someone, when safe to do so, that he or she does not like what was said or done. This action instills a sense of control as well as responsibility over one's life.

Empowering tools are particularly essential when a child works on a long term project such as a television series or a music contract with a group. The child needs to know that he or she is not without power; that inspite of what the director and producers might feel, the show does not always go on. And certainly not at the expense of the emotional well being of the child.

THOSE BRAVE ENOUGH TO DO THE RIGHT THING

Many people in the industry, agents included, would like to make you feel that they have the power to **blacklist** your child out of Hollywood with a single stroke of the pin or telephone call. Early in the history of Hollywood this was possible because only a few major studios controlled everything. Now things are highly specialized with independent production companies and movie studios too numerous to name. A person can walk away from one set and easily find work with another.

A possible exception involves union craftsmen. In the 1980's, several crew members, who testified in the helicopter deaths of children on the movie set of a popular movie got blacklisted by their union. These were not actors, but skilled craftsmen, responsible for safety measures on the set, who relied on their union for work. Out of this tragedy, however, came stricter labor laws protecting minors from hazards on the set. In the process, however, these men sacrificed their jobs and careers to testify in court.

Since no reason exists legitimately to worry about getting black-listed, teach your children to politely stop people dead in their tracks the minute they sense that a situation is getting out of hand. Give them permission to say "time out," or to walk off a set if the assistant director, actor or a crew member is overtly hostile, "unduly" rude, or signals the child out for abuse that affects his or her ability to perform in front of the camera. Mind you, most assistant directors treat everyone equally bad. In such instances, a child's innate sense of justice is not unduly shaken because the child knows that he or she is not being personally attacked. When the attack is personal the most potential for damage presents itself.

Each negative experience your child encounters, not just in show business, but in life, has the potential for a devastating emotional impact. Work hard, therefore, on not allowing your child to internalize situations negatively. Teach your child acceptance; that we have no control over other people's prejudices and shortcomings, and that the only thing we do control is our own thoughts about the situation. We can choose to wallow in the problem, or practice forgiveness and move on.

Also, encourage your child to love and take pride in his or her work while secure in the knowledge that nothing is more important to you than the child's happiness and well-being. Moreover, never let problems get out of hand, solve them the moment they occur. Most important of all, assure your child that his or her voice deserves to be heard. Just because other children and their parents are afraid to speak up for themselves, your child does not have to buy into that mentality.

BELIEVING IN A POWER GREATER THAN YOURSELF

Children who believe in a source greater than man know that their lives are being divinely directed. They intuitively search out that spark of divinity inside of everyone. Children need to be able to rely on a power greater than man to prevent feelings of powerless when confronted by people in positions of power over them. That includes their school teachers. If this concept sounds beyond you at this point in your life, then I suggest coming up with something better to fill that spiritual void within your child. It is there in all of us.

Those child actors we read about in headlines who have committed crimes or fallen prey to drugs will tell you that they were simply trying to fill the pain and emptiness inside of them that occurs when one has lost their sense of values, becomes spiritually bankrupt, does not feel unconditionally loved, or simply has a chemical imbalance in the brain that drives him or her in the wrong direction. Those who seek help, or take the time to carve out a personal belief system in alignment with the laws of the universe, are not likely to become destroyed by devastating situations because they have an inner source of strength on which to rely.

POINTS TO PONDER

1. *There is no substitute for self-esteem. If a child has a strong sense of self-worth and belief in his abilities, he or she will not feel insecure when the inevitable need arises to shoot a scene over and over.*

2. *Teach your child to detach emotionally from people and situations and to separate what a person does from who the person is. He or she can still like the person while disliking what that person does.*

3. *Instead of internalizing problems on the set negatively, come up with creative coping skills that enhance the child's sense of self.*

4. *The best defense is no defense.*

5. *Expose your child to a belief system that empowers and enables him or her to rely on a source greater than man. This will prevent development of a spiritual void inside that the child seeks to fill with the wrong substances and stimuli.*

Chapter 18

THE COMPETITION LIES WITHIN

Think of your competition. Think of what is unique about each of them. Think about what is different in you that is not in them ... The smart actor will study himself until he can see what it is that he has that is unique, special, commercial, salable, acceptable that he can develop and magnify and use better than anybody else. Martin Gage, agent The Gage Group (from "The L.A. Agent Book" by K Callan)

No one will deny that show business thrives on competition. Everyone has heard horror stories of people stepping on their mothers and killing lovers to get to the top. Ironically, when one reads the biographies of people who stepped on toes to get to the top one noticeable point pops out: the high price paid for such actions in terms of destroyed health, relationships or families. Some call it Karma or the law of reaping and sowing; others call it "what you give out you get back." The concept seems to fall under one of those inescapable universal laws of crimes against humanity and its subsequent punishment. The sad part about such behavior is that it's so unnecessary. Talent, self-confidence and a winning attitude are acquirable skills which make it unnecessary to waste time and energy blocking another person's path to success.

By no means am I implying that the entertainment field has a monopoly on bad behavior. Even an ordinary quest for academic excellence can get out of hand if one becomes obsessively competitive about it. Avoid this attitude by reminding your child that there will always be another audition. Discourage the young performer from becoming obsessed about getting each part he or she goes out for. Moreover, instead of feeling insecure, jealous or upset with whoever got the part, the child should be taught to view another person's success as an indicator that his or her opportunity is waiting around the corner; all the young talent has to do is get ready to claim it when the time comes.

Preparation for the inevitable day of success may involve study to develop a fresh approach towards dialogue, learning relaxation techniques for acting, confidence building, creating a different angle on a character, coming up with a funky look for a commercial, or simply maintaining an acceptable weight for print work. Agent Barry Freed says that *"the winning difference between two actors on the same level auditioning for a role may just be that one makes everyone in the room have a better time."* (from "The L.A. Agent Book by K Callan). One way to make a casting director feel comfortable is by being self confident.

THERE ARE NO ACTUAL OVERNIGHT SUCCESS STORIES

Even though the media loves to exaggerate "overnight success stories," as mentioned before, if one reads between the lines or listens closely, it's easy to discover that an awful amount of actual training and preparation went into getting that "overnight" break which ultimately lead to fame and fortune. Before becoming superstars these "overnight success stories" usually showcased their abilities at school talent shows, on college campuses, in small community theaters or on Venice Beach somewhere with a bucket for donations. (The Motown musical group "The Boys" were discovered on Venice Beach along with a host of other entertainers). The truth is, people want to believe in overnight success stories. In particular, those who enter this business impatient for their big break. They arrive in Hollywood with unreasonable expectations that more often than not lead to discontentment and disappointment.

FOCUS ON YOUR OWN ASSETS: QUIT WORRYING ABOUT THE COMPETITION

At auditions, choosing to see everyone in the waiting room as an enemy automatically puts one in an adversarial position. The reality is that only one person is going to get the job (unless they're looking for a group of people) so why not develop the attitude that it might as well be you, as opposed to: "How could they possibly choose me out of all the people here?" That type of attitude equates to self-defeat before beginning.

Rather, cultivate an open, friendly attitude towards the competition, especially with those more successful. Who knows, this person might willingly share winning secrets with your child. Teach children to open up to and be ready for new possibilities. Mentoring successful behavior has proven results as evidenced by biographies of millionaires and successful actors.

Even though parents already knew that actors with looks similar to their child's have distinguishing features, personality traits or abilities that separate them, it's easy to lose sight of the obvious. Always remind your child of his or her uniqueness since casting directors search for that very trait. This explains why someone with the same look might get the job over your child, or vice versa. One never knows when a variation in a look will win out if other things are pretty much equal. It all boils down to subtle little differences in character traits, personality, hair, eye color, etc.

Here in Los Angeles there must be a dozen little girls with my daughter's look. We see each other over and over at auditions with people often mistaking my daughter for someone else in a commercial or vice versa. It would be a waste of time for me to allow my child to worry about the fact that so many girls who look like her all go out for the same part. Far better to remind her, instead, that casting directors see something different in each one of them.

For my daughter, her big, hazel eyes and smile are her best asset, so I make sure that her hair doesn't get in the way of her eyes. I also encourage her to smile a lot. Often the decisive factor that landed Crystal a commercial was her big friendly eyes, warm smile, cheerful "Hello", and sincere "Thank you." Little things can mean a lot in a casting director's busy day.

THE POWER OF A SMILE

When we moved to Los Angeles from Houston I noticed right away how difficult it was to get a pleasantry, let alone a smile out of people. Children in particular. For a while I taught English and Creative Writing to fifth and sixth graders at a school in California. Besides the children's lack of decorum, the first thing I noticed was that none of them smiled or said,"Good Morning." Not even when I smiled and greeted them first.

The first thing I worked on was everyone smiling and repeating to me: "Good Morning, Mrs. Grant." Many responded with a mechanical grunt or stone face. It took almost six weeks of conditioning before the smiles became automatic and the greetings spontaneous.

Moreover, in the beginning, the children seemed startled or shocked if I acknowledged their presence outside of the classroom with a cheerful "Hello" upon running into a familiar face between classes, or in the cafeteria. By the same token, after conditioning the children to smile and say "Hello," when the transformation finally occurred, I found myself pleasantly surprised.

The beauty of it all was that the smiles and "hello's" became contagious. Pretty soon all the children at the school knew me and began speaking on campus. It visibly irritated many of the teachers when my students were lined up outside their rooms and greeted me in unison as I passed by. Putting up with other teachers was worth the transformation of those cynical, stone faced children into bright eyes and sweet smiles.

As long as there is no enemy inside, the enemy on the outside can do no harm. (Paraphrased from an African proverb)

The point of this story is that if I found spontaneous smiles and genuinely friendly faces a scarce commodity in Los Angeles, you can bet casting directors see far too many overly serious, somber and sour faces on kids who walk into auditions. When a truly happy, bubbly kid, with a heart warming smile walks into a casting director's office, it has to make their day. And after the audition, if a child walks up to the casting director with a handshake, smile and a sincere "Thank you," who do you think that casting director will remember when going over the list of possible callbacks with the client that hired him or her?

Remember that every failure has a clue to attainment if one takes the time to search for it.

Ask yourself: If you had the choice of working with someone who walked around with a black cloud of nervousness, negativity or uncertainty, as opposed to someone with a sunny, cheerful and delightful disposition, whom would you choose? Those warm, feelings we give out makes us memorable to others.

POINTS TO PONDER

1. *A warm smile, "Hello," "Please" and "Thank you" are simple refinements that will successfully take one all around the world and back. Greeting others with a pleasant face is uplifting and contagious.*

2. *Remember the old saying: "If you do what you love the money will follow." The truth of this phrase lies in teaching your child to enjoy the audition process, including all the preparation involved, and to do it because nothing else brings greater satisfaction or feels more rewarding.*

3. *The child's focus should be on DOING and BEING, not the end result because people who love what they do will win out in the end over those struggling to get there.*

4. *Remind your child that instead of worrying about someone who works more than he or she does, possesses better singing, dancing or acting skills, the child should focus on sharpening his or her own abilities and learn from those further along in their careers.*

Chapter 19

SLOW PERIODS: WORKING THROUGH THEM

Hollywood manages to keep its mind on show business even when everyone else on earth is caught up in other things.

Hollywood has always had an envious, well guarded mystique that actors become caught up in protecting or perpetuating without knowing quite the how's or why's of it all. The reality, however, is long, hot hours working on sound stages that look like big black barns, surrounded by people single minded of purpose.

Sitting in on the taping of a television sitcom can give the novice a good idea of how much work and discipline goes into the craft. Better still, visiting a set all week long to observe the raw sitcom process (from table reading to taping) would be ideal. This experience would shed light upon the entire illusion that creates willing captives to a form of entertainment that appears magical. There is nothing magical, however, in the tedious, repetitive, and confusing commands often required just to shoot one acceptable scene for print.

At times other children in the business can lead your child to feel anxious, inadequate or impatient for his or her chance at success. The obvious solution may appear to be avoidance. However, association with other actors is an inescapable part of the audition process. Children constantly go out on calls with the same actors. While one may not always know the name of his or her competitors, their faces become quite recognizable.

THE GAMES PEOPLE PLAY

Everyone has a normal curiosity about who booked the job they auditioned for, mostly to determine if they lost out to a different type, or to an actor with stronger ability or credits. Once your child books a job, it is not necessary to say a word to anyone else, others seem to know by osmosis. The underground network which spreads information and gossip throughout Hollywood continues to amaze me. Even if one books a small role or bit part on TV or film, everyone that auditioned for the part will find out who got it. Usually, someone they know will hear about it through their agent, or see your child on the show and tell someone, and they will tell someone and so on and so on. There seems to be this insatiable curiosity to KNOW who got what. Such a system automatically establishes who's hot and who's not, or more importantly, who now falls in that elite category of currently working actors. Another enigma in this "curiosity complex" involves the inexplicable elation people feel upon recognizing someone they know on the screen. Familiar faces simply pop out from the television or movie screen. When this happens unexpectedly, you will hear someone exclaim: "I know that face!"

SO, WHAT HAVE YOU DONE LATELY?

Whether one offers the information or not, others will always want to know what your child has done lately. A harmless question, right? Maybe. If one happens to be going through a dry spell, that question can put a child on the spot, create pressure, or cause performance anxiety which is the last thing a child needs while waiting to audition for a part, especially during a dry spell. The cacophony of voices in the audition room speaking proudly, nonchalantly or boastfully about their latest job can make a child feel downright desperate, or even worse, depressed.

Slow Periods: Working Through Them

Now imagine how the child feels after listening to all this talk in the waiting room only to go inside and have the casting director take a glance at his or her resume and inquire good-naturedly: "So, what have you been up to lately?" Talk about feeling put on the spot. Of course, the casting director may not even be referring to the business. She may mean vacation, school or play. But after the way your child's mind has been altered by the conversations in the waiting area, he or she will naturally assume that the casting director means jobs NOT booked lately. Take the time to explain to your child that the casting director would only ask such a question based on the child's track record; not to make him or her feel ill at ease. And to avoid feeling put on the spot again when asked that question, remind your child to refer to his or her latest job, a class or workshop enrolled in, or a new hobby.

The children of the poor have much to teach the children of privilege about the strength that comes from a journey of struggle. -Marian Wright Edelman "The Measure of Our Success" (Beacon Press)

One cannot avoid dealing with egos or insecurities at casting calls. During slow periods, a child may feel inclined to keep to himself, or to withdraw at auditions as a result of off-handed, facetious, or sly little comments spoken in jest, yet delivered with malicious intent by other children or parents. Often someone will create a conversation designed to slip in a tidbit about their latest job success. Regardless of the fact that one may feel happy for the other fellow, listening to someone volunteer self-gratifying information is boorish and no different than rich people boasting of their affluence and privileges to those poverty stricken. Encourage your child to congratulate the other person, then change the subject to something that interests them both or that makes him or her feel more comfortable. Again, remind your child, whenever possible, to refrain from speaking of his or her accomplishments unless asked. And not to mention new roles to those not currently working or to those not in the business, unless someone else brings up the conversation.

Volunteering such information can unknowingly incite jealousy, unhealthy competitiveness or rivalry.

SEEING SLOW PERIODS AS A SEAM IN THE CYCLE OF SUCCESS

One child actor, accustomed to working a lot, went over six months without booking a single theatrical audition. When he finally auditioned for and landed a guest starring appearance on a television show, the child told me that it was so nice to be acting again he would have done it for free. Just being in front of the camera was worth more than money to him. And that was saying a lot for a kid who happened to love money.

===

There is a magic in believing that transcends logic...Real power comes from your soul, your inner beliefs --Dr. Wayne W. Dyer "Real Magic" (HarperCollins Publishers)

===

During slow periods an actor can grow to feel isolated, as if no one understands or cares. After going for long stretches without even an audition, the situation compounds itself. A long dry spell can cause one to forget what he or she knew from the beginning: that the nature of this business is hot and cold, peaks and valleys, highs and lows. In spite of this knowledge, a tendency exists for actors to identify with and reward only the highs, peaks and hot periods.

While going through a valley or experiencing a low, some child actors imagine eyes of pity, satisfaction or aversion cast in their direction. And it does not matter if it is all in the mind. It seems real. In fact, such a situation makes it easy to conclude that other people are actually happy or gloating because things are not going well. Moreover, that unspoken aspect of friends and relatives who envy working actors because they, too, want to be a part of the dream-like fantasy that Hollywood has woven around stars, combined with those who disapprove of actors for choosing a fickle profession, makes the situation difficult at best to deal with. There simply may be no accounting for the public's ambivalent feelings about actors, especially within the context of a business that thrives off of insecurities. The trick then, is how to handle such situations without losing ones equanimity or belief in his or her abilities under conditions that are less than favorable?

Wealth will come into your life when you are unattached to needing it. It only eludes you if you chase it. -Dr. Wayne Dyer, Author "Real Magic" (HarperCollins Publishers)

One prominent adult actor told me that he went through a string of successful movies and then hit a three year dry spell. Every time he ran into someone who asked him what he had done lately, he felt like cringing. It was only after he ceased identifying himself with his work and got involved in other activities that he began to work again. Through that experience he came up with an answer to the question. Now, even though he is currently riding the high of a five-year roll, he told me that when people ask what he has been doing lately, he says with gusto, enthusiasm, and a great big smile: "Living."

CREATING WORK ON YOUR OWN

In between jobs, have your child volunteer his or her talents to a favorite charity or cause. That will keep the youngster busy and in the limelight, while providing a worthwhile community or social service. If your child sings or dances, volunteering to perform at benefits, parties, colleges or educational events provide an excellent forum for showcasing talent. Such organizations love to bill professionals as special guests and the free publicity is great, not to mention an excellent way to establish contacts, build a following or a fan club.

Dr. Wayne Dyer recommends that we "*strive for growth motivation which changes your inner thinking from lack to completeness.*" Doing volunteer or benefit work can fill the void of waiting on the agent to call and make the actor feel good about using his or her talents to make a difference in the community.

Dinner theaters, community theaters, college campuses, or repertory theaters also provide rewarding outlets for child actors. Many of these shows receive reviews in the papers. If your child is a strong actor and lucky enough to land a part in a well written script, he may end up with a rave review. I remember attending a play at a small theater on Melrose. The theater was only half full, but the play was truly delightful and I recognized an up and coming actor in the cast who was on a television show that had recently been canceled. His role was more of a cameo, but he stole the show and had the audience in stitches. That same weekend I saw a front page article on this very actor in the calendar section of the "Los Angeles Times" giving this actor's performance in that little play four stars.

Do not allow your child to automatically assume that because he or she just finished a film, television show, or whatever, that casting directors are going to line up outside the door offering new roles. The only time that happens is if the actor is in a blockbuster film and it truly has to be a major blockbuster for that to happen. Otherwise, each your child to enjoy the lulls and slow periods, learning to use free time constructively. Like the squirrel, prepare for, then put something away for the cold, lean winter. At the same time, Dr. Dyer admonishes us: *"not to think of yourself separately as a thinker and doer, victimized by something outside of yourself called scarcity."* Refuse to allow a fearful ego to trap your child into feeling that there is not enough business to go around, or that he or she is too good or to talented for the work available.

One would not believe how many famous people from canceled television series end up on cattle calls for commercials or theatrical auditions. They have to wait their turn outside just like everybody else. I have also heard stories about once successful actors, who felt that they were beyond going out on auditions with regular people. Guess what? They end up in the category of actors that make you wonder: "Whatever happened to so and so?" Those from canceled shows who do manage to go on to new roles do so because they refuse to buy into the belief that the former show was the only one they would ever get. Maintaining a positive attitude, a confident demeanor and a belief in an abundant universe will enable one to attract more work at the end of each job.

USING BENEFIT WORK TO CREATE YOUR OWN FACADE

During slow periods one should in no way diminish or put down plays, charity, benefit or community theater participation. Work is work. Absolutely no one need know that the child is doing it for free (if that be the case) unless there exhists a need to know. Besides, really famous actors take free or low paying theater roles between jobs for the thrill and challenge of performing in front of a live audience. There is no better training ground.

Just because your agent isn't sending the child out during slow periods does not mean that you, as a parent, cannot create work on your own. An audience filled with people that you and your friends invited to see a play that a group of you wrote, produced and had your children perform in, utilizing donated space can be one of the most rewarding and memorable experiences of your child's career, especially if the child helped create the excitement. And why not ask a friend to invite his friend (who just happens to be a newspaper critic for a local paper) to come out and cover the event? Who knows, you just might get a good review. Dr. Wayne Dyer adds a reminder: *"be your own internal standard of comparison rather than measuring yourself against others."*

WORKING YOUR WAY OUT OF LIMBO LAND

This is a peculiar business. For as much as everyone always scrambles for and fights over the latest star, Hollywood is ever intent on making stars. If your child happens to fall into that up-and-coming category, (i.e., neither a star, nor an unknown, which, incidentally is where the vast majority of actors find themselves detained for a large part of their career), the child may feel lost in the shuffle sometimes, or even worse, in purgatory. Again, one of my favorite writers, Dr. Wayne Dyer says that: *"Someone else's success should serve as a model. It is no reason for you to feel inadequate or wanting."*

There is no reason for the child to wait there in limbo, watching himself or herself get passed over in favor of someone inexperienced (and cheap) or a box office star (expensive). It could drive the child's self-confidence right out the window just pondering such madness. Not to mention how frustrated it could make the young actor feel. Why not do something about it and donate your child's talents to a children's hospital, nursing home, or orphanage, where they will be ever so appreciated and rewarded with warm thanks, hugs, smiles and autographs?

Again, Wayne Dyer reminds us that: *"Giving is the key to your own abundance."* We have to give of ourselves in order to receive those intangible rewards which money cannot buy. Besides, after performing at a charity or benefit, children often book paying jobs from someone in the audience.

Sometimes, getting back into the fast lane only requires a change in perspective or attitude. One mother that I know complained frequently about how slow things were here in Los Angeles as opposed to New York, and how the child was not working. Then, in another breath she would casually dismiss a national print job the child had just done because she felt that modeling was not in the same league as commercials, television or film. It took me a while to convince this mother that she needed to change her perspective and place modeling in the same category as other work because the competition for print jobs is even more fierce than other areas. The fact that her daughter booked print work at all in Los Angeles was a testament to the child's strength as a model. Moreover, I pointed out to the mother that it might be more productive for them to return to New York while the child's age group was in-demand. The child was still getting requests from photographers who had worked with her in New York. In Los Angeles the little girl only worked occasionally; whereas, in New York, the child worked almost everyday as a model. I felt concerned that the child would lose her client base if she stayed away from New York much longer.

Once the mother began to appreciate her daughter's value as a model and stopped placing so much emphasis on the acting end of the business, she found the courage to pack up and move back to New York. There the child immediately resumed her successful modeling career and took on more work than she could handle. Now every time I talk to this mother, I hear pride in her voice over the fact that her child is once again working regularly and they are all happy as a family.

Sometimes it takes a dry spell for us to appreciate that there was nothing wrong with what we already had. Occasionally we simply have to cross the fence to see if the grass really is greener on the other side. Again, Dr. Wayne Dyer recommends being *"at peace with your work and focus on the over riding spiritual, social or loving purpose that drives your work; then you will experience a prosperity shift."* What this parent had to do was find peace with her child's natural abilities in front of the photographer's lens. Once the little girl's mother did this, she experienced the shift that Dyer refers to.

HOW DO I HANDLE WAITING JITTERS?

The answer is simple. Get a life. Or at least a hobby that parallels or compliments the child's career. It is counter productive to sit around waiting for the agent to call. If you do that, they never will. Good things come when you least expect them, yet always while preoccupied doing something else. Moreover, the phone never rings while you sit there anxiously awaiting news that your child booked the job. Somehow, when you do that the shooting date manages to come and go without a word from your agent.

===

"Prosperity is about process; not results. And process is purpose. Purpose is loving and giving." -Dr. Wayne Dyer "Real Magic" (Harper Collins)

===

MAKE EACH AUDITION AN ADVENTURE

When we first arrived in Los Angeles it was summer time. After our last audition of the day, the kids and I would always have a little adventure planned, like a picnic, visit to the library, book store, movie or just a trip to their favorite fast food restaurant. We never rushed home to check the answering machine. I simply followed instructions from the agent to check in with her twice a day. I didn't even have a beeper then. And if we finished with our last audition after five o'clock, I never bothered to check in with the agent. Inevitably when we got home a message waited on the machine that the kids had a callback, another audition or one of them had booked a job. It was always a delightful surprise.

===

Success comes when you relax and remove the pressures from yourself. --Dr. Wayne Dyer "Real Magic" (HarperCollins Publisher)

===

After walking out of each audition we had a ritual. I allowed the kids to volunteer information about how they felt they had done on the audition. Sometimes the children would feel that they had not done as well as they would have liked. At such times I reminded them that there would always be another audition. They simply needed to learn how they could improve from this one. I let them know that all they should expect from themselves was the very best they could do at that particular time. Nothing more was necessary.

During that period the children went into each audition with no expectations. Getting the part was secondary to enjoying what they were doing, feeling proud of their efforts, and promptly putting the audition out of their minds. I made sure that we all became immediately occupied with other hobbies or activities on the way home. Using this method, my two children easily booked job after job. And we were delighted every time.

IT IS EASY TO BECOME JADED OR DISILLUSIONED

At one point the children began to expect to book every job that they auditioned for, especially when their performance was outstanding. When that did not happen every time they expected it to, they became surprised. Later, this incredulity turned to disappointment and before I knew it, both children were quickly becoming disillusioned. When that happened a reversal took place. My children became surprised when they DID get a job, not when they didn't. Thus, the results began to meet their expectations.

I remember my daughter remarking once, after I told her that she had a callback for a doll commercial, "I don't know why they always call me back when I never book any Barbie commercials." I knew then that I had allowed her to become too absorbed in the business of auditions, without enough hobbies and extra-curricular activities. It had become work, instead of an adventure. Furthermore, we had curbed our little outings after each audition to the point where I could not remember the last time we had gone on one.

===

Work at replacing those thoughts within you that reflect a scarcity consciousness. -Dr. Wayne Dyer "Real Magic" (HarperCollins Publishers)

===

Of course, none of this happened overnight. It was a gradual occurrence. I had simply become too busy rushing from one audition to the next and then running back home because my husband was expecting us or I had something else to do.

My daughter's comment served as a reality check. I knew it was time for me to recapture what had originally worked for us: making the audition process a picnic. Innately I knew that it was important to dispel negative thoughts and follow Wayne Dyer's advice to *"get on with the magic of believing, rather than the anguish of doubt."*

We went back to basics that began with an attitude adjustment. I reminded my daughter that just because she had booked a lot of commercials did not mean that every one she auditioned for had her name on it. Casting directors were always looking for fresh faces and, in particular, positive attitudes and personalities. I emphasized how important it was to reflect a friendly, relaxed, out-going, yet humble disposition. Ultimately, casting directors were going to hire the kids that they liked, those whose smiles were genuine, not jaded. I helped her to understand that they were looking for children who walked in the room filled with energy, wonder and excitement, those full of delight about being there.

With team effort and a little time, my daughter reached back to the way she was when we first came to Los Angeles. In no time at all, she began enjoying the audition process once more (rather than filling herself up inside with anxiety about not getting the part). Her new attitude showed, and she began booking jobs like before. It took talking, affirming, believing and saturating ourselves with positive thinking tapes (as we had in the beginning) to reverse this negative pattern we had allowed into our lives. Fortunately, children are resilient and bounce back easily with guidance and encouragement. In the process, we learned that when one lets up on positive thinking, negative ones automatically creep in to fill the void.

POINTS TO PONDER

1. *To motivate your child during slow periods reread this chapter. I would also recommend reading the book,"Real Magic" by Dr. Wayne Dyer (Harper Collins Publishers) or buying the tapes and playing them in your car on the way to auditions.*

2. *Do not allow the success of other actors to depress you or your child; use theirs as a model for your own success.*

3. *When going through a slow period and another actor asks you or your child what he or she has been doing lately, answer: "Living," with a warm smile.*

4. *During slow periods participate in theater work, charities, benefits, or put on a show yourself.*

5. *After an audition, immediately occupy your time and your child's time with something else instead of waiting, worrying or wondering if he or she got the job. The news never comes if you sit waiting on it, it always arrives when least expected.*

Chapter 20

OUT OF TOWNERS: MAKING THE MOVE TO L.A.

You need to know how the town works. Success is reached over time. Great success begins with a series of little successes. That begins with getting in town and being financially secure. -Brian Thomas, Spotlight Entertainment, Ltd. (from "The L.A. Agent Book" by K Callan)

I have witnessed out-of-towners come and go in Los Angeles. Mostly go. Whenever that happens I am reminded of Gladys Knight's song "Midnight Train to Georgia." L.A. can prove "too much" for most people.

The decisive factor in making the radical decision to take a leave of absence from my job in Houston, and move to Los Angeles, was my son's age. Several agents advised that it was "now or never." Salim was ten, soon to be eleven and there was no way of knowing what might happen to him physically or emotionally as a teenager. We had reached that critical window of opportunity wherein, like those time travelers, if they do not exit at a particular moment in time, they end up stranded. Furthermore, I did not want my son coming to me years later saying: "If only you had let me take that chance when I was ten." As for my daughter, Crystal was six-and-a-half years old, the perfect age for entering the Los

Angeles kid market. Both children were already working regularly in Houston and Dallas when I signed Salim up for an acting workshop in Dallas sponsored by Linda Seto. Two Los Angeles chose Salim. Crystal was spotted by one of the agents, Mary Grady, while in the Hotel lobby. Mary Grady asked Crystal if she wanted to come with her brother to Los Angeles for the summer. The agents and I felt that both children had an excellent chance of doing well in Hollywood since they already had a track record in Texas.

PREPARING FOR OUR SUMMER IN LOS ANGELES

We began making preparations for the summer stay in Los Angeles early in the spring of 1988. A leave of absence from my job at a law firm was no problem. That spring Salim had booked a lead in a Disney film as well as the then new, "Barney And The Backyard Gang" series of edutainment videos in Dallas. With my savings, and part of Salim's earnings, we arrived in Los Angeles with approximately ten thousand dollars to make it through the summer. The three of us flew to Los Angeles. My husband drove my car from Houston so that we would not have the added expense of car rentals.

The day we stepped off of the airplane the children and I fell in love with the weather in Los Angeles, especially Torrance, California where we went to stay with my husband's cousin. Being close to the beach made day time temperatures about ten degrees cooler than Los Angeles. And we loved the fresh, brisk, breezes at night. To our amazement the air was wonderfully dry and free of the humidity that ruined my hairdo's in Houston. The smog seemed a small price to pay for forever sunshine, "purple mountains majesty" and beaches for as far as the eyes could reach.

The only problem was the drive from Torrance into the media district every day. It was quite demanding; and even more so since I took surface roads all the way. I had a difficult time making sense out of the freeways and never could seem to find my way back on to one once I exited. The freeways here do not have feeder roads running alongside them for easy entrance and exit the way they do in Texas.

It did not take me long to discover that between what I paid my husband's cousin to live with them in Torrance, along with food, gas and maid service, it was more convenient to get our own furnished studio at Oakwood Apartments in Toluca Hills. It offered a much closer location for auditions. It was, however, nice being with my husband's cousin that first month because they knew their way about the city, could map out the place for me, and answer many of the questions I had about Los Angeles.

Salim and Crystal were delighted to move to Oakwood Apartments, which caters to relocated business professionals and people in the entertainment industry. Approximately 98% of their more than 1,200 units are furnished. The majority of their residents are on month to month rental (which is much more expensive than a lease) because they do not know how long they will be in Los Angeles filming or to find a permanent home.

The children and I loved Oakwood because of the security, social life and the amenities. Every Sunday morning management provides a complimentary brunch. Most weekends the social director puts on a party of some type in one of the two Club Houses. Moreover, Salim and Crystal were excited about joining over a dozen other children from Dallas, Texas who had also come down for the summer with Linda Seto and were staying at Oakwood. After running around all day at auditions the kids found it relaxing to lie out by the pool or hot tub, take a swim, play tennis, volley ball or basketball. I preferred walking up and down the hills of the huge complex or reading a book out by the hot tub. With a convenience store, dry cleaners, beauty salon and a shoe repair place within the complex, there was no reason to leave unless we wanted to.

The three of us felt pretty cozy in the contemporary, bleached wood decor of our little studio. A mirrored, double sized Murphy bed folded down at night. Crystal slept with me. Salim took the couch. In addition, we had plenty of room for our clothes, television, computer and Nintendo. We even had a large walk in closet, built in bookshelves and more than adequate drawer and shelf space.

My biggest culture shock was the outrageous price of apartments in Los Angeles. Because we got a corporate rate through Linda Seto's acting workshop, and paid month to month, we ended up with the highest rate possible for our little studio apartment: $965.00 per month. Electricity and phones were extra. Because the children and I called home every night, rent, lights and phone combined cost us a minimum of $1,500.00 month. We spent another $500.00 or more for food. After adding in gasoline and entertainment our total expenses ran around $2,500.00 per month, not including extraordinary expenses such as car repairs, dental, medical or clothes (luckily we came out with new clothes and did not have to buy any for a while). This amount was in addition to the regular expenses my husband covered to maintain our home in Houston.

As human beings our greatness lies not so much in being able to remake the world -- that is the myth of the 'Atomic Age' -- as in being able to remake ourselves. -Gandhi

Needless to say, it did not take long before our nest egg was almost gone. But that didn't bother us because the children were booking non-union jobs pretty regularly. Of course the jobs did not pay that much, but they added up. At about the time we were to return home, Salim was up for a television series. The agent asked if we could stay on for a few more months. We did not hesitate to accept.

My husband was willing to wait it out in Houston for six months, paying the bills there and sending enough to cover the rent in Los Angeles, but we had to take care of food and gas. To earn extra income I immediately took the state examination for teachers and got a job right away as an Artist In Residence at the school where my husband's cousin taught.

My daughter, Crystal, was really missing her father, so I encouraged my husband to take a couple of weeks vacation to visit California and look for a job. He works in management in microelectronics and got an offer from Hughes Aircraft. After accepting the job my husband flew back home, gave away or sold most of our furniture and put the rest in storage for his company to move to Los Angeles, and leased our home.

Of course we had to immediately look for a larger place. Even though we loved Oakwood, their largest unit was only two bedrooms and we needed three. We hated to move because there was something contagious in the attitude of everyone at Oakwood that encouraged us to take the time to lie out by the pool and just relax -- something we rarely found time for in Houston. There were hours when we just sat in the hot tub, gazing out at the beauty of the hills and lush green foliage while basking in the foothills of the bright California sun. When we moved to a nearby apartment complex, the view of the mountains from our bedroom window was enough to justify leasing our home and moving into a three bedroom apartment barely the size of our downstairs in Houston. The children missed Oakwood so much that we ended up moving back a year later into a two bedroom. My son was willing to sleep on a sofa bed in the living room just to be back at Oakwood.

BEFORE DECIDING TO MAKE THAT MOVE

Every year I meet mothers who move here from all over the country. Often I find that the difference between those able to make it and those forced to go back home hinges on adequate planning and support, usually from a husband or family back home. Those mothers whose husbands could not afford to pay the bills back home and the rent in Los Angeles, had no choice but to go home, in particular if the mother could not come up with a flexible job that allowed her to work and take the children on auditions. In addition, the sporadic nature of work in the entertainment industry can drive mothers to distraction. Unless the child is a regular on a television series or currently working on a feature film, one can hardly count on a regular pay check. Furthermore, until eligible to join the union (SAG or AFTRA) the client who hires your child can take up to three months to mail the child's check to the agent. Once the child joins SAG, however, checks have to be mailed to the agent within two weeks or face a penalty. After the agent receives the check he or she has to mail it to the client within seven days.

Because parents have to make themselves available after school to take the child on auditions, and the parent must accompany a child on the set whenever a child works, a regular nine to five job just won't do the trick. Options for single, or working parents are discussed in detail in the next chapter: "What If I'm A Single Parent?"

There is nothing like the desperation in the eyes of people I have met who come out here without getting an agent or manager ahead of time. In the very least, get a friend, relative, or acquaintance to refer you to someone who can legitimately hook you up with a franchised agent.

If you move to Los Angeles anyway without an agent do yourself a favor and purchase a copy of *"The L.A. Agent Book" by K Callan* (Sweden Press, 1990) first thing. Out of towners can order a copy from the following address: Sweden Press, Box 1612, Studio City, CA 91614. Or call 818-995-4250. It's an indispensable item for anyone in search of an agent. Callan did exhaustive interviews and researched the best and most reputable agents in L.A., coming up with a book that includes *"background on the agents, histories of the agencies and information regarding size and quality of the client lists."* The book also *"helps you evaluate your present agent and your mutual contributions to your problems or success."* Moreover, Callan's book provides an excellent source for selecting the agents that best fit your child's needs.

After narrowing down your list of agents, send them copies of your child's picture, resume and videotape of any work, including live theater or public performances. Since many agents do not like to receive phone calls inquiring about new submissions, one might wait a couple of weeks, then call and explain that you submitted pictures and would like to know if they could recommend you to another agency in the event that they do not have a spot for your child. If you get a referral mention that in the cover letter to the new agent. This could become the push needed to get your child's foot in the door.

NECESSITIES ONCE YOU'VE ARRIVED IN THE CITY

Once you've found an agent willing to represent your child (remember that firm representation is usually contingent on an actual interview after arriving in town), the first thing you need to do is buy a ***Thomas Guide Map Book*** (already mentioned earlier in this book). After all, you will have to find your way to the agent's office for a meeting. And if the agent wants to send you out on auditions right away, you will need to quickly find your away around Hollywood, Burbank, Culver City, Century City and Santa Monica, (i.e., the "Media District") where most of the auditions take place. The book can be purchased for approximately $25 at any bookstore or major supermarket.

We are actors and we are our own instrument. If the instrument is not in tune, it's impossible to play it successfully. Living in a dump or out of a suitcase is like leaving your violin out in the rain. Get a good case for it and polish it and there's a much better chance for it to shine. *K Callan, author "The L.A. Agent Book"*

A pager and an answering service are also a necessity to insure that your agent can reach you at all times. Since one has to have a phone anyway, I would recommend Pacific Bell's electronic voice mail answering service. Approximately $5.00 per month will buy you an answering service that dates and times your calls and allows retrieval of messages from remote locations. For an additional small fee, Pacific Bell can forward urgent calls directly to your pager. A car phone is also helpful when the agent pages you in the middle of traffic.

HOUSING:

Oakwood Apartments in Toluca Hills offer month to month rentals and come completely furnished with everything from dishes to towels and maid service. The rates are cheaper if you sign a six month or one year lease. Keep in mind that orporate or monthly rates are more expensive than individual rates.

Adjacent to the brand new Academy of Television Arts and Sciences in North Hollywood is *Academy Village Apartments*. Ideally suited for those in the entertainment industry, it offers one and two bedroom units with or without furniture. This elegant, modern mid rise offers a wide range of amenities such as rehearsal studios, beautifully furnished meeting rooms, and personal trainers. It's location puts you within minutes of major studios, the Burbank Airport and major freeways. Short term leases are available.

The Royal Equestrian apartments on Riverside in Burbank, offer prices that are a little more competitive than Oakwood, however, only a few of the units are furnished. They only offer studios and one bedroom apartments. The complex is small and intimate with a clubhouse, pool, spa and exercise facility.

On Hollywood Way in Burbank is *Parc Point Apartments*. They are the only complex in this group to offer 3 bedroom and 2 bedroom-den units. Nicely situated between a small shopping center and a park with a jogging trail, Parc Point also has most of the amenities. Does not offer furnished units.

Granted, there are any number of nice apartment complexes in Burbank, North Hollywood, and Studio City. It's just that the ones mentioned above all cater to the entertainment profession, have the all important amenities, and keep their prices affordable for families. Moreover, thoses who work in the industry often prefer such complexes because they offer residents the comfort and convenience of a network of people with similar interests, goals and pursuits.

CULTIVATING THE RIGHT ATTITUDE TOWARDS THE CITY

Before we moved here my children had never seen an actual gang member and were terrified of the prospect. Because of that fear, I taught the children to become fearless by looking for the humanity that lies deep in the eyes of everyone. Naturally, we still practiced common sense, like locking our doors, making sure that the car was serviced regularly and always had enough gas. I also did my best to keep my son in neutral colors to avoid mistaken gang identity. In addition, we learned that if a gang member asks you where you are from to answer: "No where," indicating none affiliation with local gangs.

It goes without saying that if one makes the effort to move to L.A, it helps to actually like the city, or at least be willing to overcome any fears or phobias about the place. I have met people from smaller towns or suburbs who are petrified of L.A. and afraid to venture out into the city alone. Those who protest about how much they dislike the city are the worst. I have found that people who constantly complain about L.A., the traffic, the smog, earthquakes, etc., while glorifying the wonderful things and people back home, quickly end up back home. I remember a couple of months after the Northridge Earthquake, my son went back to Houston for a week. He called me his last night there and said that he was being smothered by humidity, spring pollen and too many relatives. It had gotten the best of him. He confided that he could not wait to return to "Shakey Town."

An important aspect of making a total commitment to success is to immediately acclimate yourself to Los Angeles, leaving everyone and everything back home to take care of themselves. Be focused and of one mind. There's an old saying that a house divided against itself cannot stand. When you arrive here it is important to begin seeing L.A. as home. With that settled in your mind, one finds it much easier to concentrate on getting a new house and career in order.

Of course, everyone has heard stories of how people struggled to make it in Los Angeles. Anyone who brings children to this city, however, should not embrace that as their story to live or tell. The move to Los Angeles needs to be as pleasant as possible for the children in order for them to maintain the necessary innocence, naiveté and wonderment to carry them through the audition process. Believe me, casting people can read desperation in the eyes of children. It's a frightening turn-off.

Moreover, if the family is stressed out worrying about how they will pay the rent and uncertain how much longer they will be able to stay in L.A. before forced to go back home (with nothing to show for the trip) the child certainly will not be at his or her best on auditions. In fairness to everyone, under such circumstances, do not even bother coming out to Los Angeles, in particular, if one does not have enough money to pay rent for at least six months in advance.

With children, as long as the parents are happy and they feel loved, kids can easily make the transition from a sixteen-room house to a three-room studio without complaint, as mine did. Life should provide one big adventure after another for kids. That's what the move to Los Angeles should be. Otherwise, do yourself a favor and stay home.

POINTS TO PONDER

1. *If you have a child and are thinking about giving L.A. a trial run, do not wait until the child has passed his or her biggest window of opportunity, between the ages of 6 and 10. If the child is older than that, be sure that he or she is small for their age group, (height and weight wise) not an early developer, already has a nice resume, or can sing or dance well; otherwise keep the child in acting, dance or voice classes and consider coming out as a teen once the child has out grown that awkward stage of puberty (usually around fifteen or sixteen).*

2. *Should you decide to move to L.A. anyway be certain that you already have an agent and adequate funds in the bank for at least a six month stay. Have a nest egg to fall back on. It is impossible for a child to be comfortable and relaxed at an audition if he or she is desperate about getting the job out of fear that if he or she doesn't the family will have to return home too soon, and empty handed, no less.*

3. *Forget about your hometown and focus on becoming comfortable here in the city. If you are afraid of L.A. and constantly comparing it to home, with L.A. coming up short, guess where you're bound to end up? (That's right, back at home.)*

Chapter 21

WHAT IF I'M A SINGLE PARENT?

Genius ... means little more than the faculty of perceiving in an unhabitual way. William James

HOW I MADE IT WORK AS A WORKING MOTHER

In actuality, it does not matter if one is single or married as long as both parents have to work, the challenge of how to get the child to auditions during work hours presents a problem. For seven of the ten years that my children worked in the entertainment field, I had a full time position inside of an office.

In the beginning, I continually called on favors from friends and relatives to get my two children to auditions. At the time I was living in Houston, surrounded by family and friends which was by no means an ideal situation, since most were unreliable and fickle. At times I had to bribe relatives and pay my friends.

Each time a call came in from my children's agent I would go into a mild panic, immediately dialing the numbers of everyone I knew, who did not work, to see if anyone was available. If no one could do it I would take off of work myself.

I learned from dealing with my husband never to make a request to my boss. I would simply go in and announce that I had to take an extended lunch break then offer to work overtime or to come in early the following day to make up the lost time. Nine times out of ten, the attorney I worked for would immediately go into distress about some filing deadline we had to make that very day. To circumvent these situations (everyday in the life of the attorney I worked for was an emergency or last minute deadline) I became adept at drafting and editing documents at lightening speed. Or asking other people in the office to finish something for me in exchange for helping that person out in an emergency. Usually, I ended up paying three fold for these favors, but I did not mind as long as my children did not have to miss an audition or a job they had booked.

Eventually, my boss became involved in the children's activities and we ended up striking a nice working arrangement. In exchange for all the overtime she wanted (which was considerable) I earned the ability to leave whenever the agent called for an audition. Of course, this still included not taking a lunch that day or coming in extra early (if I knew in advance) in order to complete a document that needed filing.

Even with this arrangement, the attorney I worked for would attempt to hold me over with last minute emergencies. At such times, I called on my stand-bye's in the office to finish the work for me.

Eventually my boss became involved in the children's careers and delighted in their successes often getting a kick out of opening the *"Houston Post"* or *"Houston Chronicle"* and seeing my children's faces in the editorial ads. Once she even had her husband stand-in as my son's father in a television movie.

After moving to Los Angeles I lost my support base of friends, relatives and a cooperative boss. Moreover, I had to work to make ends meet by teaching school to free up audition hours after school. That worked out for a while, but had its drawbacks too, because the school where I taught was an hour away (in no traffic).

On a regular basis I encounter many single parents who express a strong desire to get their child in show business yet feel constrained by the demands of a regular nine-to-five job. Since auditions take place between three and six in the afternoon during the school year and all day in the summers, flexibility at work presents a problem.

YES, SOME SINGLE STAGE PARENTS WORK

Many single parents do manage to rearrange their lives and work schedules to accommodate a child in the industry. Here's how some do it:

(1) own businesses outside or inside of the home that allow flexibility for auditions.

(2) work in sales, marketing or other positions outside of an office where they arrange their own schedules to call on clients. Such jobs allow parents to arrange their appointments and days off to coincide with audition schedules.

(3) flex hours on the job which allow parents to make auditions. Other parents save up and use vacation or sick time for days when the child works. Other "flex hour" arrangements allow for coming in early and working through the lunch hour on the day of an audition or saving up overtime to be used later as "comp" time for auditions.

(4) teaching, nursing, or consulting

(6) friends or relatives take the child out on calls, or

(7) hire a transportation service or someone to take the child out on auditions.

A mind at peace, a mind centered and not focused on harming others, is stronger than any physical force in the universe. The entire philosophy of aikido and the Oriental martial arts is based not on external power over the opponent, but on becoming one with the external energy to remove the threat. -Dr. Wayne Dyer, author of "Real Magic" (HarperCollins Publishers)

AUDITION DRIVERS/SET-SITTERS

When I left my teaching assignment to take a job at a law firm that paid more money, I ended up hiring an audition transportation service and registered with a second one as a back up. I found out about the transportation services through my agent. Some services have a registration fee, others do not. Most charge mileage along with a flat hourly rate (I paid $12.00 per hour).

The guy who ran the primary service I used was a single parent with a young son in the business. He was great. He combed my daughter's hair, made sure that the children remembered to change into audition outfits after school, ate only wholesome snacks, and always got them to the audition on time.

With two children going out on a lot of auditions, however, the process eventually became cost prohibitive, especially when one takes into consideration that a great deal of auditions end up in callbacks, not actual bookings. Sometimes, hiring a transportation service is the only alternative, however, for working parents.

After dropping the audition service I took a job closer to home at a small law office that permitted me to take the children to auditions then come back later and finish my work. That job would have been ideal if not for the fact that my son ended up filming a movie that took almost five months to complete. In the beginning of the film I had a nice little arrangement with the director, assistant director, and studio teacher. I could stay on the set a few hours in the morning to get Salim settled in. Then I would go to the office for a few hours and return to the set to pick Salim up. If I had a lot of work to do that day, I would go back to the office that evening to complete my work. Since Salim was not the typical twelve year old who ran around all over the place (he stayed in his dressing room or the school room until needed on the set), he was not in anybody's way. Eventually, politics and a stressed out Assistant Director on the set made me decide that I needed to spend all day with my child to keep him from getting emotionally caught up in the negative atmosphere.

HOLLYWOOD SCREEN PARENTS ASSOCIATION

For an annual membership fee, The Hollywood Screen Parents Association (HSP) offers up-to-date information on audition drivers and set-sitters through their newsletter. HSP publishes booklets that provide current, detailed listings of children's agents, performing arts programs, as well as information on workshops and seminars. They also have an extensive library of published books, magazine and newspaper articles. To join Call 818-955-6510, or write Barbara Schiffman, President, Hollywood Screen Parents Association, Box 1612, Burbank, Ca 91507.

GUARDIANS ON THE SET PITFALLS TO WATCH OUT FOR

Due to the uncertain nature and sporadic quantity of acting roles for children, most single mothers simply cannot quit their jobs to sit with their child, even when the child has a regular role on a television series. One never knows from season to season if the show will get picked up again. One mother explained that she preferred having her own money rather than dependence on the child's income. Furthermore, this mother did not want to give up a job that offered her security and retirement benefits as well as the flexibility of working out in the field, calling on clients. Her job lends adaptability to arrange or rearrange her appointments around the child's audition schedule. In fact, before her son got a television series and was only doing guest spots here and there, she would show up on the set to get him settled in, sign a sheet of paper that the studio teacher can provide which grants temporary guardianship to one of the other mothers, or to the studio teacher, then go back to work and return in time to pick him up at the end of the day. After the teen landed a television series, she hired a guardian full time. At that point the mother only came by on the day of *taping*.

The most important thing to remember about hiring a guardian on the set is that California has strict laws regarding workman's compensation and disability insurance for anyone who does not fit completely within the category of contract worker. Most people assume that babysitting is contract work, since the babysitter works for herself. Well, technically she is self-employed. Under California Law, however, one must carry workman's compensation insurance (quite inexpensive in California) on anyone required to be at work on a regular basis at a certain time every day, or for a specified length of time. The fact that the guardian does not control or set her own hours is the loophole that can end up costing you an arm and a leg should an accident or injury occur on the set. Call the Labor Board in your area and obtain detailed information on the requirements for workmen's compensation insurance before hiring a guardian on the set.

One parent I know quite well was sued by a set-sitter, who won a judgment against the parent when the sitter fell on the set. The State of California considered this sitter an employee because the child was a regular on a television series, which demanded the sitter's presence every day for specific hours. The mother had to pay the judgment out of her pocket; whereas, if she had known to buy workmen's compensation insurance she would have been covered by the small fee paid to worker's compensation.

POINTS TO PONDER

1. *The following kinds of jobs offer single parents the best chance of getting their child to auditions: sales, nursing, teaching, marketing, self-employment, work at home, flexible hours, or a job that allows the employee to leave and make up the time when he or she returns.*

2. *For those who must work a regular job, keep in mind that many bosses are understanding or supportive as long as you get your work done. Instead of asking your boss for the time off, tell him or her you have to take off, then offer to make up the time.*

3. *The Hollywood Screen Parents Association is a good resource for finding audition drivers, set-sitters, and for staying abreast of what's going on with the children's entertainment industry through their newsletter.*

4. *Remember that even though a parent or guardian is mandatory on Hollywood sets, rarely is it appreciated. Parents are the only people on the set required to be there but not paid for their presence.*

Chapter 22

CONTRACTS: KNOWING WHAT TO ASK FOR UP FRONT

The teacher is everywhere. The assistance you need will be provided by the universe as soon as you convert your readiness to willingness. Once you are willing you will find teachers in every niche of your life. -Dr. Wayne Dyer REAL MAGIC

NOTE: The information in this chapter is not intended to take the place of advice from an experienced entertainment attorney, it is designed to offer insight into the most common complaints I've encountered in the contract negotiation process and to avail the reader of what, if any, options are available.

First, of all, do not assume that just because you have an agent that the agent will take care of all the fine details when negotiating a contract. Although agents do negotiate the price of the job, in general, attorney's handle fine details of contract negotiations. Remember, the agent's primary focus is booking the job so that agent and client can both make money.

Some agents will simply accept whatever offer comes in from the client out of fear they will lose the booking. Other agents take pleasure in the negotiation process, developing reputations as tough customers who demand and receive top dollar for their talent. It would behoove each parent to investigate their agent's reputation and consciousness about money before signing with that agency. Inquire ahead of time which end of the money spectrum your agent falls under: a SAG-AFTRA minimum agent or one who will fight for more than that. For example, immediately before a child goes to network on the final callback for a television series, the child has to sign a contract with that network for a specific amount of money, whether the child gets the job or not. At this point, the selection process has already been narrowed down to a handful of kids, all of whom must sign a contract. The network does this to prevent the actor's agent from coming back and asking for more money once network has chosen who they want. When the initial offer comes in, an agent who is an effective negotiator will fight for more than minimum rates, particularly if the client has done guest television spots or film work. Moreover, once a child has gone to network and a price established, even if the child does not get the job, when that child goes to network again, network cannot offer the young performer less than the last amount offered because a precedent has been set in writing.

If your agent decides to accept and settle for SAG minimum even after a higher precedent has been established, then your child takes a step backwards and gets stuck with the lower rate.

SMALL CONSIDERATIONS CAN BECOME MAJOR ISSUES

Little frills, such as **billing** or a private dressing room on a movie set are not automatically granted. They require negotiation ahead of time. The production company can and will grant such considerations up front if you ask for them but will flat out refuse to even consider extras if you try to come back later and request them after the contract is already signed. Furthermore, do not count on your agent to remember to ask for specific items other than what's offered in the standard SAG contract since most agents focus on booking the job. Moreover, things like screen credits or dressing rooms add nothing to the overall price an agent can get for the client, so they are not exactly on the top of an agent's list of priorities.

In general, SAG contracts set the standard for concessions and serve as the bottom line in negotiations. Moreover, many details in standard SAG contracts are left up to the *"producer's discretion."* That term covers a wide variety of details, such as whether you will receive a honey wagon shared by all of the extras, or your own dressing room; a director's chair with your name on it, or for that matter, a chair at all. The chair issue may seem too minor to bother with in a contract until you have to stand all day on location.

Occasionally, one may receive nice little extras without asking for them. (But don't count on it.). For instance, in a Japanese movie that my son filmed, he received star billing in Japan as a standard clause in the contract without his agent having to fight over billing credits. This was not, however, a SAG contract. Further, in this same movie deal my son's agent also negotiated for him to get paid the day he completed filming, which was unusual.

BILLING AND SCREEN CREDITS

Take nothing for granted in this business. Do not assume you will receive billboard credits unless negotiated in writing ahead of time. In another film my son did, his face was all over the billboards as well as other publicity items, without his name appearing on the billboard credits. I discovered too late that this fell under *"producer's discretion."* Even when we inquired about it later, the studio would not give in because the consideration was not negotiated up front by the agent. Further, in the opening credits of this same movie, my son had what was called a *"shared card,"* or screen credit where one's name appears on the screen along with someone else's name instead of by itself.

My point is that it does not make sense to accept less than one can easily negotiate up front. By the same token, anything one fails to specify up front will most likely prove next to impossible to obtain later, regardless of how small, even if you are one of those people who knows how to charm your way around. Hollywood can prove a challenge to anyone's charm.

DAY PLAYER VS. PRINCIPAL PLAYER

One thing many agents will automatically negotiate up front is a guarantee that the client will work a minimum number of weeks. Since this clause ultimately adds more money to the agent's commission, it is understandable that the agent would want to include that in the contract, when possible. Besides, it is important not to sign up as a *"day player"* where one only gets paid for actual days worked, as opposed to a full week's pay for any portion of that week worked. *Principal players* who work any part of a week get paid for the entire week.

Once hired as a regular or principal player, as opposed to a day player, the studio will tie your child up for the entire shoot whether the child works every day or not. This means that the child will not be free to film a one day commercial, for instance, without the express approval of the studio because that item also falls under "producer's discretion." Under such circumstances it is, therefore, only fair that the child receive compensation for the time not available to work anywhere else.

SINGERS: DEMO SPEC AGREEMENTS

Under a Demo Spec Agreement, the producer gets paid after a record deal is signed. The most obvious advantage to the artist is that he or she does not have to come out of pocket to pay for studio time, which can be expensive, ranging anywhere from $35.00 an hour (for a four or eight track studio) up to $400.00 an hour (for a state of the art 48 track studio).

A Demo Spec Agreement gives the producer a chance to have his or her work presented to A&R people at record labels, along with an opportunity to have songs appear on the artist's album. A Demo Spec Agreement specifies how much the producer will get paid for each song, how many songs will appear on an album, and the number of producer points. For producers who own their own recording studios, it is easy for them to offer a demo spec agreement because they do not have to pay out of pocket to rent a recording studio. Such producers can be hard to come by, however, because everybody is in the business to make money and demos are a calculated risk at best. For example, A&R people may hear the demo and say: "Clearly you can sing, but I don't like the songs." There is no accounting for taste, which is why many producers are unwilling to take the risk of the artist getting a deal anyway, inspite of the fact that the record label did not like the producer's music or style. Which brings me to Production Contracts:

SINGERS: PRODUCTION COMPANY CONTRACTS

If possible, try to sign your child directly to a record label as opposed to a record label via a production company, which puts you under the control of the production company (who acts as a middle man) as opposed to the direction of the label. The exception would be if someone of the Quincy Jones, Jimmy Jam & Terry Lewis (of Janet Jackson Fame) or L. A. & Baby Face caliber wants to sign your child to their production companies. Producers of this stature usually have their own record labels, major distribution, and hit after hit to their credit as well as high profiles and major clout in the industry. Which means that they also have the money behind them to back up their artists.

Moreover, many giants in the record industry work with production companies because they save the label a lot of time. For example, the production company writes the material, produces the music, records the songs, and submits the finished product to the record label which saves the record label considerable time and expense. The label will either accept or reject the material. Since there is a tendency in the industry to use various producers on one album in order to get as many hit singles as possible, the record label may not use all or any of the music that the production company submits, especially if the album is produced entirely by one person or team. Therein lies the problem.

Contracts: Knowing What To Ask For Up Front

If your child is signed to a production company and that production company has signed to the record label, regardless of how much or how little work the production company actually does, your child's money goes directly to the production company who takes 50% off the top and then distributes what's left, AFTER production costs, to the artist. Which means that your child may never see a dime. Since the artist has no control over production costs, if one happens to sign with a money hungry or dishonest producer, the balance sheet can get written in such a way that production costs always exceed actual income. If that happens, one has no recourse through the record label because their contract is with the production company, NOT the artist. Therefore, when problems arise, the record label will tell you to work it out with the production company because they do not want to get caught in the middle.

The other problem with signing to a production company is the fact that trends are always changing in the record industry. Only a few big names hold strong year after year. If you happen to be signed to a production company who is no longer hot in the industry, has not produced any hits in a while, has developed a bad reputation with their artists or the record label, then there won't be a thing you can do except ride out the terms of the contract or pay dearly to buy yourself out of it.

Of course producers will urge you to sign a production company agreement because the contracts are a win-win situation for them. They protect the production company, allowing them 50% of your child's money, regardless; even if someone else produces all the songs and the production company does not end up with a single song on the album.

On the other hand, one may want to sign with a production company if the producer already has an independent label with major distribution, current hits, or have strong songs on albums with major artists or by "up and coming artists."

Sometimes an artist will sign to a production company that does not have its own record label to save the cost of paying for a demo or the trouble of shopping that demo to record labels since the production company handles it for him or her. However, this only works with strong songs or a producer who has current working relationships with major labels. If so, the producer has only to walk the artist through the door with a demo tape and negotiate the deal.

Keep in mind that producers currently working in the industry and doing well will not necessarily press an artist to sign to a production company because they have confidence that their music will find acceptance by whatever label ends up signing the artist they produced. On the other hand, a producer who has artists picked up by a record label that rejects the songs they produced will not want to take that risk. This type of producer will pressure the artist to sign a production company contract out of fear that the artist will make it and he or she won't.

To avoid this scenario, sign a Demo Spec Agreement ahead of time, which insures that the producer will get paid for time and effort expended once the artist signs to a record label, which is fair for both parties because they share the same risks. If, however, the producer is greedy or really insecure about his or her ability to write hit songs in the future, that will not be enough. Such producers will block the artists from getting a deal unless they sign to their production company, which takes 50%. I had this happen once with Salim. Our attorney and the producer's attorney had agreed to the terms of a Demo Spec Agreement before the producer walked Salim into two different labels on the strength of one song and Salim's ability to perform live. The song was awesome and Salim had done a great job in the studio. Both labels wanted to sign Salim. The producer got so excited he decided to go to a third label and start a bidding war over Salim, but not before putting pressure on me to sign Salim to his production company. I refused, inspite of the producer's loud protests, anger and manipulation, especially since we had gone into the deal with a different agreement. Moreover, I could not understand why the producer was willing to loose the deal completely when he was assured the prospect of working on Salim's album via the Demo Spec Agreement. He refused to do the deal except through his production company. We had to walk away from both offers.

Contracts: Knowing What To Ask For Up Front

Later, I found out that the reason the producer was so adamant about signing to his production company was because he had not written the song that Salim recorded. We met the producer who had actually written and composed the song. The former producer had simply engineered the song and added a couple of lines to the bridge so that he could get a percentage of the publishing. Therefore, what actually made this producer desperate was the fact that he had been unable to get any of his songs on the albums of several acts that he had produced and gotten signed to record labels. Salim simply met him at a time when he felt frustrated, desperate and insecure about his abilities.

I felt relieved over the fact that I followed my instincts and did not allow myself to sign with someone who could not live up to an agreement we had ahead of time. How could someone like that be trusted to handle your money? Remember, there are sharks everywhere. Always test the water before jumping in. And make sure you have a good entertainment attorney who knows how to revise your contract to insure that your child does not get shelved by the record label, that production costs have a cap on them and that the child receives all royalties from sale of records.

SINGERS: POINTS, MERCHANDISING AND PUBLISHING CONTRACTS

Typically, record labels leave a ten point spread available for negotiation with artists. Since ten is usually tops, it is reserved for hot prospects, or after an artist has proven himself or herself in the industry in terms of "money in the bank." New artists tend to receive between five to eight points. Remember that groups divide the points evenly among them. A solo artist gets to keep all the points. Basically a point is the equivalent of one percent of 100.

Bear in mind that contracts favor the record label. Not surprisingly, the label will try to keep all the merchandising and publishing they can get away with. In fact, in the much publicized case of New Kids On The Block, (who made more money off of merchandising than album sales) they signed away merchandising rights. Because of the publicity surrounding this case, it is now easier to share in merchandising.

The same goes for publishing, which allows a company to make money off a song for as long as the copyright exists (usually 75 years). Record companies used to negotiate hard and fast to keep all of the artist's publishing rights or to give up as little as possible. Now record companies are separating themselves from the music publishing business and allowing artists to own their publishing income. So be sure to request that publishing be excluded from the record contract so that you can seek a separate publishing deal if your child writes. Of course it matters not if the artist has no inclination or ability to write, but if the artist does, he or she could be signing away the most money the singer will ever make. In fact, when Motown was sold, Barry Gordy kept Jobet Publishing, which was worth infinitely more than the record company itself because of all the hit songs Motown had over the years that have been re-recorded by other artists over and again.

It's important to point out that you should also shop around for a good entertainment attorney who will not play both sides of the fence (i.e., some of them will claim to work for you when they are actually being paid more money by the other side to see that you do not get a fair deal). Interview your attorney carefully, check references and hire somebody who has an impeccable reputation in the business. Keep in mind that many attorneys will represent an artist on spec, taking five percent of the up front money from the record deal. That's the best deal.

DURATION OF MANAGEMENT CONTRACTS

Most managers prefer a three year contract because it compensates them for the time they have to put into developing a client's career. Each client comes to a manager at different stages of development, however. Therefore, if you already have an established track record (or have gotten work on your own) and come to the manager ready for shopping to an agent or record label, ask for a shorter contract.

ORAL CONTRACTS

In a court of law, verbal agreements or oral contracts with a manager or agent are just as binding as written ones, especially where money has exchanged hands or witnesses know of the arrangement. Once a client accepts the services of a manager or agent, he or she automatically engages the terms of a contract to pay for services rendered. Obtaining work through a manager's efforts without paying a commission amounts to theft. The manager can take the client to court to obtain the fee owed plus attorneys' fees in conjunction with compensatory or punitive damages to prevent a person from attempting the same thing with someone else.

Moreover, before deciding to act unethically, keep in mind that such actions will haunt you in this business, or in life for that matter. Taking of anyone's time, talents, contacts and efforts in your behalf and not paying for it, denies that person the right to earn a livelihood.

When I first began managing children I had oral agreements until I ran across too many parents who thought nothing of using my time, knowledge and expertise and later refused to pay a commission after their child gained work through an agent that I placed them with. Usually these were the parents who took up the most of my time.

CANCELING CONTRACTS

A minor can get out of any contract after a ninety day waiting period, provided the contract has not been approved and ratified by the court. In that case, the parent needs to prove that staying in the contract would be harmful or detrimental to the child's physical or emotional well being in order to get out of it.

SAG contracts (which are what franchised agents use) have a ninety day clause that allows one to cancel an agency contract after 90 days if the child has not worked at least ten full days during that period.

Moreover, in any contract, it does not hurt to request a thirty day notification period upon which one may cancel the contract. A confident, competent and capable manager will not be intimidated by such a request because all earnings accrued during the notification period are subject to commission.

Note that when you sign a contract with a manager most contracts state that all of your earnings are subject to a management fee, whether the manager obtains the work for you or not. If you have a problem with that clause, be sure to stipulate in the contract that the manager is only entitled to a percentage of the earnings received through that manager's efforts or contacts, not work the child obtains on his or her own.

WEIGH ALL OFFERS CAREFULLY

I have turned down contract offers that would have tied my client up for an extended time without adequate compensation. For example, one movie wanted my son for six months as a dancer. We passed up this offer because he prefers acting roles. If we had not done so we would have missed out on a much better movie role he received a month later, which we accepted.

Remember to keep a clear head when negotiating contracts. Usually, when your child gets an offer and your agent calls, both of you are excited. So much so that sometimes you overlook important details. Do not think that the production company isn't aware of this. They generally do not allow a lot of time for you to mull over the offer. And with good reason. This would allow you the extra time to permit the initial elation to sink in and common sense to surface. Therefore, at such times it helps to be able to think on your toes. If you are not that type of person, however, tell your agent that you will call back in fifteen minutes. Explain that you simply HAVE to discuss this with your spouse, manager, attorney or whoever. Take a moment to consider the points I have highlighted in this book along with any notes added from information gained along the way or through your attorney. Then call the agent back. In so doing, you will be able to adequately cover

Contracts: Knowing What To Ask For Up Front

all the bases, and perhaps come back with a counter-offer, or at least some intelligent options.

A wise poet once said that you only get what you expect or ask for from life. Therefore, if your expectations are low and you are satisfied to work with stars for free or at minimum wage then that's all you'll get. Several people have told me that they would work with some of the stars that my children worked with for free. Consider the following: we've done enough freebies in this business to know that if everyone else is in it to make a profit and you go into it for free, you won't like yourself very much in the end if you get nothing out of it for all the time you invested. After all, time is money and everyone has to put a certain dollar value on their time. Otherwise, you will find people lined up to waste your time and talent. Besides, why demean or diminish your child's talent when you can expend your energy in profitable and worthwhile pursuits that will make the child feel good? While my children do their share of free work, you can bet it is for a reputable cause or charity that I believe in.

Moreover, children have an inborn sense of self worth. Before reaching grade school they are already out of the dollar mentality and are thinking in terms of twenty's or hundreds. So, don't play your child's career cheap by short changing the youngster. Every time I decide to have my children perform at public events I evaluate the worth in terms of the type of charity and effort required. And the benefit must be mutual. If someone wants my child to give his or her time free, that person is simultaneously asking for my time as well (not to mention my family's time too). It, therefore, has to be worth it for all concerned before we will decide to get involved.

Once your child has reached a certain celebrity status you will have people coming out of the woodwork asking you to do something for nothing. Just make sure that when you do get involved with a charity that it is a legitimate one, and that it does not require more than one rehearsal and a performance. Also insure that your child will receive some type of acknowledgment for his or her efforts. Be sure to ask for what you want up front in writing.

POINTS TO PONDER

1. *SAG contracts leave many important items to the producer's discretion, which can be quite broad. Standard SAG contracts set the standard to go by. Everything is negotiated UP from there.*

2. *If you do not specifically ask for items or special considerations up front, in writing, you won't get them later. So don't accept any offer without first finding out about billing, screen credits, dressing rooms, director's chairs, etc. Otherwise you could end up with your face on the billboard with no credits; a honey wagon shared by everyone, and standing on location all day because a director's chair went unasked for.*

3. *If at all possible, stay away from production company contracts unless offered by a big name in the industry who has current hits, a good reputation, and a proven track record.*

4. *With contracts, remember that everything is negotiable. If you are not a good negotiator, or do not know what to ask for up front, get an attorney who will fight for your child to obtain the best options possible.*

5. *Unless the contract is ratified by the court, after 90 days a minor can break any contract. All he has to assert or prove is that fulfilling the terms would cause undue stress, strain or emotional injury.*

Chapter 23

SO, YOU'RE THINKING ABOUT CHANGING AGENTS?

The biggest problem in the actor/agent relationship is lack of communication. *-Martin Gage- THE GAGE GROUP (from "The L.A. Agent Book")*

As soon an actor develops a name or gets a lead role in a hit movie or television series that talent is usually snatched up the larger more prestigious agencies who wait in the wings. And with good reason. At that point the actor is no longer a risk, so naturally, everyone wants to share a piece of the pie. Keep in mind, however, that agents and managers who start the child out in the business deserve a certain amount of loyalty for the time and energy put into developing the child's career. Without that original push, the child would never have gotten a big break. So, if you are fortunate enough to find an agent or manager who's willing to work hard for your child, even during slow periods, keep that person. On the other hand, if you, as the parent, had to do a lot of pushing and prodding to get the agent to send your kid out, or if you and your manager bring in most of the leads, then that's another story. You should change agents as opposed to allowing the agent to capitalize off of your efforts.

The agent-client relationship is a partnership that begins with understanding the basic nature of an agent's job. For the most part, agents submit names or pictures and resumes of clients to casting directors based on listings from the Breakdown Service or through calls that come in directly to their office. Clients are then chosen according to their type, look or skill level. After submissions go out, the agent waits to hear which client, if any, is chosen for the audition or booking, then calls and notifies that client. At other times, certain agencies receive exclusive bookings from clients or casting agencies. In that instance the agent selects the actor or actress who best suits the breakdown and then phones in those names. Anything other than the above tends to fall under the "above and beyond category."

Since the client-agent relationship involves an agreement that both partners will do everything possible for their mutual success, at times actors have a right to expect agents to go above and beyond the requirements of their office if the situation calls for it.

Before deciding to change your child's current agent, based on information gathered from other parents, books and articles, determine what characterizes a good agent. Then formulate clearly in your mind those needs and expectations most important to you as a parent and communicate those feelings to your child's present agent. This conversation may clear up gray areas that your agent may not have known existed. Children's agent, Bob Preston, of Cunningham, Escott & Dipene defines a superior agent as someone, *"who's willing to work hard for his client, willing to take a risk on someone brand new, has a good rapport with casting directors and who's proven in terms of the kids he's developed in the past. It's also someone who's willing to convince a casting director to give his client a chance, when the kid may not be what the casting director had in mind initially."* (See Kyle Count's "Hollywood Reporter Article")

I would expand the definition of a superior agent to include someone who believes in the client enough to look for, or create opportunities where none exist (i.e., instead of waiting for job listings through the Breakdown Service). For example, an agent who takes time to access and evaluate the particular strengths of a client when nothing in that category has shown up for a while, then takes the initiative to call casting directors or producers directly to set up appointments for a general reading. For works in progress, these readings provide a jump start for the actor with projects that have not made it to the Breakdown Service yet. During such readings, the producer may see something special in an actor's performance, or simply take a liking to the performer that could eventually lead to creating a role for that actor in a new or existing show. The fact that an agent thought enough of the client to set up an appointment for a general reading with a new producer, director or casting director might impress the other person enough to take notice.

If someone from our agency goes out, they usually get it, because we push only on those things the client is right for. -Pat Amaral AMARAL TALENT AGENCY (K Callan, The "L.A. Agent Book")

Unfortunately, there are only a few children's agents who actually take the time or have the clout to package and promote their clients. Usually, the needs of the many outweigh the needs of the few. Often, it's all the agent can handle just to keep up with submissions on clients who fit the specifications requested from casting notices on the Breakdown Service.

REMEMBER TO DO YOUR PART TO HELP THE AGENT HELP YOU

Since most agents have their hands full just running the agency, clients need to work with the agent to develop their career. Meaning that one has an obligation to himself to be out there on his or her own mingling and selling himself in social settings as an actor. Chapter 19 of this book, titled "Slow Periods--Working Through Them" covers the aspect of creating work on your own. Any agent knows the importance of visibility for her client. As mentioned in Chapter 19, parents should encourage children to showcase their abilities in small community theaters, or weddings and private parties. Actors who cannot sing could combine their talents with those of musicians, singers and comedians to create entertaining little skits that friends, relatives and acquaintances truly appreciate. Such forums not only create new contacts, but establish a network that promotes name recognition.

Agents appreciate having an ambitious, hard working parent who creates opportunities to promote the child. And most of them are more than willing to come out and support your efforts. Depending on the agent, it can take several invitations before they will actually come to a performance. Get to know your agent and the type of social activities preferred. In that way one will automatically know what places and forms of entertainment would be exciting and appealing enough for the agent to want to give up evenings or weekends to attend. Remember, agents have more than one client. If they attended the performances of all of them, they would have no life. Initially, do not grow discouraged or disappointed if the agent is unable to make all of your functions.

Agents who do not come out to see their talent perform, should in the very least, review their work on videotape to keep abreast of that client's growth, diversity and ability to handle live audiences, the camera, etc. Moreover, when the agent cannot attend live shows, then make videotape available for the agent, and follow up to see if the agent took time to view the tape.

After doing your part in keeping your agent informed about the work your child obtains on his own, and your agent continues to show no interest, or is not motivated to follow your example of creating opportunities for the child, one should consider changing to an agent who has more time or interest, combined with a willingness to push for the child. Some agents only bother to meet or cater to the demands of those clients currently earning money. Select an agent who does not mind nurturing talent. Children's agent, Evelyn Schultz says, *"I love kids. It's fun to discover young talent, develop it and watch it grow. I think that's probably my greatest satisfaction as an agent."* (See Kyle Count's Hollywood Reporter article)

DOES YOUR AGENCY MAKE YOU FEEL LIKE A LITTLE FISH IN A BIG POND?

Many people come to small agencies looking for personalized attention as opposed to the impersonal feel of a large agency that offers more diverse opportunities. Certain personalities tend to fare better with the informality, openness, and accessibility of a small agency. Others need the more rapid pace and competitiveness of a larger agency. A mid-sized agency that offers the best of both worlds might prove a good compromise. Regardless of the agency size everyone needs an agent that not only makes them feel wanted, valued and respected as a client, but one who gets clients out on calls right for them.

Bonnie Ventis of JHR, works for a large, multi-service agency, yet feels the need to keep her client list manageable. She says, in Kyle Count's article: *"We don't take people just to take them on, and we don't allow dust to collect on anyone's picture. Jody (her partner) and I go through [our client list] several times a year. For whatever reasons -- maybe the chemistry between us and X person is not happening -- we will release them. On purpose, we've kept our client list incredibly small because we enjoy good communication with our clients."*

On the other hand, Bob Preston feels that having a large client base does not prevent him from giving his clients the attention they need. He feels that large client lists are *"a famous line that managers use, 'to get their clients to work with a smaller agency.* He points out that *"ICM and the William Morris Agency don't have just one client. They have hundreds, too. You've got to consider a talent agency like a grocery store. When you work in commercials, for instance, you've got to have your shelves stocked full of talent."* (See Kyle Counts' "Hollywood Reporter" article)

WHAT IF THE AGENT WON'T TAKE MY CALL?

Whether your agency rates as large, small or mid-sized, the most important question to answer involves accessibility. Can you get through to your agent when you need to? Is the agent accessible? If so, then the size of the agency really does not matter. Even a small agency, if under-staffed, can be too busy to talk to you when you call. John Kimble at TRIAD said: *"If your agent won't return your phone calls or have a meeting with you, you need another agent."* (K Callan, "The L.A. Agent Book")

Regarding phone calls to your agent, avoid nuisance calls. Frequent telephone calls to your agent cuts down on actual time that the agent can spend working for you. Phoning or dropping by briefly, once a week, will serve most purposes. Also, when calling the agent, keep your attitude positive, upbeat and constructive, unless you have a legitimate complaint about something that happened on an audition or a job. Do not burden your agent with unnecessary personal problems. Keep the agent informed regarding the following:

1. Car repairs with no rental car available. In such situations one may need to request a longer lead time for getting to auditions in a cab, on the bus, or with someone else;
2. Illness or family problems;
3. Vacations, or business out of town; no need to go into laborious details when you call, facts will sufficient.

PRACTICAL CONSIDERATIONS BEFORE CHANGING AGENTS

If you want to look for another agent after only a few weeks, most likely the problem lies with your impatience and unreasonable expectations, rather than the new agent. Not allowing a reasonable amount of time in which to make a go of the relationship with a new agent proves an injustice to both parties. Slow periods come and go regularly in show business, you may have signed up during one. Evelyn Schultz hit the nail on the head in Kyle Counts' article when she said that *"the client has to be able to trust that their agent is doing the best job possible for them."* If, however, you've honestly given the agent a reasonable opportunity to prove otherwise, only then should one begin looking for another agent.

The three reasons most frequently cited for wanting to change agents involve:

(1) Not going out on enough auditions;
(2) Not booking a job at all since signing with the agent; or
(3) The agent has not sent them out on any auditions at all.

As noted in the Chapter 10 titled "Teenagers," the agent's attitude about work available for teens is important. If an agent holds an innate belief that a child's career pretty much stands still between the ages of thirteen and sixteen, that agent will not actively seek work for your child. Instead, the parent will hear excuses. Even though work can slow down during this period because many adolescents become overweight, develop acne, or their features grow out of proportion to their face, this does not happen to all teens. Since one cannot change another person's innate belief system, in such a situation, changing agents would put the child back in business rather than waste time sitting out an agent's belief system for three years. It matters not that the same agent worked well for the child in previous years.

A parent's intrinsic belief system serves as a guide in making the decision to leave an agent. One reminder, however, SAG contracts do require staying with an agent for at least 120 days if the contract is not a renewal. One only has to stay ninety days on a renewal contract.

If, after carefully weighing the situation, you decide to cancel your agency contract, then send a certified letter to the agent stating that you're canceling under SAG guidelines that require an actor to work at least ten full days out of the preceding 90 day period. This applies to theatrical and commercial contracts. For commercial contracts only, if one has earned over a certain amount of money even though the performer has not worked the full ten days, the child will have to wait for the next 90 day cycle. Call SAG and find out the current cut-off amount. With theatrical contracts, the amount earned does not matter if the child has not worked for ten full days within the last 90 day cycle.

Send a copy of the cancellation letter to SAG so that they can note your new agent in their computers. Sometimes a casting director will try to locate a particular client who booked a job with them a while ago and will call SAG to contact that person through the agent. Of course they will first call the original agent you were with at the time of the booking. However, that agency may now have new people working for them who do not remember your child. If SAG has the new agent's listing they will give out your current agent's name and number to casting directors, producers or people searching for your child.

POINTS TO PONDER

1. *Before deciding to change agents, allow the agent sufficient time to make the relationship work. Sometimes the client signs with a new agent during a slow period.*

2. *Check in with your agent once a week via the phone or drop by the office if they have an open door policy. Anything more than that is too frequent.*

3. *Notify your agent of transportation, illness or vacations that might prevent you from going out on a call.*

4. *If the agent will not take your call, of if you discover your child has missed out on more than a few auditions for his or her age group or type, one should think about looking for a new agent.*

5. *Choose an agent who has an open door policy, believes in his or her clients and works hard for them. Get recommendations from other actors who have good relationships with their agent.*

Chapter 24

YES, RACISM IS ALIVE AND WELL

You might have had an opportunity to do a great role in one picture, but that would be the end of it. Whereas, on the other side of the coin, if you had been a white actor or actress and you had done such a role (i.e., "To Kill A Mockingbird"), that could be the start of your career. They'd be shopping around for projects to take advantage of your talent." -Brock Peters SAG's 199 Achievement Award Winner (quoted from "Screen Actor" Summer 1991, Vol.30, No. 1, The Screen Actors Guild)

Racism appears destined to follow us well into the twenty first century. Even though children, in their innocence, hold the key to locking up and abolishing ideas that no longer serve us, we as adults, rarely take time to learn from them. Moreover, children do not readily recognize racism when confronted by it, nor do they ever really become comfortable with a concept that defies rationalization, though they many end up adopting the ideas of their parents. Even as children develop into good little racists, in the silence of their own understanding, something deep inside of them knows better. The pettiness of narrow minds that carefully disguise self hatred as racism does not escape the notice of children who innately know, or have been taught the truth: that all races sprang from one race; and no man can hate another they do not even know, without first loathing or fearing something within himself.

Marian Wright Edelman in her wonderful book "The Measure of Our Success" (Beacon Press) admonishes us not to *"tell, laugh at, or in any way acquiesce to racial, ethnic, religious, or gender jokes or to any practices intended to demean rather than enhance another human being."* She instructs her children to *"walk away from them. Stare them down. Make them unacceptable in your homes, religious congregations, and clubs."* Edelman also encourages us to make a deliberate effort *"through daily moral consciousness [to] counter the proliferating voices of racial and ethnic and religious division that are gaining respectability over the land ... Let's face up to rather than ignore our growing racial problems, which are America's historical and future Achilles' heel."*

The biggest factor that enables the continued acceptance and spread of racism is the denial we practice when confronted with it. At times we are so shocked by it's covert and often overt tones, we do not want to accept it at face value. Unfortunately, pretending that racism is actually something else or simply calling it by another name only enables those who practice it to continue doing so unchallenged.

TOO APATHETIC TO DO ANYTHING

As long as enough minorities willingly portray limited, one dimensional characters that continue to denigrate ethnic races, executives in the board room will not come up with anything better, in particular, if no one complains or refuses to eat from the menu served. As a result, minorities share mutual blame and responsibility for the type of roles created and offered up to Ethnic Americans in show business. Moreover, many ethnics in Hollywood who make it big often find it easy to overlook wrong treatment or to remove themselves from the situation, particularly in lieu of the fact that once a minority miraculously reaches celebrity status, that person becomes green, the color of money. At which point, the celebrity no longer has to worry about being treated poorly due to race because fans will overlook matters of race, creed or color.

Even though African Americans are gaining ground in television and film, Hispanics and Asians still have a ways to go to make up for the disparity in prime time programming. One has to look hard to find even one or two Asian or Hispanic's guest starring on prime time network television. Moreover, rarely is more than one prime time show picked up at a time with an Asian or Hispanic in a starring role. Surely this is not simply a figment of my imagination. And I do hope that I am not the only one who takes note of such things. Or am I?

To add insult to injury it was almost shameful the way the Academy Association totally over looked the wealth of brilliant Asian actors and cogent screen-writing displayed in the feature film "The Joy Luck Club." Not only did the movie reflect a positive and important message for women in general, but it contained the most impressive caucus of Asian talent to come across the big screen in recent years. Even though years earlier the Academy willfully ignored the slew of nominations Steven Spielberg received for Alice Walker's Pulitzer winning novel "The Color Purple," the film *was* nominated. Whereas, "The Joy Luck Club," in spite of it's critical acclaim and rave reviews, did not receive a single nomination. The worst part, however, was the fact that not one group or high profile minority opened their mouths or pulled out their pens in protest; a clear indication of the state of denial and apathy that ethnics are in today.

To further illustrate my point: When I first heard that the Governor was supporting abolishment of Affirmative Action in California, I thought to myself: "Women, homosexuals, and each minority ethnic group will finally come together on this issue like they did in the 60's against segregation." I grew concerned, however, when I assigned my college English students to write a paper on Affirmative Action and more than half of them did not know what it was, while the majority of the other half was against it, point blank. The fact that those against it were women or minorities moved me from concern to alarm. At that point I knew that the state would prevail in getting Affirmative Action abolished. Anytime society gets to a critical mass where college students can't find it within themselves to rally against deep societal ills like discrimination or racism, then we're headed for real trouble and unrest. After all, if inequity was not engrained within the fabric of our culture we would not have needed Affirmative Action in the first place to protect the rights of minorities. Of even greater concern is the lack of concern on the part of minorities who either think they are insulated from discrimination, or who feel powerless to protect themselves from it. There appears to be no happy medium.

With the abolishment of Affirmative Action in the State of California college system, it should be interesting to see what happens to enrollment based on grade point average and entrance exams in the years to come. Since Asians consistently tend to score higher than any other group academically, whites might end up in the minority, unless of course, the school decides to lower its standards to increase white enrollment. But then again, couldn't that be viewed as discrimination?

TWO SHADES TOO LIGHT OR TWO SHADES TOO DARK

The anomaly of racially mixed children, who catch flack from both ends, serves as both a testament and a contradiction. How well I know. The fact that my two children book any jobs at all, in spite of the fact that they are either two shades too light or two shades too dark, serves as an affirmation in and of itself. In reality, very few roles are open for my son to actually audition for. We have to look for parts that could be played by any ethnicity (i.e. orphans, or children's stories that do not have adults in them). Or for roles that require his specialties like singing, dancing, or martial arts, which could be played by any ethnicity.

I've often discussed the big screen void of ethnic teenage male heart throbs with the agents I work with. The fact that so few wholesome, big screen roles are available or written for handsome and intelligent minority teenager boys does not mean that no need exists. Hollywood continues to covet the role of teen heart throb (on the big screen) as white domain. The roles available are, for the most part, negative, stereotypical, or hard-core street thug types.

The sad part is that this conspiracy continues to persist through the silence acquiescence of minority races.

When Salim was cast as himself on NBC's Saturday morning teen show "Saved By The Bell" I complimented the producers and writers for their vision and courage. One of the writers did remind me, however, that they were worried that Salim was too nice looking for the role. Thank goodness the Executive Producer did not concern himself with that.

It was also fortunate for Salim and others like him, that the music industry has always had an open door policy towards attractive young ethnic males, which is why I encouraged Salim to pursue singing along with his acting career. Interestingly enough, it was not surprising that a well known Senator got so fired up against rap music -- too many young whites were idolizing black gangster rappers!

Ironically, my daughter, Crystal, who looks just like Salim, except for her hazel eyes, does not have as hard a time with her looks as he does. Of course she still cannot land roles where a real ethnic look is called for, but still, the situation is not as bad for her as Salim. Traditionally, the ethnic female received better treatment and press than ethnic males in American society. Aided by historical white propaganda, ethnic males became re-created in the minds of white America as a threat to white females, no doubt as a cover up for white male guilt over taking ethnic females as trophies for themselves. Explaining why, for the most part, my daughter's exotic looks act as an asset to her, while my son's serve primarily as a hindrance, particularly after the age of ten. Regrettably, the onset of puberty in ethnic males tends to incite white fear.

TIMES, THEY ARE A CHANGIN'

According to Nina J. Easton in the May 3, 1991 issue of "Los Angeles Times," in an article titled: "New Black Films, New Insights," things were looking up for African American actors in the movie business with twenty black films released in 1991. Although the numbers tend to fluctuate each year since '91, African American films do sell, which helps these figures hold steady. Still, such numbers have to be put into perspective when one considers that there were over 400 films released that year. Admittedly, it is a lot better than when Salim was seven years old. There were none. And when he landed the role of Danny in "Ghost Dad," a collective sigh of relief was released because it had been years since a black film had been shot. Unfortunately, Asians and Hispanics have a lot of ground to make up since they continue to be under-represented on the big screen with only one or two major features released during a good year.

RACISM WITHIN RACES

For as much as it wounds me to witness it, and as much as I hate to admit its sad existence, I am probably more troubled by the racism that African Americans have against each other over skin color, than the other kind, because it is so insidious, divisive, and destructive. More often than not, there is a strong, underlying resentment of racially mixed African American's by those with darker skin. This practice might defy explanation if one were not familiar with the history of slavery in America (more on that later). Further, the entire concept would be laughable were it not so serious, especially since African Americans come in all colors. Essentially, the one drop rule (i.e., that one drop of black blood makes you black) means that most of white America would have to be reclassified as African American if one bothered to research family trees to dig up the dark skinned relative hidden or buried underneath.

This bias against light skinned African Americans trickles down indirectly to Caucasians who readily cash in on the benefits of divisiveness (i.e., minorities can't get ahead while fighting among themselves). One sees reflections of the problem in the insignificant number of light skinned African Americans on television and film. Especially light skinned Black males. Essentially, racially mixed features do not fit the stereotypical image of African American men. These standards were set with the knowing complicity of both races denying the existence of mulattos.

Of particular note is that the popularity of dark skinned vs. light skinned African American entertainers in Hollywood seems to be cyclical, coming and going as if it happens to be something that can be changed, like a new fall outfit. Why not, in t.v. and film, regularly reflect the variety of skin tones that exist within all races, not just African Americans?

The mere fact that African Americans continue to make distinctions among themselves (and draw lines within the race based on color) is a direct result of the fact that many influential African Americans continue to perpetuate outdated ideas that create disharmony and destruction among the race.

The publication of an article by a popular black magazine questioning whether the children of interracial marriages are black or white, illustrates my point perfectly. The article accused biracial actors and actresses in Hollywood of down-playing or denying their black roots. At the same time, a high profile African American authority on race relations stated in that article that biracial people resented their blackness, preferring to be identified as something other than black, such as Greek or Italian. This authority further proclaimed that biracial people did not like, or were ashamed of, the African American half of themselves.

As I read these quotes I could not help but wonder who these people were that the writer of the magazine article and the authority on race relations referred to. All of the mixed people listed in that magazine article spoke about the positive advantages of being from two different cultures, or of embracing all their cultures. In fact, Jennifer Beals, from the movie "Flashdance" was accused in that article of denying her mixed racial identity. I did some research and found a feature article published in *The Houston Post* on August 28, 1985 wherein biracial actress Jennifer Beals states: *"So many Americans are of mixed backgrounds, and it means they don't quite belong to either cultures. But they belong to America as Americans."* I hardly see a denial of her Black heritage in that statement. That same article also referenced Beals having a Black father. Moreover, Beals explained how being mixed made her feel unable to fit in anywhere, only on the "periphery" of society. She added that she feels (and infact is) no more Caucasian than African American, explaining why she chose to mark "other" on her application to Yale University. From the way I see it, the choice of "other" is the act of embracing all that mixed raced people are as opposed to a denial.

Moreover, having founded an organization for Biracial Children with memberships from around the country, my interviews and research did not turn up a single mixed child who was hesitant to tell others that they were half African American. In fact, I could not believe it when the Anglo interviewer of a television talk show we appeared on asked two of the children in my organization why they chose to identify as black when they could so easily pass for white. In light of the facts, I felt the same disbelief when I read the aforementioned magazine article, accusing mixed actors and actresses of denying their black side.

Children of a mixed marriage opting to refer to themselves as "biracial", "mixed", "other", or "Omni-racial", as Rae Dawn Chong calls herself, (November 6, 1985 issue of *The Houston Post*) is not a denial or rejection of their black blood, but a simple acknowledgment of all that they are. Frankly, I find no fault in Jennifer's willingness to embrace herself as an "American"; as well as Rae Dawn Chong's ability to relate to people of all races as *"a gift only a multiracial person has."* In fact I perceive their views as much more progressive or enlightened than the narrow, biased and unsubstantiated notions of the authority on race relations in the article mentioned above. In fact, such articles only serve to further divide the African American community along the unnecessary, yet ever present, color line.

In fact, another article, in a different African American magazine, also explored the issue of skin color. This magazine was owned by the same company previously mentioned and, not surprisingly, printed a continuation of the light skin/dark skin divisiveness among African Americans. The story proudly pointed out the predominance of darker-skinned role models, international power models, and dark skinned campus queens as the norm, hailing this as a great mile stone. The article noted that a few decades ago, it was all but impossible to elect a darker-skinned college queen. The article also went on to bemoan the fact that African American couples expressed an overwhelming preference for light-complexioned or mixed-race babies for adoption.

Although African American publications perform an important service to the black community by profiling and publicizing the accomplishments of black people, such publications have an innate responsibility to their readership to be unbiased and thorough when presenting research material. Particularly since the written word has the power to either persuade one to see all sides of an issue and move on to a more open, enlightened perspective; or, to keep the public mired within the same narrow frame of reference, leaving no hope of overcoming disharmony between or within the races.

In respect to the foregoing, the underlying reason for the resentment of light-skinned blacks was indicated in a poll administered by the same magazine article mentioned above. This poll reflected that there was clear support for the position that preferential treatment was given to light skinned blacks by whites in America. What the article did not explain to the reader is that this concept is grounded in slavery, and has no place in today's society. Particularly in light of the fact that as soon as the racial identity of a light skinned black is established, whites automatically switch to treating them the same as they would other African Americans. Since it is difficult for someone on the outside looking in to accurately perceive a situation; for the most part, only those light skinned blacks who have actually experienced this shift can attest to its reality and validity, thus rendering this "perceived" preferential treatment conditional and tenuous at best.

In Hollywood, African American directors appear to be divided along the dark skin/light skin color line. Debbie Allen and Spike Lee represent notable positive exceptions. If one reviews the productions they direct, it is easy to find a wide variety of African American skin tones.

On the other hand, Black director, Bill Dukes felt an obvious need to explain his blatant lack of light skinned Blacks in his movie "A Rage in Harlem." The movie had a large cast with huge ballroom and night club scenes filled with dark skinned blacks. With the considerable influence that mulattos had during the Harlem Renaissance it struck me as oddly out of character to have to look hard in order to find only one light skinned black in the whole room.

Duke explained that he consciously cast Robin Givens' lover (played by actor Badja Djola) as a tall, dark-skinned man with the kind of looks that *"scare most white people."* Further, Duke added: *"I show he can love people and people can love him."*(*Los Angeles Times*, May 3, 1991, Nina J. Easton, "New Black Films, New Insights").

Duke's point is well taken and no doubt Hollywood needs to see African American men beyond the mythical boundaries created for them. I simply see no reason why the point has to be made at the expense of fellow blacks who happen to be fairer of skin.

What we need is more minorities on television and the big screen PERIOD, no matter what their skin tone. And an end to discrimination and racism among the races as well as within the races. It is past time for African Americans to discard mental remnants held onto since the abolition of slavery.

It is important to know and understand the historical nature of traditions that were created and perpetuated during slavery and later accepted without question by succeeding generations who did not stop to examine their significance or origin. It reminds me of the following story: A mother was questioned by her young daughter as to why she always cut off the leg of the ham at Thanksgiving and threw it away. The mother told her little girl that she did it that way because that's what her mother did. So the little girl when to her grandmother and asked why she cut off the leg of the ham and threw it away. The grandmother repeated the same answer. So the little girl went to her great-grandmother, who was sitting in her rocker, and asked why she always cut off the leg of the ham and threw it away. The great-grandmother chuckled and said: "I cut off the leg because I didn't have a pan big enough to fit the whole ham in and couldn't afford to buy another one." The moral of this story is that sometimes we need to stop and question traditions, especially when they make no obvious sense.

After one recognizes that certain intra-racial beliefs are nothing more than false concepts created during slavery to justify its existence, only then can they can be laid to rest. Especially when one sees that certain concepts were designed to perpetuate a system designed to feed upon and destroy others in order to exist. This included whites enslaving their own blood (i.e. the offspring of slave-master relationships), all in the name of profit, since the more slaves a master owned the more the plantation was worth. So what if the master happened to father some of them?

If you truly wished to find out what is best for the country you would listen more to those who oppose you than to those who try to please you. -Isocrates, Athenian Orator

African Americans today bear reminding that jealousy, enmity and conflict arose between dark skinned and light skinned blacks because of the seemingly preferential treatment house slaves received over field hands. Yet when one takes into consideration that many of the house slaves were in actuality the bastard sons and daughters of the master, can one really find favoritism in such a weak gesture? Further, need one wonder why those related by blood might receive such token preferential treatment?

Moreover, the question remains: how special was this treatment, if one stayed a slave, forced to serve and clean up after half brothers and sisters? Of course, at times, benevolent masters made exceptions. In particular, the illegitimate slave offspring of President Thomas Jefferson who received education and freedom. The majority of house servants, however, rarely received an education, let alone a chance at freedom. Dark skinned Blacks might also ask themselves: what is so privileged about being born into a society where neither race accepts racially mixed people unconditionally for who they are?

The truth is, no valid reason exists today or tomorrow for enmity between blacks based on skin tone. In fact, there never was. When one considers the history of why and how blacks became divided among the color line, it hardly seems intelligent to dignify perpetuating such denigration.

By no means am I implying that interracial strife or racism within the race is endemic to Blacks. My husband used to manage a large number of Asians on his job. He had Koreans, Japanese,

Chinese and Vietnamese who have to work together on projects. Most of them broke off into ethnic cliques and complained about each other. For example, if my husband hired a Chinese supervisor, the Vietnamese, Japanese and Koreans felt that they were being discriminated against by the Chinese who gave them more difficult tasks to do while the Chinese received the easiest work, and vice versa. Many times my husband had to mediate and see to it that the work was distributed fairly.

It is past time for Americans to move beyond divisions over skin tone, race or creed. Until every race begins to appreciate themselves as unique and worthwhile individuals, acceptance of and by those who hail from different cultures, religions and walks of life cannot become a reality. We will remain a divided nation. And we all know that a house divided against itself cannot stand for long on its own. Marian Wright Edelman, eloquently summed up the urgency of our need for unity when she said that, *"young white people who have been raised to feel entitled to leadership by accident of birth need to be reminded that the world they face is already two-thirds nonwhite and poor and that our nation is every day becoming a mosaic of greater diversity ... As our fate becomes more and more intertwined with that of non-English speaking people of color ... personal, economic and world survival will depend on awareness of and respect for other races and cultures."* That same concept applies to respect for each other within the race.

In conclusion, a city with the ethnic diversity of Los Angeles has an obligation to honestly reflect that truth through television, which has the single most significant impact on the lives of Americans. Children who watch television each day come to believe that what they see is an accurate reflection of the racial makeup of their country. What message then, does that send out to the millions of Hispanic, Asian, Native American and African American children who have to diligently search, or wait for certain days of the week to find someone who looks like them on prime time t.v.? It's an invalidation of their own uniqueness and significance. Is that the subliminal message Hollywood wants to send ethnic children -- that they are unimportant, or worse yet, invisible?

POINTS TO PONDER

1. *Racism is alive and well in Hollywood.*

2. *As long as minorities continue to accept and play stereotypical roles that denigrate themselves, Hollywood will continue to serve what they know will be eaten up.*

3. *African Americans, Hispanics and Asians have to split among themselves the approximate 12% of roles made available to minorities in the business. Hollywood still has a long way to go in terms of offering up to the public a realistic portrait of the ethnic diversities of our cities.*

4. *For African Americans, racism within the race only supports racism outside of the race. There is no reason to perpetuate a divisive mentality that developed during slavery between dark-skinned blacks and mulattos.*

5. *The blatant discrimination of light skinned Blacks is a validation of Hollywood's unwillingness to let go of stereotypes and finally acknowledge the existence of mixed race people.*

Chapter 25

HOLLYWOOD CASTE SYSTEMS

A radical is one who speaks the truth.
-Charles A. Lindbergh, Sr.

DISREGARD FOR MOTHERS ON THE SET

Parents are the only non-paid entities on the set whose presence is required. As a result of historic umbrage against stage moms, carried over from the old studio era, disregard for mothers on the set still runs rampant. For the most part mothers are expected to be seen and not heard, to relinquish parental authority to the director or assistant director, and to act as if her child belongs to the studio. For example, a mother may be told not to talk to or touch her child's clothing or hair while the child is on the set, even though hair and wardrobe personnel often fail to do their job. At other times, the mother may be told that there is not enough room for her on the set. At this point the mother will be asked to leave which violates SAG rules that provide for a parent or guardian to be within sight or sound of the child at all times. Even under crowded conditions the parent still has the right to be within hearing of her child.

Ironically, in general, stage fathers are not treated with the same disregard. For instance, when my husband joins me on the set he is greeted with automatic respect by the crew. Moreover, when I send him on the set alone he often receives preferential treatment, as opposed to the casual inattention and neglect that awaits most stage moms who are usually ushered off to the **green room** or dressing room the instant they enter the set.

There have been many times when I could not help but feel the sting of a system that stigmatizes parents for "living" off of their child, while making it virtually impossible for that parent to work and have a child on the set. Especially when a studio teacher is provided who does not have to teach anyone but your child. Certainly that is a far cry from having to teach 30 or more children all day. Furthermore, I see no difference in leaving a child at school all day with the teacher, as opposed to leaving him or her on the set with the teacher hired to protect the child's welfare. In addition, while regular teachers deal with a high student-to-teacher ratio everyday, the studio teacher can bring in help if he or she has more than ten children on the set. In actuality, the odds are much more favorable for a child on the set than in a regular classroom setting.

It bewilders me as to why parents in this country, (especially L.A. and N.Y.) have not gotten together and done something about the way parents are treated on the set and the fact that they lose money by being there. From what I can see, far too many parents are too grateful for their child being "the chosen one" to do anything that will jeopardize that position, even if it means dealing with unfair or arbitrary rules that impose a financial hardship or burden. I think it is past time for parents to abandon this attitude of gratitude that sets them and their children up for misuse of power.

Even if one comes to terms with the issue of race and gender discrimination in Hollywood, the problem of caste systems crop up. These have no color lines. They are based upon your clout, prestige, or lack thereof as an actor. In effect, a pecking order takes place on sets.

First and foremost, everyone caters to the star of the show. He, of course, receives preferential treatment; from the largest dressing room, to his own personal wardrobe and makeup person. Not to mention private studio teacher.

The next in line is the co-star, who garners a measure of respect and attention from the crew, meted out in strict accordance with the actor's current status, number and type of acting credits, and current salary. (Somehow, salaries are the first bits of information that go public. Contracts are signed, filed and on record with the Screen Actors Guild). Plus, quite a few people on the set have access to this information, so word gets around easier than one would imagine.

Following the co-stars are actors with principal speaking roles (anywhere from one scene to several). These people receive a measure of respect, but that all depends on the decided graciousness of crew members. At times, crew members (in particular hair and make up or wardrobe personnel) take vicarious delight in meting out the merits of this caste system; reserving service or favors strictly for those in the upper echelon. This type of caste system becomes clearly evident to new arrivals on the set for guest spots; in particular actors whose faces have not yet become household names. Let me explain. On one popular television show where my son made a guest appearance, the wardrobe person refused to iron his shirt, exclaiming, in a haughty manner, that he did not iron for extras. When we told him that Salim was a featured guest, he offered a quick apology and ironed the shirt.

That incident made a lasting impression on me. It is not easy to forget the denigrating tone of voice this wardrobe person used in the presence of my child. K Callan, in "The L.A. Agent Book," offered some pretty sound advice on how to internalize such situations. She said: *"If you are employed in the business in any visible way, people are usually nice to you and validate your existence. If you are not, the lack of respect is appalling. Keep your wits about you and this type of treatment (though never welcome) can help you keep perspective. I am the same individual when I'm out of work as I am when I am working."*

EXTRAS, YOUR VOICE DESERVES TO BE HEARD

On most sets extras are crowded together into the same dressing room or honey wagon and forced to eat from segregated snack tables away from the rest of the actors. Naturally the best food remains reserved for those with speaking lines. This separate table of inferior food for extras is mindful of the old segregated "White Only" signs.

On one television set where my son worked, I was shocked to see a tiny table with a metal canteen of water and a canteen of kool-aid set up with a sign saying "EXTRAS ONLY." Not far away, stood several large tables with every conceivable fruit, vegetable, pastry, drink or snack. Extras were not allowed to eat from those tables.

And once, on a made for television movie set where my son worked, there were two catering trucks set up on location. Extras had to pay for their breakfast from a limited menu, while the cast and crew got theirs free. Moreover, a big mean looking biker type stood guard over the main catering truck. If an extra or someone off of the street came by, his job was to chase them off. Amazingly few complain and the few who do fail to do so to the appropriate people who can do something about the situation.

The only thing necessary for the triumph of evil is for good men to do nothing. -Edmund Burke

My observations on the treatment of extras in this business lead me to conclude that anyone planning on becoming an actor should work in that capacity just once. This experience will quickly open ones eyes to an antiquated system resurrected from the Middle Ages that allows flagrant disregard for human dignity. After working as an extra more than likely, an individual will discover that once is enough.

Unless stars and actors with clout or influence speak out against such tasteless conduct, or until extras band together, demanding that they receive the same food and treatment as the rest of the crew, demeaning caste systems will continue to flourish right along side the glitter and glamour that is Hollywood.

I doubt that any of us would stay for dinner if forced to eat inferior food in the back kitchen while our more privileged guests ate the finest food served on china in the dining room. If we would not put up with such nonsense in our homes, why tolerate it on movie sets?

Moreover, if we discard race discrimination only to embrace social and caste distinctions, how can we ever come to recognize that common thread of humanity that links all of us together?

POINTS TO PONDER

1. On the set, for the most part, extras and mothers are treated like second class citizens.

2. In many instances extras are not even allowed to eat the same food or from the same snack table as the crew and regular cast.

2. Moreover, the cast and crew tend to look down on extras.

3. Until actors, and stars in particular, speak out or take a stand against the shameful caste system that still exhists on Hollywood sets, demanding that extras eat and drink the same food as everyone else, this denigrating system will continue to flourish.

ROZ STEVENSON, SR. PUBLICIST
UNIVERSAL PICTURES HOLLYWOOD
Reveals Valuable Insights on Publicity For Children In Film.

As a senior publicist at Universal Pictures, Roz Stevenson has worked successfully with many children and teens as well as the young performer's parents, managers, agents and publicists. Some of the children's films that Roz has handled the publicity campaigns on include "Beethoven," Heart and Souls," "Matinee," "Problem Child 1 and 2," "Kindergarden Cop," "Ghost Dad," "Crooklyn," "The Flintstones," and "The Little Rascals."

A good relationship with the publicist on a film is important. The publicist's interaction with the parent and performer can effect how well the child does throughout the publicity campaign of a project. The publicist will want all publicity efforts to go through her, and this may bother some parents. However, the publicist does this because she is held accountable by the studio for all media exposure the film receives. What she needs most from the parent is help in easing the performer's anxiety about interviews and television appearances. The most valuable help a parent can give a child is to set a positive tone and be supportive of the child's efforts.

During the taped publicity interview, the publicist will normally want the child to act as natural as possible. If a parent openly criticizes something the child says, this can make the child uneasy with interviews and damage future publicity efforts. The publicist usually prefers that the parent to be within earshot but out of sight of the child. This prevents the child from looking to the parent for approval, which distracts from the success of the interview.

Another common problem arises when a child is part of an ensemble cast. Many times a parent feels concerned that her child is not getting the same media attention as other cast members. These concerns should be taken directly to the publicist in private without the child. Keep in mind that a publicist's choice of which actor to use for a particular interview is based on several variables: the child's role in the film, age, and ability to speak concisely and clearly about himself or herself and the role. Many times a child, who is an excellent performer may be very uncomfortable in interview situations.

After a film is completed the parent should be in touch with the studio publicity department and keep the department abreast of the child's new projects or activities which may be helpful in promoting him or her in the film. The publicity department does not mind parents inquiring about the publicity campaign. However, the studio does have to be careful about parents working with the press on their own. The main concern involves having information go out incorrectly and unprofessionally. Also, if the performer is in a film with a major star, that star may have legal approval over any art containing his or her likeness. As a result, the studio has an obligation to protect those rights. This is why when art is approved for the purpose of publicity, the studio prefers to be responsible for its placement.

Soon after production is completed parents should set an appointment to pick out photos of studio approved art. Parents can make selections for personal use, but it is not wise to tell the studio that you want to do your own publicity. Also available at this time are the preliminary production notes. These notes provide important written information, detailing correct facts regarding the production, filmmakers and cast.

The publicity staff should welcome inquiries about the publicity campaign. If you do not receive cooperation from one member of the staff feel free to go to someone in a higher position. A parent should ask if the publicity will involve coverage in the following types of publications; children's, educational, teen and parenting magazines. Other questions parents might ask are: Will ethnic press be serviced? Are there plans for fashion layouts? Will press and promotion activities involve the child?

Closer to the time of the film's release a full press kit with black and white and color selections will be available to the parent. At this time the parent may also want to ask for clips (footage) of the child from the film. If the scene that the parent wants is not on the prepared clip reel, the parent can request the specific scene at no cost prior to the release of the film. However, a couple of months after the film's release clips are difficult to get and may incur cost. Keep in mind that if you don't ask for these items, no one will offer them. And remember, when asking for film clips, it's a good idea to request the master on Beta or 3/4" because of broadcast quality. Moreover, duplication copies on to VHS will be sharper from Beta or 3/4." Copies taken directly from VHS tend to lose their sharpness. Obtaining videotape of your child is valuable for putting together a product reel for future presentations.

If a parent feels their child has reached a certain level in his or her career, she should consider hiring a professional entertainment publicist. For referrals ask your agent, manager or the parents of other child actors who have publicists. They can help you find someone who is affordable and competent enough to sell the child to the right print media, radio and television shows. The fee for a professional publicist can start as low as $600.00 a month, if the parent shops around. Of course many parents question the high cost of publicity because they cannot always see a tangible value in the work that a publicist does, unless the child actually book jobs as a direct result of publicity appearances or media coverage. However, parents should keep in mind that it takes at least six months to develop a campaign for a new client. This process entails numerous phone calls, pictures and mailings in order to obtain placement for new talent. Even with all the work involved on the part of the publicist, many still question why they should pay a publicist. Few appreciate the effort it takes for a publicist to get a new face out there.

Moreover, many parents are unaware that a publicist nurtures relationships with members of the press. A good publicist can sell the performer more effectively since the publicist is in constant contact with the media and knows, for instance, when theme stories are being done that may be the perfect publicity vehicle for an actor. Publicists also know of events, award shows, premiers and charities where the performer may gain good exposure. Legitimate, high profile organizations also contact publicity firms, looking to use their clientele for certain events. Overall, hiring a reputable publicist is the best investment in avoiding shoddy and unethical hustlers who tend to prey on budding performers.

Chapter 26

PUBLICITY AND PUBLIC RELATIONS

"Without publicity a terrible things happens: Nothing" - Mike Hughs, Publicity Express (From "The Zen of Hype" by Raleigh Pinskey)

Parents should be aware that for an up and coming child actor, obstacles can and do present themselves in the promotions department. The information outlined above represents the best possible scenerio, which can happen for some children. However, television and movie studios generally reserve their publicity efforts almost exclusively on behalf of the star of the show. Parents that I interviewed revealed lack of support or cooperation when they attempted to obtain press kits or publicity material to promote a child on a new television series or film. Frequently, attempts to promote a child's part in a movie or television series is blocked completely by the television or film studio; met with lack of cooperation and support; or the publicity materials delayed for so long that they become worthless by the time the parent receives the press kit. Part of the problem resides with the negative stage mom image discussed in earlier chapters of this book. Another publicist that I spoke with suggested that parents might stand a better chance of obtaining press materials from a studio publicity department if the request came from the child's agent, manager, or a hired publicist. This suggestion amounts to a direct admission of the negative bias against stage moms.

Keep in mind that if your child is a regular on a television series or a co-star in a feature film, one needs publicity photos (with the studio logo, or the television logo on the picture) and a press release on company letterhead in order to generate publicity. Without either of these essential items one cannot even consider obtaining magazine, newspaper, or television coverage. Face it, networks and print media cannot afford to publicize anything not authenticated by company logo or letterhead. The Catch 22 is that some studios or television shows will not release publicity photos or press releases to co-stars in a timely enough fashion for them to serve any useful purpose other than a scrapbook.

For example, most teen magazines require at least a three to four month lead time for a story to go to press. Since the publicity department of movie studios sometimes will not release material to co-stars until a few weeks before the film is released, magazine coverage becomes a moot issue. As you know, timing is everything. In addition, a feature article on a new television series is timed for release right before the series airs, not three months after the show's debut. Who wants to cover old news?

Naturally, the novice automatically assumes that any and all publicity would be welcome because of the obvious fact that it promotes the movie or television show, or adds to the overall viewing audience. True. However, those in power sometimes find themselves caught up in a caste system that sacrifices the good of the many for the needs of the few (i.e., the star). Therefore, publicity that takes attention or focus away from the star may not meet with support or approval unless the star feels comfortable with the move. Remember, children and pets are not the favored choice of some adult stars because of the age old fear that the child will upstage the older actor.

Now that children are becoming profitable as well as popular in Hollywood, television and studio executives are beginning to take chances on child co-stars that they think have the potential to make it big. Occasionally they will promote the child right along with the star of the show. While such situations are ideal, do not automatically expect them because they are not yet the norm.

Since stars are made, not born, publicity is everything, explaining why so much control is exercised over who gets to do the interview and who doesn't. Things can and do get political. Moreover, publicity photos chosen for billboards, as well as *clips* selected for *trailers* (shown to promote movies) often follow a political decision making process. One high profile example that caught my attention involves the movie "The Good Son" starring Macauley Culkin. While Culkin received top billing and his was the only face on the billboard, I personally felt that the real star of the movie was Elijah Wood, (i.e., "Avalon," "Huck Finn," "Forever Young," "Radio Flyer," among others) who, at the time of the movie's opening, had appeared in at least eight feature films (about as many as Culkin had done to date). Culkin, however, had a block buster film to his credit. While most of Elijah's films did well, none were as phenomenal as "Home Alone." So, even though the storyline of the movie opened with Elijah and totally revolved around him, once again, box office dollars pushed Culkin's face to appear solo in the promos. But that's Hollywood, folks! You learn to love the good and bad or leave it all together.

POINTS TO PONDER

1. *Obtaining permission to publicize a co-starring or strong supporting role in a feature film or new television series can be difficult at times because movie studio and television executives have to obtain the star's permission to release the art work.*

2. *Appearing in a television series that airs on a cable channel, as opposed to a network show, will not pay as much money, nor will it afford the same level of exposure or publicity that a network show can generate.*

3. *Hiring a good publicist may be the best investment a parent can make in promoting the child's career.*

Chapter 27

BRACES, WORK PERMITS, AND UNEMPLOYMENT FOR MINORS

CLEAR AND REMOVABLE BRACES:

Since bright, straight beautiful teeth are a definite asset for show business kids, getting crooked teeth straightened as soon as possible at the onset of a problem is a sound investment. Since clear or removable braces only cost a couple hundred dollars more than regular metal braces, it makes sense to go for the alternative. Clear braces photograph well and pose no problem for television cameras. Furthermore, clear or removable braces can keep a child in the business who would otherwise have to go on hiatus with a mouth full of heavy metal.

FLIPPERS:

A flipper is a cosmetic tooth that children's dentist use as a replacement for a missing tooth while waiting for the permanent tooth to grow in. Usually flippers are only required for the middle four top and bottom teeth, since side teeth do not pose much of a problem for the camera. *CAUTION:* A flipper cannot be used for eating purposes; they are cosmetic only. Children flip them in right before the audition and take them out immediately afterwards. For food commercials, in particular, a full set of teeth are required. Some commercials or television shows think that missing teeth are cute or natural looking and will not require a flipper.

For younger children who are still losing teeth, casting directors will ask if the child has a flipper. This question is usually included on the size sheets one has to fill in at auditions. Many parents answer "yes" to the flipper question because they know that a flipper is readily obtainable, often with as little as a days notice to a children's dentist that works with show business kids. A flipper cost approximately $200.00 for the first tooth and about $85.00 thereafter for each additional tooth.

In the Los Angeles area contact: Dr. Robert Smith, 9201 W. Sunset, West Hollywood, California. Phone: 310-273-5775

WORK PERMITS:

Any child intending to work in the state of California must obtain a work permit prior to employment. Work permits are valid for six months. If the child is school age, one must obtain a *first timer's application form* from the address listed below and have it signed by the child's school. For first timers only: include a copy of the child's birth certificate along with a copy of his current report card, if school is out of session. During sessions, the school must approve the form.

Previously, parents were allowed to walk in anytime to local offices and obtain a work permit the same day. Now that service is available only for emergency work situations on certain days of the week at specific hours. Otherwise this process is handled by mail, so allow a couple of weeks for processing. Once the form is filled out and signed, mail it, along with aforementioned attachments and a *self-addressed stamped envelope* to the following address: Entertainment Permit Section, Labor Standards Enforcement 5555 California Avenue, #200, Bakersfield, CA 93309

FOR EMERGENCY WORK SITUATIONS:

Call the following number: (818) 901-5484 or you can write or go by: Entertainment Work Permit Section, Labor Standards Enforcement, 6150 Van Nuys Blvd., #200, Van Nuys, Ca 91401

FOR RENEWALS ONLY:

During the school term, send a copy of the old work permit, along with the renewal application, signed by your child's school. When school is out, send a copy of the report card. No need to include a copy of the birth certificate for renewals. Also, enclose a self-addressed stamped envelope. A new renewal form is returned with the work permit. There is no charge for the renewal. One month prior to expiration (no sooner) mail the renewal form to the Bakersfield address.

UNEMPLOYMENT BENEFITS FOR MINORS:

In the state of California, minors who work in the entertainment industry pay for unemployment insurance benefits which are taken out of the check along with social security and federal withholding taxes. As a result, whenever a minor is between jobs he or she is eligible to file for unemployment compensation. The child has to earn a minimum amount of income in order to qualify. To apply, take the child's birth certificate, work permit, social security card and canceled check stubs to your local unemployment office. With their computers and the child's social security number the office can access exactly how much the child is qualified to receive.

Once a child has accumulated unemployment benefits, even if the family moves to another state, the child is still eligible to receive those benefits earned while working in California. Call the unemployment office for your state and see if child actors are eligible.

APPENDIX:

HOLLYWOOD SCREEN PARENTS ASSOC.
(A National Organization for Show Biz Kids)
Barbara Schiffman, Founder
P. O. Box 1612
Burbank, Ca 91507-1612
818-955-6510

PERFORMING ARTISTS UNIONS:
SAG - National Headquarters
5757 Wilshire Blvd.
Los Angeles, Ca 90036
213-954-1600

AFTRA -National Headquarters
260 Madison Avenue, 7th Floor
New York, NY 10016
212-532-0800

AFTRA - L.A. Office
6922 Hollywood Blvd
Hollywood, Ca 10016
213-462-8111

ON LOCATION EDUCATION
The Beekman School of New York
Alternative Education for Young Performers
800-800-3378

THE STUDIO ACADEMY
(Run by Studio Teachers)
North Hills Prep
9433 Sepulveda Boulevard
North Hills, California 91343
818-894-8388

PERFORMING ARTS PROGRAMS
FOR THE LOS ANGELES AREA

Beverly Hills Parks Department
330 N. Foothill Road
Beverly Hills, Calif.
(310)-550-4753

Richard Brander Acting Studio
Film Actors Workshop
12445 Moorpark Street, Suite B
Studio City, Ca.
(818)-509-1064

Burbank Parks & Recreation Dept.
Box 6459
Burbank, Ca
(818) 953-9506

Center Stage
Kevin McDermott, Director
P. O. Box 1368
Culver City, Ca 90232
(310)-837-4536

Cold Reading Workshop
Kathy Messick, Teacher
c/o Brian Reese Studios
7945 Fountain, Hollywood, Ca
213-462-6565 or 213-466-6057

Universal Dance Studio
Paul & Arlene Kennedy, Directors
6009 W. Olympic Blvd.
Los Angeles, Ca
213-938-6508

Divisek Commercial Workshop
7715 Sunset Blvd. #100
Hollywood, Ca
818-509-1096

Jewish Center for Performing Arts
Temple Israel
7300 Hollywood Blvd
Hollywood, Ca
213-874-0894

Professional Artists Group (PAG)
845 Highland Blvd.
Los Angeles, Ca
213-871-2222

Lavern Reed Dance Company
10834 Hortense #5
No. Hollywood, Ca 91601
818-980-3077 or
818-752-4999

Glorious Players
12111 Ohio Avenue
Los Angeles, Ca
213-826-1626

Lee Strasberg Theater Inst.
Joyce Foley, Dir.
7936 Santa Monica Blvd.
Los Angeles, Ca.
213-650-7777

Crossroads Arts Academy
Marla & Angela Gibbs
3870 Crenshaw Blvd.
Los Angeles, Ca.
213-291-7321

Arts Of The Dance Academy
11144 Weddington Avenue
North Hollywood Ca
818-760-8675

Young Actors Space
5918 Van Nuys Blvd.
Van Nuys, Ca.
818-785-7979

L. A. Commercial Workshop
6607 Moore Drive
Los Angeles, Ca
213-930-1003

Kids on Stage
Elaine Hall, Director
West Los Angeles
213-473-5204

Hollywood Film School
Westlake Village
805-496-5306
818-706-8422

Madelyn Clark Studios
10852 Burbank Blvd.
N. Hollywood, Ca
818-506-7763

Debbie Reynolds Dance Studios
6514 Lankershim Blvd.
North Hollywood, Ca
818-985-3193

Tepper Gallegos Workshop
Casting for Commercials
611 N. Larchmont
Los Angeles, Ca
213-469-3577

Young Actors Workout
4739 Lankershim Blvd
North Hollywood, Ca
818-985-0731

Tracy Roberts Actors Studio
141 S. Robertson Blvd.
Los Angeles Ca
213-271-2730

R. Kirby Commercial Workshop
368 N. LaCienega Blvd.
Los Angeles, Ca
213-657-8556

Weist Barron Hill
4300 W. Magnolia Blvd.
Burbank, California
818-880-5141

Idyllwild School of Music&Arts
P.O. Box 38cA
Idyllwild, Ca 92349
714-659-2171

Screenland Dance Studios
3800 W. Burbank Blvd.
Burbank, Ca.
818-843-2262

Moro Landis Studios
10960 Ventura Blvd.
Studio City, Ca
818-753-5081

Appendix

Acting for Kids
4414 Laurelgrove Ave.
Studio City, Ca
818-760-3656

Act I Theater
9214 W. Pico Blvd.
Los Angeles, Ca
213-395-9258

Pamela Campus Commercial Workshops
8833 Sunset Blvd. #305
Los Angeles, Ca 213-659-5013

BOOKS, MAGAZINES AND TAPES RECOMMENDED READING LIST

ACTOR'S SOURCE DIRECTORY (Box 57049, Tarzana, Ca 91357)

AFTRA-SAG Young Performer's Handbook (Screen Actor's Guild)

Belshe, Judy *IT'S A FREEWAY OUT THERE:* A Parent's Guide To The Commercial & Film Industry (Small Doggie Publishing, 4731 Laurel Canyon Blvd #3, N. Hollywood, Ca 91607)

Black, Shirley Temple: *CHILD STAR* (McGraw-Hill)

Callan, K: *THE L.A. AGENT BOOK* (Sweden Press)

Carson & Fawcett, *KIDBIZ: How To Help Your Child Succeed In Show Business* (Warner Books)

Chopra, Deepak *MAGICAL MIND MAGICAL BODY* (Nightingale Conant Corporation, Tape Series)

"Daily Variety" *Kids in Show Business Issue*

Dwyer, Dr. Wayne W.: *REAL MAGIC: Creating Miracles In Everyday Life* (HarperCollins Publishers)

Edelman, Marian Wright: *THE MEASURE OF OUR SUCCESS* (Beacon Press)

FLORIDA ACTORS HANDBOOK (5210-12th Ave. North St., St. Petersburg Florida 37210-5901)

Gold, Aggie: *FRESH FACES* (Career Press)

Gwen Glasel Gendler, *KIDS ON CAMERA* (GGG Enterprises)

Appendix

"Hollywood Reporter" *Annual Show Biz Kid's Issue*

Johnson, Vernee Watson: *"COMMERCIALS, JUST MY SPEED,"* and *"KIDS IN THE COMMERCIAL BIZ,"* (650 Alexander Street, San Fernando, Ca 91340)

Pinskey, Raleigh: *THE ZEN OF HYPE* (1991 A Citadel Press Book, Published by Carol Publishing Group)

"Screen Actor" (The Screen Actors Guild)

Shinn, Florence Scovel: *YOUR WORD IS YOUR WAND* (DeVorss)

THE AGENCIES: *What The Actor Needs to Know* (Acting World Books, Box 3044, Hollywood, Ca 90078)

THE AGENCY GUIDE (Breakdown Services, 1121 S. Robertson, 3RD Floor, Los Angeles, Ca 90035)

THE BLUE BOOK (I.A.T.S.E. Local 884, Studio Teachers Union, Box 461467, L.A. 90046)

THE HOLLYWOOD PROFESSIONAL DIRECTORY (P. O. Box 36l161, Los Angeles, Ca 90036-9561)

THE WORKING ACTOR'S GUIDE (Paul Flattery Productions, 3620 Fredonia Dr., Suite 1, Los Angeles, Ca 90068)

THE YOUNG PERFORMER'S GUIDE (Padol & Simon, Editors - Betterway Publications)

WEST COAST AGENCY GUIDE (Paul Flattery Productions, 3620 Fredonia Dr., Suite 1, Los Angeles 90068)

Williamson, Marianne: *"A RETURN TO LOVE"* (Harper Audio)

GLOSSARY OF TERMS

AFTRA: The American Federation of Television and Radio Artists.

ALTERNATE: A person who takes the place of someone chosen for a part in the event the person cast for the role is unable to accept the job, or perform to the producer's liking.

A&R: Artist and Repertoire. Usually, the person at a record label responsible for recruiting and developing new talent.

ASCAP: The American Society of Composers, Artists and Producers.

ATMOSPHERE: Extras in a scene who fill up the space surrounding the principal actors to make the scene look real or believable.

AUDITION: An opportunity to try out for a television or film role, usually for a casting director.

BILLING: The order and placement of names at the opening of a film or television show.

BLACK LIST: A process used to discriminate against another due to a personal grudge by creating or promoting propaganda that prevents an individual from gaining employment in a specific area.

BLOCKING: Physical movement by actors in a scene.

THE BLUE BOOK: A booklet published by the Studio Teachers Union that outlines SAG AFTRA rules of conduct on the set regarding the education and safety of minors.

BLUE SCREEN: Used to create special effects in a scene.

BOOKING: A term used to mean that a performer has gotten a job that entails a firm commitment for a specific task.

BREAKDOWN: A detailed listing of current casting roles available.

CALLBACK: A subsequent or follow-up interview or audition.

CALL TIME: The time a performer is scheduled to appear on the set or for a casting call.

CASTING DIRECTOR: A representative hired by the producer who is responsible for choosing candidates for the consideration of the producer.

CATTLE CALL: Usually an open call available to anyone who wants to audition. These often turn into massive crowds of people.

COLD READING: The unrehearsed reading of a scene, usually at an audition.

COMMISSION: The percentage of a performer's earnings paid to a manager or agent for services rendered.

COMPOSITE: Several photographs on one single 8 x 10.

CONFLICT: Being paid by an advertiser for a commercial that prohibits the performer contractually from performing services for a competitor.

COPY: The printed material or script used for a film, commercial or television series.

CREDITS: The opening names listed in a film or television show. Also a listing of work experience by a performer.

CUE: A hand signal by an Assistant Director or Stage Manager.

COSTUMER: The person hired to select wardrobe on the set.

DAY PLAYER: A performer hired and paid to work on a daily basis as opposed to a long term contract.

DEMO: An audition tape.

DEMO SPEC AGREEMENT: A contractual arrangement between a performer and a producer that specifies the terms of payment for services rendered by the producer for a demo tape used in shopping a record deal.

DIALOGUE: The words on a script exchanged by actors.

DIRECTOR: The person who coordinates the technical and creative aspects of a production.

EDITORIAL: A modeling job for a print medium such as newspapers or magazines.

EMANCIPATED MINOR: A child given the legal status of an adult by a Judge.

EXECUTIVE PRODUCER: Person responsible for funding the production.

EXTRA: Background talent used in non-speaking or non-principal roles.

FLIPPER: False teeth for children that are easily removed and used strictly for cosmetic purposes.

FRANCHISED AGENT: An agent approved by SAG or AFTRA to solicit work for their clients.

GLOSSY: A shiny photo finish on a photograph.

GUARANTEED BILLING: A position of credit negotiated by an agent prior to signing a contract.

HEAD SHOT: Usually an 8 x 10" still photograph that includes the head and shoulders.

HONEY WAGON: A towed vehicle containing more than one dressing room.

INDUSTRIAL: Non-broadcast tape or film used primarily for educational purposes.

MEAL PENALTY: A fee paid by the producer for not setting aside specific meals or breaks included in the contract.

MEDITATION: The process of sitting or lying still and quieting the mind while focusing on one single thought or issue, or nothing at all.

OPEN CALL: An audition that is open to everyone.

PILOT: Usually an hour long episode for a new television series designed to test the waters to see if the show will get picked up by a network.

PRIME TIME: Network programming aired between 8:00 and 11:00 p.m. or 7:00 to 10:00 p.m. for Central or Mountain time.

PRINCIPAL: A performer with speaking lines or special business that advances the story line.

PRODUCER: The person who takes care of and is responsible on a daily basis, for the decision making process involved in a production.

PRODUCER'S DISCRETION: Those items in a contract that a producer has the right to grant or disallow.

PROFICIENCY TEST: An advance placement test taken by a high school student to graduate from high school early.

PROOF SHEET: An 8 x 10" sheet that displays the printed negatives from a roll of film.

RATINGS: Public surveys used to determine the percentage of listening or viewing audiences for radio and television.

RESIDUAL: A fee paid to a performer for the reuse of a commercial, film or television show.

RESUME: A listing of work experience or credits.

SAG: Screen Actor's Guild

SCALE: The least or minimum amount paid for a job.

SCREEN TEST: The filming of an audition on tape.

SCRIPT: The written form of a screenplay for film or television; or a play for radio or theater.

SESSION FEE: Payment for the initial performance in a commercial.

SET: An indoor location, usually within a studio.

SHOWCASE: A performance by an artist attended by industry people for the purpose of obtaining an agent, manager, record deal, etc.

SIDES: A scene or pages from a script used for auditions.

SIGHT AND SOUND: Parent's right under union contract to be within sight of their child at all times.

SOUNDTRACK: The audio portion of a television show or film.

SPECIAL BUSINESS: Action that is specially directed to be performed by an extra or atmosphere.

SPOT: A randomly booked commercial message.

STUDIO TEACHER: A teacher or tutor hired by the studio to teach minors and to enforce child labor laws under the guidelines of union contracts.

SUBMISSION: Performers selected by an agent for a casting director's consideration for a particular role.

TAFT-HARTLEY: A federal statute that allows a performer 30 days after booking a union job before he has to join the union.

TAKE: A shot that is written on a clapboard as "taken" or printed.

THEATRICAL: Work in film or on television as opposed to commercials.

TRACK: On an audio tape, the different channels that vocals and instruments are recorded on.

TRAILER: A series of clips used to promote a film or television show.

TRIPLE THREAT: A performer who can sing, dance and act well.

WARDROBE: The outfit a performer wears in front of the camera.

WARDROBE FITTING: A paid session, prior to the shoot, used to select clothing the performer will wear.

Appendix

SAG FRANCHISED AGENTS LOS ANGELES AREA

Fall -1995
National List and Updates Available Free For SAG Members - Small Fee For Non-Members
Note: This Is a Complete List That Contains Adult and Children's Agencies
Most Adult Agencies Now Have Children's Divisions

(List Alphabetical From Left to Right)

A S A
4430 Fountain Avenue, Suite #A
L.A., CA 90029
213-662-9787

ABOVE THE LINE AGENCY
9200 Sunset Boulevard, Suite 401
LA, CA 90069
310-859-6115

ABRAMS ARTISTS & ASSOCIATES
9200 Sunset Bl. #625
L.A., Ca 90069
310-859-0625

ABRAMS-RUBALOFF
8075 W. 3rd Street, Suite 303
LA, CA 90048
213-935-1700

ACME TALENT & LITERARY
6310 San Vicente Blvd., Suite 520
LA, CA 90048
213-954-2263

AFH MANAGEMENT, TALENT
7819 Beverly Blvd
LA, CA 90036
213-658-9152

AGENCY FOR PERFORMING ARTS
9000 Sunset Blvd., Suite 1200
LA, CA 90069
310-273-0744

THE AGENCY
10351 Santa Monica Blvd, #211
LA, CA 90025
310-551-3000

AIMEE ENTERTAINMENT
13743 Victory Blvd.
Van Nuys, CA 91401
818-783-9115

ALLEN TALENT AGENCY
11755 Wilshire Blvd., Suite 1750
LA, CA 90025
310-474-7524

ALLEN TALENT, BONNI
260 S. Beverly
Beverly Hills, CA 90212
310-247-1865

ALLIANCE TALENT, INC.
8949 Sunset Blvd., Suite 202
West Hollywood, Ca 90069
310-858-1090

ALVARADO AGENCY, CARLOS
8455 Beverly Blvd. Suite 406
LA, CA 90048
213-655-7978

AMBROSIO/MORTIMER
9150 Wilshire Blvd, Suite 175
Beverly Hills, CA 90212
310-274-4274

SHOW BIZ KIDS

AMSEL, EISENSTADT & FRAZIER
6310 San Vicente Blvd, Suite 401
LA, CA 90048
213-939-1188

ANGEL CITY TALENT
1680 Vine Street, Suite 716
LA, CA 90028
213-463-1680

APODACA AGENCY, CHRIS
2049 Century Park East Suite 1200
LA, CA 90067
310-284-3484

APODACA/MUNRO TALENT
13801 Ventura Blvd.
Sherman Oaks, CA 91423
818-380-2700

ARTHUR, IRVIN ASSOCIATES, LTD
9363 Wilshire Blvd., Suite 212
Beverly Hills, Ca 90210
310-278-5934

ARTISTS MANAGEMENT
4340 Campus Drive, Suite 210
Newport Beach, Ca 92660
714-261-7557

ARTIST NETWORK
12001 Ventura Place, Suite 331
Studio City, CA 91604
818-651-4244

ARTISTS AGENCY
10000 Santa Monica Blvd, # 305
LA, CA 90067
310-277-7779

ARTISTS GROUP, LTD
1930 Century Park West, Suite 403
LA, CA 90067
310-552-1100

ATKINS & ASSOCIATES
303 S. Crescent Heights
LA, CA 90048
213-658-1025

B O P - L. A. TALENT AGENCY
1467 N. Tamarind Avenue
LA, CA 90028
213-466-8667

BAMM TALENT AGENCY
8609 Sherwood Drive
West Hollywood, CA 90069
310-652-6252

BADGLEY & CONNOR
9229 Sunset Blvd, Suite 311
LA, CA 90069
310-278-9313

BAIER-KLEINMAN INT'L
3575 West Cahuenga Blvd, #500
LA, CA 90068
818-761-1001

BALDWIN TALENT, INC.
500 Sepulveda Blvd., 4th Floor
Los Angeles, CA 90049
310-472-7919

BALL, BOBBY TALENT
8075 W. 3rd Street, Suite 550
Los Angeles, CA 90048
213-964-7300

Appendix

BARR, RICKEY TALENT
1010 Hammond, Suite 201
LA, CA 90069
310-276-0887

BAUMAN, HILLER & ASSOC.
5757 Wilshire Blvd, Penthouse 5
LA, CA 90036
213-857-6666

BDP & ASSOCIATES TALENT
10637 Burbank Blvd
N. Hollywood, Ca 91601
818-506-7615

BENNETT AGENCY, SARA
6404 Hollywood Blvd., Suite 327
LA, CA 90028
213-965-9666

BENSON, LOIS J
8360 Melrose Avenue, Suite 203
LA, CA 90069
213-653-0500

BERZON, MARIAN TALENT
336 E. 17th Street
Costa Mesa, CA 92267
714-631-5936

BIGLEY, AGENCY THE
6442 Coldwater Canyon Ave. #211
N. Hollywood, CA 91606
818-761-9971

BIKOFF AGENCY, YVETTE
621 N. Orlando, Suite 8
West Hollywood, CA 90048
213-655-6123

BLAKE AGENCY, THE
415 N. Camden Dr., Suite 121
Beverly Hills, CA 90210
310-246-0241

BLOOM, J MICHAEL
9255 Sunset Blvd, 7th Floor
LA, CA 90069
310-275-6800

BORDEAUX, NICOLE TALENT
1503 N. Gardner, Suite 12
LA, CA 90046
310-289-2550

BORINSTEIN ORECK BOGART
8271 Melrose Avenue, Suite 110
LA, CA 90046
213-658-7500

BRAND MODEL AND TALENT
17941 Skypark Circle, Suite F
Irvine, CA 92714
714-251-0555

BRANDON & ASSOC., PAUL
1033 N. Carol, Suite T-6
LA, CA 90069
310-273-6173

BRANDON'S COMMERCIALS
9601 Wilshire Blvd.
Beverly Hills, CA 90210
310-888-8788

BRESSLER, KELLER, ET AL
15760 Ventura Blvd., Suite 1730
Encino, CA 91436
818-905-1155

BREWIS AGENCY, ALEX
12429 Laurel Terrace Dr.
Studio City, CA 91604
818-509-0831

BRUSTIN COMPANY
2644 30th Street, 1st Floor
Santa Monica, CA 90405
310-452-3330

BURKETT TALENT AGENCY
1700 E. Garry, Suite 113
Santa Ana, CA 92705
714-724-0465

C La VIE MODEL & TALENT
7507 Sunset Blvd., Suite 201
LA, CA 90046
213-969-0541

CACTUS TALENT AGENCY
13601 Ventura Blvd, Suite 112
Sherman Oaks, CA 91423
818-986-7432

CAMERON & ASSOC. (BARBARA)
8369 Saulsito Avenue, Suite A
W. Hills, CA 91304
818-888-6107

CAREER ARTISTS INTERNATIONAL
11030 Ventura Blvd., Suite 3
Studio City, CA 91604
818-980-1315

CARROLL AGENCY, WILLIAM
139 N. San Fernando, Suite A
Burbank, CA 91502
818-848-9948

BRIDGES, ENTERPRISES (JIM)
5000 Lankershim, Suite 7
N. Hollywood, CA 91601
213-962-6075

BUCHWALD & ASSOCIATES
9229 Sunset Blvd.
W. Hollywood, CA 90069
310-278-3600

BURTON AGENCY (IRIS)
1450 Belfast Dr.
LA, CA 90069
310-652-0954

CL, INC.
843 N. Sycamore Ave.
LA, CA 90038
310-556-4343

CAMDEN
822 S. Robertson Blvd. #200
LA, CA 90035
310-289-2700

CAPITAL ARTISTS
8383 Wilshire Blvd, Suite 954
Beverly Hills, CA 90211
213-658-8118

CARGLO TALENT AGENCY
703 S. Glendora Avenue, Suite 6
West Covina, CA 91790
818-960-2770

CASTLE-HILL TALENT
1101 S. Orlando
LA, CA 90035
213-653-3535

Appendix

CAVALERI & ASSOCIATES
6605 Hollywood Blvd, Suite 220
LA, CA 90028
213-683-1354

CHASIN AGENCY, THE
8899 Beverly Blvd., Suite 713
LA, CA 90048
310-278-7505

CHUTUK & ASSOCIATES (JACK)
2121 Avenue of the Stars Suite 700
LA, CA 90067
310-552-1773

CIRCLE TALENT ASSOCIATES
433 N. Camden Dr. Suite 400
Beverly Hills, CA 90212
310-285-1585

CLER MODELING, COLLEEN
120 S. Victory Blvd, Suite 206
Burbank, CA 91502
818-841-7943

COLOURS MODEL & TALENT MGT
7551 Melrose Avenue, Suite 6
LA, CA 90046
213-658-7072

COPPAGE COMPANY, THE
11501 Chandler Blvd.
N. Hollywood, CA 91601
818-980-1106

COSDEN AGENCY, THE
3518 West Cahuenga Suite 216
LA, CA 90068
213-874-7200

CENTURY ARTISTS, LTD
9744 Wilshire Blvd, Suite 308
Beverly Hills, CA 90212
310-273-4366

CHATEAU BILLINGS TALENT
5657 Wilshire Blvd., Suite 340
LA, CA 90036
213-965-5432

CINEMA TALENT AGENCY
2609 Wyoming Avenue
Burbank, CA 91505
818-845-3816

CLARK COMPANY (W. R.)
2431 Hyperion Ave.
LA, CA 90027
213-953-4960

COAST TO COAST TALENT
4942 Vineland, Suite 200
N. Hollywood, CA 91601
818-762-6278

CONTEMPORARY ARTISTS
1427 Third Street Promenade #205
Santa Monica, CA 90401
310-395-1800

CORALIE JR. THEATRICAL
4789 Vineland Avenue, Suite 100
N. Hollywood, CA 91602
818-766-9501

CRAIG AGENCY, THE
8485 Melrose Place, Suite E
LA, CA 90069
213-655-0236

CREATIVE ARTISTS AGENCY
8930 Wilshire Blvd.
Beverly Hills, CA 90212
310-288-4545

CROW & ASSOCIATES, SUSAN
1010 Hammond Street, Suite 102
W. Hollywood, CA 90069
310-859-9784

CUMBER ATTRACTIONS, LIL
6363 Sunset Blvd., Suite 807
LA, CA 90028
213-469-1919

CUNNINGHAM, ET AL (CED)
10635 Santa Monica Blvd, #130
LA, CA 90025
310-475-2111

DH, TALENT AGENCY
1800 N. Highland Avenue Suite 300
LA, CA 90028
213-962-6643

DZA TALENT AGENCY
8981 Sunset Blvd., Suite 204
LA, CA 90069
310-274-8025

DADE/SHULTZ ASSOCIATES
11846 Ventura Blvd., Suite 201
Studio City, CA 91604
818-760-3100

DAVIS, MARY WEBB
515 N. LaCienega Blvd.
LA, CA 90048
310-652-6850

DEVROE, THE
6311 Romaine Street
LA, CA 90038
213-962-3040

DURKIN ARTISTS
12229 Ventura Blvd., Suite 202
Studio City, CA 91604
818-762-9936

DYTMAN & SCHWARTZ
9200 Sunset Blvd, Suite 809
LA, CA 90069
310-274-8844

EFENDI, TALENT AGENCY
1923 1/2 Westwood Blvd #3
LA, CA 90025
213-957-0006

ELITE MODEL MANAGEMENT
345 N. Maple Drive, Suite 397
Beverly Hills, CA 90210
310-274-9395

ELLIS TALENT GROUP
6025 Sepulveda Blvd, Suite 201
Van Nuys, CA 91411
818-997-7447

EMERALD ARTISTS
6565 Sunset Blvd., Suite 312
LA, CA 90028
310-271-7120

EPSTEIN, WYCKOFF, ET AL
280 S. Beverly Dr., Suite 400
Beverly Hills, CA 90212
310-278-7222

Appendix

ESTEPHAN TALENT AGENCY
6018 Greenmeadow Road
Lakewood, CA 90713
310-421-8048

FARRELL, EILEEN/COULTER, KATHY
18261 San Fernando Mission Rd.
Northridge, CA 91326
818-831-7003

FELBER & ASSOCIATES (WILLIAM)
2126 Cahuenga Blvd.
LA, CA 90068
213-466-7629

FIELDS TALENT AGENCY, LIANA
3325 Wilshire Blvd., Suite 749
LA, CA 90010
213-487-3656

FIRST ARTISTS AGENCY
10000 Riverside Dr., Suite 10
Toluca Lake, CA 91602
818-509-9292

FONTAINE AGENCY, JUDITH
9255 Sunset Blvd.
LA, CA 90069
310-285-0545

FRESH MODEL MANAGEMENT
6399 Wilshire Blvd., #8
Los Angeles, CA 90048
213-655-5367

FUTURE AGENCY
8929 Sepulveda Blvd., Suite 314
Los Angeles, CA 90045
310-388-9602

FPA TALENT AGENCY
12701 Moorpark Suite 205
Studio City, CA 91604
818-508-6691

FAVORED ARTIST AGENCY
8150 Beverly Blvd., Suite 201
LA, CA 90048
310-247-1040

FERRAR-MAZIROFF
8430 Santa Monica Blvd. #220
LA, CA 90069
213-654-2601

FILM ARTISTS ASSOCIATES
7080 Hollywood Blvd., Suite 1118
LA, CA 90028
213-463-1010

FLICK EAST & WEST
9057 Nemo Street, Suite A
W. Hollywood, CA 90069
310-271-9111

FREED, BARRY COMPANY
2029 Century Park East #600
LA, CA 90067
310-277-1260

FRIES, ALICE AGENCY
6381 Hollywood Blvd., Suite 600
Los Angeles, CA 90028
213-464-6491

GAGE GROUP INC.
9255 Sunset Blvd., Suite 515
Los Angeles, CA 90069
310-859-8777

GARRETT TALENT AGENCY, HELEN
6525 Sunset Blvd. 5th Floor
Los Angeles, CA 90028
213-871-8707

GARRICK, DALE
8831 Sunset Blvd., Suite 402
Los Angeles, CA 90069
310-657-2661

GEDDES AGENCY, THE
1201 Green Acre Avenue
West Hollywood, CA. 90046
213-878-1155

GELFF ASSOCIATES, LAYA
16133 Ventura Blvd.
Encino, CA 91436
818-713-2610

GERARD TALENT AGENCY, PAUL
2918 Alta Vista Dr.
Newport Beach, CA 92660
714-644-7950

GERLER-STEVENS & ASSOC.
3349 Cahuenga Blvd., Suite 1
Los Angeles, CA 90068
213-850-7386

GERSH AGENCY, THE
232 N. Canon Dr.
Beverly Hills, CA 90210
310-274-6611

GERSHENSON, DAVID S.
11757 San Vicente, Suite 2
Los Angeles, CA 90049
310-207-1345

GILLEY, GEORGIA TALENT
8721 Sunset Blvd., Suite 104
LA, CA 90069
310-657-5660

GOLD/MARSHAK & ASSOC.
3500 West Olive Ave, #1400
Burbank, CA 91505
818-972-4300

GOLDEY COMPANY, INC.
116 N. Robertson Blvd., Suite 700
LA, CA 90048
310-657-3277

GORDON COMPANY TALENT
15250 Ventura Blvd., Suite 720
Sherman Oaks, CA 91403
818-907-0220

GORDON, MICHELLE & ASSOC.
260 S. Beverly Drive, Suite 308
Beverly Hills, CA 90212
310-246-9930

HWA TALENT REPS., INC.
1964 Westwood Blvd., Suite 400
LA, CA 90025
310-446-1313

HAEGGSTROM OFFICE
8721 Sunset Blvd., Suite 103
LA, CA 90069
310-289-1071

HALLIDAY, BUZZ & ASSOC.
8899 Beverly Blvd., Suite 620
LA, CA 90048
310-275-6028

Appendix

HALPERN & ASSOCIATES
12304 Santa Monica Blvd., #104
LA, CA 90025
310-571-4488

HAMILBURG AGENCY, M. J.
292 S. La Cienega, Suite 312
Beverly Hills, CA 90211
310-657-1501

HART & ASSOCIATES, VAUGHN D.
200 N. Robertson Blvd., Suite 219
Beverly Hills, CA 90211
310-273-7887

HEADLINE ARTISTS AGENCY
16400 Ventura Blvd., Suite 324
Encino, CA 91436
818-986-1730

HECHT AGENCY, BEVERLY
8949 Sunset Blvd., Suite 203
LA, CA 90069
310-278-3544

HENDERSON/HOGAN AGENCY
247 S. Beverly Dr.,
Beverly Hills, CA 90212
310-274-7815

HERVEY/GRIMES TALENT
14200 Ventura Blvd., Suite 109
Sherman Oaks, CA 91413
818-981-0891

HOLLYWOOD CNTV TALENT
1680 N. Vine Street, Suite 1105
LA, CA 90028
213-463-5677

HOUSE OF REPRESENTATIVES
9911 Pico Blvd., Suite 1060
LA, CA 90035
310-772-0772

HOWARD TALENT WEST
12178 Ventura Blvd., Suite 201
Studio City, CA 91604
818-766-5300

HURWITZ ASSOCIATES, MARTIN
427 N. Canon Dr., Suite 215
Beverly Hills, CA 90210
310-274-0240

IFA TALENT AGENCY
8730 Sunset Blvd, Suite 490
LA, CA 90069
310-659-5522

IMAGE TALENT AGENCY
259 S. Robertson
Beverly Hills, CA 90212
310-277-9134

INNOVATIVE ARTISTS
1999 Avenue of the Stars, #2850
LA, CA 90067
310-553-5200

INTERNATIONAL CREATIVE MGT (ICM)
8942 Wilshire Blvd.
Beverly Hills, CA 90211
310-550-4000

IT MODEL MANAGEMENT
526 N. Larchmont
LA, CA 90004
213-962-9564

JACKMAN & TAUSSIG
1815 Butler Avenue, Suite 120
LA, CA 90025
310-478-6641

JENNINGS & ASSOCIATES, THOMAS
28035 Dorothy Drive, Suite 210 A
Agoura, CA 91301
818-879-1260

KARG/WEISSENBACH & ASSOC.
329 N. Wetherly Dr. #101
Beverly Hills, CA 90210
310-205-0435

KALMAN/ARLETTA
7713 Sunset Blvd.
LA, CA 90046
213-851-8822

KERWIN WILLIAM AGENCY
1605 N. Cahuenga, Suite 202
LA, CA 90028
213-469-5155

KLASS, ERIC AGENCY
144 South Beverly Dr., #405
Beverly Hills, CA 90212
310-274-9169

KRUGLOV & ASSOC., VICTOR
7060 Hollywood Blvd., Suite 1220
LA, CA 90028
213-957-9000

LA ARTISTS
2566 Overland Ave., Suite 550
LA, CA 90064
310-202-0254

JAY AGENCY, GEORGE
6269 Selma Avenue, Suite 15
LA, CA 90028
213-466-6655

KAPLAN-STAHLER AGENCY
8383 Wilshire Blvd. #923
Beverly Hills, CA 90211
213-653-4483

KAZARIAN/SPENCER & ASSOC
11365 Ventura Blvd., Suite 100
Studio City, CA 91604
818-769-9111

KEMP, SHARON TALENT
9812 Vidor Drive
LA, CA 90035
310-552-0011

KJAR AGENCY, TYLER
10653 Riverside Drive
Toluca Lake, CA 91602
818-760-0321

KOHNER, PAUL INC.
9300 Wilshire Blvd., #555
Beverly Hills, CA 90212
310-550-1060

LA TALENT
8335 Sunset Blvd., 2nd Floor
LA, CA 90069
213-656-3722

LW 1, INC.
8383 Wilshire Blvd., Suite 649
Beverly Hills, CA 90211
213-653-5700

Appendix

LAINE, LAUREN TALENT AGENCY
1370 N. Brea Blvd., Suite 200 D
Fullerton, CA 92633
714-441-1140

LAWRENCE AGENCY, THE
3575 Cahuenga Blvd. W., Suite 125-3
LA, CA 90069
213-851-7711

LENHOFF/ROBINSON TALENT & LIT.
1728 S. La Cienega Blvd.
LA, CA 90035
310-558-4700

LEVY, ROBIN & ASSOC.
9701 Wilshire Blvd., Suite 1200
Beverly Hills, CA 90212
310-278-8748

LIGHT AGENCY, ROBERT
6404 Wilshire Blvd. Suite 900
LA, CA 90048
213-651-1777

LOFT AGENCY, THE
369 S. Doheny Dr., Suite 203
Beverly Hills, CA 90211
310-576-9012

LOVELL & ASSOC.
1350 N. Highland Ave.
LA, CA 90028
213-462-1672

MGA/MARY GRADY AGENCY
4444 Lankershim Blvd., Suite 207
North Hollywood, CA 91602
818-766-4414

LANE TALENT, STACEY
13455 Ventura Blvd., # 240
Sherman Oaks, CA 91423
818-501-2668

LEE & ASSOC., GUY
4150 Riverside Dr., Suite 212
Burbank, CA 91505
818-848-7475

LEVIN AGENCY, THE
9255 Sunset Blvd., Suite 401
West Hollywood, CA 90069
213-653-7073

LICHMAN CO., TERRY
4439 Worster Ave.
Studio City, CA 91604
818-783-3003

LINDER & ASSOC., KEN
2049 Century Park East, #2750
LA, CA 90067
310-277-9223

L. A. PREMIERE ARTISTS
8899 Beverly Blvd., Suite 510
LA, CA 90048
310-271-1414

LYNNE & REILLY AGENCY
6735 Forest Lawn Dr., # 313
LA, CA 90068
213-850-1984

MADEMOISELLE TALENT
8693 Wilshire Blvd., Suite 200
Beverly Hills, CA 90211
310-289-8005

MAJOR CLIENTS AGENCY
345 Maple Drive, Suite 395
Beverly Hills, CA 90210
310-205-5000

MARTEL AGENCY, THE
1680 N. Vine Street, Suite 203
LA, CA 90028
213-461-5943

MEDIA ARTISTS GROUP
8383 Wilshire Blvd., Suite 954
Beverly Hills, CA 90211
213-658-5050

MIRAMAR TALENT AGENCY
9157 Sunset Blvd., Suite 300
L A, CA 90069
310-858-1900

MOORE ARTISTS, TALENT
1551 S. Robertson Blvd.
LA, CA 90035
310-286-3150

MOSS & ASSOC., H. DAVID
733 North Seward St., Penthouse
LA, CA 90038
213-465-1234

NATHE & ASSOC., SUSAN
828 Melrose Ave.., Suite 200
LA, CA 90046
213-653-7573

ORANGE GROOVE GROUP
12178 Ventura Blvd., Suite 205
Studio City, CA 91604
818-762-7498

MARSHALL MODEL & COMM.
23900 Hawthorne Blvd., Suite 100
Torrance, CA 90505
310-378-1223

MAXINE TALENT AGENCY
4830 Encino Avenue
Encino, CA 91316
818-986-2946

METROPOLITAN TALENT
4526 Wilshire Blvd.
LA, CA 90010
213-857-4500

MITCHELL AGENCY, PATTI
4605 Lankershim Blvd., Suite 201
North Hollywood, CA 91602
818-508-6181

MORRIS AGENCY, WILLIAM
151 El Camino Drive
Beverly Hills, CA 90212
310-274-7451

MURPHY AGENCY, MARY
6014 Greenbush Avenue
Van Nuys, CA 91401
818-989-6076

OMNIPOP INC.
10700 Ventura Blvd., 2nd Floor
Studio City. CA 91604
818-980-9267

OSBRINK TALENT, CINDY
4605 Lankershim Blvd., Suite 401
North Hollywood, CA 91602
818-760-2488

Appendix

OTIS, DOROTHY DAY
13223 Ventura Blvd., Suite F
Studio City, CA 91604
818-905-9510

PARADIGM TALENT AGENCY
10100 Santa Monica Blvd., Suite 2500
LA, CA 90067
310-277-4400

PARTOS COMPANY, THE
3630 Barham Blvd., Suite Z 108
LA, CA 90068
213-876-5500

PLAYERS TALENT AGENCY
8770 Shoreham Drive, Suite 2
West Hollyhood, CA 90069
310-289-8777

PRIMA EASTWEST MODEL MGT.
933 N. La Brea Ave., Suite 200
LA, CA 90038
213-882-6900

PRO-SPORT & ENTERTAINMENT
1990 S. Bundy Dr., Suite 700
LA, CA 90025
310-207-0228

RAEL COMPANY, GORDON
9255 Sunset, Suite 425
LA, CA 90069
213-969-8493

ROGERS & ASSOC., STEPHANIE
3575 West Cahuenga Blvd., Suite 249
LA, CA 90069
213-851-5155

PAKULA KING & ASSOC.
9229 Sunset Blvd., Suite 315
LA, CA 90069
310-281-4868

PARAGON TALENT AGENCY
8439 Sunset, Suite 301
LA, CA 90069
213-654-4554

PERSEUS
3807 Wilshire Blvd., Suite 1102
LA, CA 90010
213-383-2322

PREMIER TALENT AGENCY
2001 Wilshire Blvd., 6th Floor
Santa Monica, CA 90403
310-453-6886

PRIVILEGE TALEN AGENCY
8170 Beverly Blvd., Suite 204
LA, CA 90048
213-658-8781

PROGRESSIVE ARTISTS
400 S. Beverly Drive., Suite 216
LA, CA 90212
310-553-8561

RENAISSANCE TALENT & LIT.
8523 Sunset Blvd.
LA, CA 90069
310-289-3636

ROMANO, CINDY
414 Village Square West
Palm Springs, CA 92262
619-323-3333

ROOS WEST LTD, GILLA
9744 Wilshire Blvd., Suite 203
Beverly Hills, CA 90212
310-274-9356

ROSSON AGENCY, NATALIE
11712 Moorpark Street, Suite 204
Studio City, CA 91604
818-508-1445

SANDERS AGENCY, THE
8831 Sunset Blvd., # 304
LA, CA 90069
310-652-1119

SAVAGE AGENCY, THE
6212 Banner Ave.
LA, CA 90038
213-461-8316

SCHECHTER COMPANY, THE IRV
9300 Wilshire Blvd., # 410
Beverly Hills, CA 90212
310-278-8070

SCHNARR TALENT, SANDIE
8281 Melrose Ave., # 200
LA, CA 90046
213-653-9479

SCHWARTZ ASSOC., DON
8749 Sunset Blvd.
LA, CA 90069
310-657-8910

SCREEN CHILDRENS TALENT
4000 Riverside Drive., Suite A
Burbank, CA 91505
818-846-4300

ROSENBERG OFFICE, MARION
8428 Melrose Place, Suite # B
LA, CA 90060
213-653-7383

S D B PARTNERS, INC.
1801 Avenue of the Stars, # 902
LA, CA 90067
310-785-0060

SARNOFF COMPANY, INC.
3900 West Alameda Ave.
Burbank, CA 91505
818-972-1779

SCAGNETTI TALENT, JACK
5118 Vineland Ave., Suite 102
North Hollywood, CA 91601
818-762-3871

SCHIOWITZ/CLAY/ROSE, INC.
1680 North Vine, Suite 614
LA, CA 90028
213-463-7300

SCHOEN & ASSOC., JUDY
606 North Larchmont Blvd., # 309
LA, CA 90004
213-962-1950

SCREEN ARTISTS AGENCY
12435 Oxnard Street
North Hollywood, CA 91606
818-755-0026

SELECTED ARTISTS AGENCY
3575 Cahuenga West, 2nd Floor
LA, CA 90068
213-368-1271

Appendix

SHAPIRA & ASSOC.
15301 Ventura Blvd., Suite 345
Sherman Oaks, CA 91403
818-906-0322

SHOWBIZ ENTERMAINENT
6922 Hollywood Blvd., Suite 207
LA, CA 90028
213-469-9931

SHUMAKER TALENT AGENCY, THE
6533 Hollywood Blvd., Suite # 301
Los Angeles, CA 90028
213-464-0745

SIERRA TALENT AGENCY
14542 Ventura Blvd., Suite 207
Sherman Oaks, CA 91403
818-907-9645

SINDELL, RICHARD & ASSOC.
8271 Melrose Ave., Suite 202
LA, CA 90046
213-653-5051

SLESSINGER ASSOC., MICHAEL
8730 Sunset, Suite 220
LA, CA 90069
310-657-7113

SORICE TALENT AGENCY
16661 Ventura Blvd., Suite 400-E
Encino, CA 91436
818-995-1775

STAR TALENT AGENCY
4555 1/2 Mariota Ave.
Toluca Lake, CA 91602
818-509-1931

SHAPIRO-LITCHMAN, INC.
8827 Beverly Blvd.
LA, CA 90048
310-859-8877

SHREVE AGENCY, DOROTHY
2665 North Palm Canyon Drive
Palm Springs, CA 92262
619-327-5855

SIEGEL ASSOCIAES, JEROME
7551 Sunset Blvd., Suite 203
LA, CA 90046
213-850-1275

SILVER MASSETTI & ASSOC.
8730 Sunset Blvd., Suite # 480
LA, CA 90069
310-289-0909

SIRENS MODEL MGT
6404 Wilshire, Suite 720
LA, CA 90048
213-782-0310

SMITH & ASSOC., SUSAN
121 N. San Vincente
Beverly Hills, CA 90211
213-852-4777

SPECIAL ARTISTS AGENCY
335 North Maple Drive, Suite 360
Beverly Hills, CA 91602
310-859-9688

STARWILL TALENT AGENCY
6253 Hollywood Blvd., # 730
LA, CA 90068
213-874-1239

STERN AGENCY, CHARLES
11766 Wilshire Blvd., # 760
LA, CA 90025
310-479-1788

STONE MANNNERS
8091 Selma Ave.
LA, CA 90046
213-654-7575

TGI-BLOOM
6300 Wilshire, # 2110
LA, CA 90048
213-852-9559

TALON THEATRICAL AGENCY
567 South Lake
Pasadena, CA 91101
818-577-1998

THOMAS TALENT AGENCY
124 S. Lasky Drive
Beverly Hills, CA 90212
310 247-2727

TISHERMAN AGENCY, INC.
6767 Forest Lawn Dr., Suite 101
LA, CA 90068
213-850-6767

TURTLE AGENCY, THE
12456 Ventura Blvd, Suite 1
Studio City, CA 91604
818-506-6898

UMOJA TALENT AGENCY
2069 W. Slauson Avenue
LA, CA 90047
213-290-6612

STEVENS, STEVEN R.
3518 West Cahuenga Blvd., # 301
LA, CA 90068
213-850-5761

SUTTON, BARTH & BENNARI
145 South Fairfax Ave., #310
LA, CA 90036
213-938-6000

TALENT GROUP INC.
9250 Wislhire Blvd., # 208
Beverly Hills, CA 90212
310-273-9559

TANNEN & ASSOC.
1800 N. Vine Street #120
LA, CA 90028
213-466-6191

THORNTON, ARLENE
5657 Wilshire Blvd., #290
LA, CA 90036
213-939-5757

TOTAL ACTING EXPER., A
20501 Ventura Blvd, #112
Woodland Hills, CA 91364
818-340-9249

TWENTIETH CENTURY
15315 Magnolia Blvd, #429
Sherman Oaks, CA 91403
818-788-5516

UNITED TALENT AGENCY
9560 Wilshire Blvd., 5th Fl
Beverly Hills, CA 90212
310-273-6700

Appendix

WAIN AGENCY, ERIKA
1418 N. Highland Ave #102
LA, CA 90028
213-460-4224

WALLIS AGENCY
1126 Hollywood Way #203-A
Burbank, CA 91505
818-953-4848

WALLS & ASSOCIATES, CURRY
9107 Wilshire Blvd., Suite #602
Beverly Hills, CA 90210
310-858-0085

WATT & ASSOC., SANDRA
7551 Melrose Avenue, #5
LA, CA 90046
213-851-1021

WAUGH TALENT AGENCY, ANN
4731 Laurel Canyon Blvd. #5
North Hollywood, CA 91607
818-980-0141

WEBB ENTERPRISES, RUTH
7500 Devista Drive
LA, CA 90046
213-874-1700

WEST MODEL MGT, TALENT
7276 1/2 Melrose Avenue
LA, CA 90046
213-525-3355

WHITAKER AGENCY, THE
12725 Ventura Blvd., Suite #F
Studio City, CA 91604
818-766-4441

WILSON & ASSOCIATES, SHIRLEY
5410 Wilshire Blvd., Suite 227
LA, CA 90036
213-857-6977

WITZER AGENCY, TED
6310 San Vicente Blvd., #407
LA, CA 90048
310-552-9521

WORLD CLASS SPORTS
9171 Wilshire Blvd., #404
Beverly Hills, CA 90210
310-278-2010

WORLD WIDE ACTS
5830 Las Virgenes Rd., #492
Calabasas, CA 91302
818-340-8151

WRIGHT ENTERPRISES, CARTER
6513 Hollywood Blvd, Suite 210
LA, CA 90028
213-469-0944

WRITERS AND ARTISTS
924 Westwood Blvd., #900
Los Angeles, Ca 90024
310-824-6300

ZADEH & ASSOCIATES, STELLA
11759 Iowa Avenue
LA, CA 90025
310-207-4114

ZEALOUS ARTISTS P., INC.
139 S. Beverly Drive #222
Beverly Hills, Ca 90212
310-281-3533

About The Author

Ruthie O. Grant runs her own talent management agency where she has discovered, taught and nurtured young actors who star in television series, movies, commercials, and national print ads. She conducts show biz kids workshops and seminars and has been interviewed by *Hard Copy, Inside Edition, American Journal, L.A. Parent* and *Celebrity News Magazine* in segments about child actors. She interviews regularly on radio stations across the country.

Grant graduated with honors from the University of Houston with a B.A. in English Literature. She teaches part-time at Pasadena City College and Los Angeles Valley College. Her poetry and short stories have won national awards. A suspense novel of Grant's made it to the finals out of 5,000 entries in Amblin's Chesterfield Film Project sponsored by Universal Studios. Grant is working on a women's self help book titled: *Breaking Away.*